# RADICAL PHILOSOPHY

## 2.03
Series 2 / December 2018

| | |
|---|---:|
| Starting again from Marx | |
| **Antonio Negri** | 3 |
| The Palestinian Museum | |
| **Hanan Toukan** | 10 |
| *Dossier*: Economies and Times of Deportation | 23 |
|     The deportation power | |
|     **Nicholas De Genova** | 23 |
|     Deportation, nation state, capital | |
|     **Clara Lecadet** | 28 |
|     Expulsion, power, mobilisation | |
|     **William Walters** | 33 |
|     Stolen time | |
|     **Shahram Khosravi** | 38 |
| Fallen angel | |
| **Peter Hallward** | 43 |
| The politics of miscarriage | |
| **Victoria Browne** | 61 |
| Agustín García Calvo in our time | |
| **Vicente Ordóñez** | 73 |
| Forgetting Vietnam | |
| **Trinh T. Minh-ha with Lucie Kim-Chi Mercier** | 78 |
| Reviews | 90 |
|     Pierre Charbonnier et al., *Comparative Metaphysics* | |
|     **Miri Davidson** | 90 |
|     François Cusset, *Le déchaînement du monde* | |
|     Elsa Dorlin, *Se défendre* | |
|     **Emmanuel Jouai** | 93 |
|     Laura Briggs, *How All Politics Became Reproductive Politics* | |
|     **Sophie Jones** | 98 |
|     Galen Strawson, *Things That Bother Me* | |
|     **W. Thomas Pepper** | 101 |
|     Jasbir K. Puar, *The Right to Maim* | |
|     **James Eastwood** | 106 |
|     Theodor W. Adorno, *Aesthetics* | |
|     **Louis Hartnoll** | 108 |
|     Clare Hemmings, *Considering Emma Goldman* | |
|     **Victoria Hesford** | 111 |
|     Jean-Paul Sartre et al., *It is Right to Rebel* | |
|     **Jussi Palmusaari** | 114 |
|     Tom Bunyard, *Debord, Time and Spectacle* | |
|     **Eric-John Russell** | 116 |
|     Kuhar and Paternotte, eds, *Anti-Gender Campaigns* | |
|     **Eva von Redecker** | 120 |
| Stanley Cavell, 1926-2018 | |
| **Daniele Lorenzini** | 122 |
| Paul Virilio, 1932–2018 | |
| **Paolo Fabbri** | 127 |

**Editorial collective**
Claudia Aradau
Brenna Bhandar
Victoria Browne
David Cunningham
Peter Hallward
Stewart Martin
Lucie Mercier
Daniel Nemenyi
Hannah Proctor
Rahul Rao
Martina Tazzioli
Chris Wilbert

**Engineers**
Austin Gross
Daniel Nemenyi
Alex Sassmanshausen

Creative Commons BY-NC-ND
Radical Philosophy, December 2018

ISSN 0300-211X
ISBN 978-1-9999793-2-4

# Starting again from Marx
Antonio Negri

Let us start again from Marx.* Why? Is it because we are communists? No, this answer is not convincing. We could start again from somewhere else, from Lenin, or Mao; or, we could believe that current feminist or anti-racist struggles have no need for Marx; we could even think that Marx's Eurocentrism makes him an enemy. Writing an apology for Karl Marx is not what I wish to do here. It is not my style. For too long I have hated tenured Marxists and every call for a reading of Marx that turns him into a closed system, so closed that to put it forward in its perfection one has to engage in nonsense in-fighting with other communists. Instead, here I would just like to clarify why, in my view, if we are communists we cannot do without Marx – and, in fact, why Marx can be a formidable means of promoting communism. Communism sustains the belief that this world is intolerable because it forces us to work in order to enhance the power and wealth of a master, and shows us that the contradictions of capitalist expropriation can never be 'fixed', and ultimately lead to war, environmental destruction and the misery of workers. But it also sustains the belief that it is possible to subvert this world, to liberate the productivity of workers from the slavery of labour, create common institutions of freedom, peace and wellbeing.

Let us begin with the argument of *why* and *how* one starts again from Marx. First, one must do so because too many people who used to call themselves Marxists have repented and, turning coat, now declare Marxism *passé* [*inattuale*]. It is obvious that the Russian Revolution has been defeated and that social democracy is in agony; but the problems that made Marx construct a communist perspective are still before our eyes, aggravated by scandalous neoliberal policies and bourgeois hypocrisy. As such, Marx's teachings, and debate with Marx, seem to me still essential for three reasons.

The first reason is *political*. Marx's materialism helps us to demystify all progressive and consensual notions of capitalist development, and affirm, in opposition to them, its antagonistic character. Capital creates an antagonistic social relation. A subversive politics lies *within* this relation and involves the proletariat, the militant and the philosopher, in equal measures. The *Kampfplatz* [battleground] is 'within and against' capital. This 'within and against' means that we are inside a power relation, an asymmetrical and irreducible relation of two forces, capital and labour power; and, because of this, capital is defined not only as an object of study but also as an enemy confronting us. A political reading of capital requires that research and knowledge are expressed as a class 'standpoint', as the knowledge and the power of the class standpoint, and thus that *class is affirmed as a subject*.

Many comrades are, quite understandably, upset by the terrible effects of exploitation. In the course of the crisis that has been upon us since 2007, we have been witness to such a degradation of the conditions of the reproduction of life, and to such a worsening and shrinking of 'necessary labour', as to render plausible a protest against the suffering and misery imposed on the proletariat and the working class. This protest or denunciation is certainly not one that we reject. However, given these conditions, it would be easy to forget Marx's teaching that the worker is always powerful. Without the worker's activity, there

---
* This is a translation of the paper, '*Ricominciare da Marx, sempre di nuovo*', presented at, 'The (re)Birth of Marx(ism): Haunting the Future', Maynooth University, 4 May 2018. A video of Negri's original presentation is available via the conference's website.

is no production of value. Capitalism does not exist without workers' productive power. I am not saying this to deny the suffering of labour and of non-labour, but to emphasise the force that the proletariat is, even in the worst conditions of its exploitation. The fables being told about the worker reduced to 'bare life' are gloomy; yet every inquiry, every moment of participation in workers' lives, every struggle, furnishes the opposite image: an image of resistance, antagonism and hatred for the enemy. To affirm the *class as a subject*, to build it in a process of subjectivation, is the first and most important of Marx's contributions, to anyone becoming aware of exploitation and who is willing to fight it.

We inhabit capitalist despotism as it unfolds both in the factory and society, yet capital cannot eliminate the use value of workers' labour, of labour power – even less so as the social character of the productive power of labour increases. Because of this, the capitalist relation is always subjected to this contradiction, one that can explode at any time, one that confronts us every day, in a banal but effective way, in the wage question. As soon as the process of buying labour power on the capitalist market is determined, it is immediately obvious that there is no equal exchange: the exchange is antagonistic. We are all familiar with the moment in the first volume of *Capital* where Marx describes the shift from absolute to relative surplus value and analyses the formation of large-scale industry. This shift is punctuated by workers' struggles around the 'working day' and gives rise to a veritable antinomy: 'right against right'. As Marx concludes: 'Between equal rights, force decides',[1] and that is class politics. Said in the even stronger and more precise terms of his critique of political economy,

> With the division between surplus-value and wages, on which the determination of the profit rate essentially depends, two quite different elements are involved, labour-power and capital. It is the functions of two *independent variables* [emphasis added] which set limits to one another, and the *quantitative division* of the value produced emerges from their *qualitative distinction*.[2]

It was in seeing the wage as an 'independent variable' within the capitalist relation that I learned to do politics, as did many others also. The discovery of this ever more invariable and ever less docile antagonism, of this contradiction without reconciliation that could nonetheless be actualised from the standpoint of labour power as a whole, the working class – it was this that represented the necessary instrument to carry out political research, or rather, co-research with the exploited, capable of branching from questions of the organisation of struggles in the factory to struggles in society at large, from the objectives of wage demands to the fight for welfare, from protests against the curtailing of freedom imposed on workers' struggles to the revolution in the conditions of the reproduction and freedom of life ... There were no objective laws to abide by, but there was to be developed that independent variable (both material and political) which was determined by the subjectivation process of revolutionary struggle: constituent projects to be realised always in the context of a liberation *of / from* labour, which in itself constitutes society and history.

The second reason we cannot give up Marx is *critique*. Marx carries forward his critique of capitalism in a historical ontology that is construed and always renewed by class struggle. Critique takes on the standpoint of the oppressed working class and puts it in *motion*. Thus, the critical perspective is necessary as an analysis of the relationship between capital and labour power / the working class in movement. It makes it possible to follow the capitalist cycle and grasp its development and crisis, so as to help us comprehend the metamorphoses of capital and working class, to describe, in unique temporal and spatial contingencies, the 'technical composition' of the exploitative relation of the oppressed working class and, eventually, to helps us organise its 'political composition' from the perspective of resistance and revolution. The autonomy and transformations of the working class standpoint are central to critique. Critique puts forward the class standpoint as movement.

At this point, I would like to tell you of 'another time' when we decided to 'restart with Marx'. In the 1960s and 1970s [in Italy], faced with the opportunism of trade union confederations and the dogmatic decadence of the communist thought of the Soviet Union and the International, we began to attack, from a working class standpoint, the corporative enclosure of the worker under the command of the trade union in the factory. We had already realised whilst reading *Capital* and the *Grundrisse* that working class labour was twofold, and consisted in two activities, one opposed to the other: it was exploited labour power (as *variable capital*) and *living labour* creative of value. In order to free labour from exploitation, the struggle needed to begin in the factory against the oppressive regime that the master imposed and that social democracy legitimated. It was from there, in industrial relations, in the immediacy of working conditions that a constructive form of resistance had to emerge. We detested the apologies of suffering and piety that induced solidarity, mere solidarity, and, although we too were poor, we wanted to make the wealth of the worker, the surplus [*eccedenza*] of productive labour, visible. This was a discovery of living labour as a force, a power, a subjectivity, as the only chance both for productivity and for revolution. The discovery allowed us to provide the bases for, and carry out the beginnings of, a working class insurrection. Later, when in the 1970s new industrial relations policies aimed at emptying out and destroying industrial sites and displacing the working class, building industrial districts based on family labour and the near-enslaving conditions of the exploitation of migration, we were confronted with a process similar to another 'primitive accumulation' in Marx's terms. It was this shift from a formal to a real subsumption of society under capital that prompted us to start broadening our notion of the working class. Again, this was always done in Marx's terms, because the concept of 'class' and it alone could represent the point of rupture, where capitalist valorisation took place. It was necessary to define both its place and its reach, its temporality and intensity. Now, as exploitation became social and spread to services, the reproduction of life and the circulation of commodities, as the extraction of surplus value no longer occurred only in the factory but spread throughout society, the concept of working class had to be broadened; we created, then, the notion of the 'socialised worker'.

With this notion, we also directly took issue with the limitations of the traditional concept of the working class in terms of *race* and *gender*. Comrades belonging to the groups in which I was a militant, *Potere Operaio*, began the movement for 'Wages for Housework'; the first campaigns to demand a wage detached from factory work. The issue concerned more than a simple polemic against a 'factory-centred' notion of the functioning of the law of labour power: it attacked the relation of production-reproduction as it had been traditionally understood by Marxist dogmatism. This relation needed to be reformed if it was to function. When renewed, it became open to the perspectives of broader social struggles around welfare, and, more immediately, when it came to women, it included, back in the far away 1960s, the issue of abortion, health and children's education.

The same applied to migrants' labour: both domestic migrants and those who integrated the exploitation of industrial, agricultural, or domestic labour with the adventure of continental migrations. We theorised and defended, with the 'right to flight' from misery, the struggles for wage equality between national and migrant workers, the struggles to abolish wage differences between the North and the South of Italy; and we moved on the paths (that would later become motorways) of European migrations. By developing the concept of socialised worker in this way, we sensed the dangers of seeing a new concept of class become a mere 'container' of different identities, of turning a renewal of the concept of working class into a figure that might function as a mere assemblage of differences that are ontologically fixed in advance. But we soon overcame this danger. In fact, we did not need [new] figures to substitute for the working class, a concept that, though inclusive of differences, remained the same. The forms and objectives of the struggles organised by the 'socialised worker' demonstrated, instead, that the transformation of the concept was neither mystified nor artificial. We were moving from struggles over the wage to struggles over income, from factory strikes to social strikes, to *mareas*, and so on; welfare objectives became more central as a terrain on which both the wage contract and class war would be played out. In that period, between the 1960s and the 1970s, class war was renewed and manifest in the active participation of other classes, beyond the worker, those involved in services and reproduction. In Italy, a ferocious repression annihilated the chance for this shift from mass to socialised worker to take on an organisational form. However, in France it was punctuated, as is customary there, by great episodes of mobilisation and struggle: 1986 in schools; 1990 in hospitals, by nurses; 1995 the railway workers, etc. There was also a manifest transformation of the 'forms' of struggle as they moved from factories to squares and gave power to social movements.

The third reason to stay with Marx, and to start again planning struggles for the present, is that his *theoretical* contribution makes it possible, and has done so for the past century, to follow the deepening of the crisis of mature capitalism and its two-fold form, both liberal and socialist; it makes it possible to trace the emergence of an adequate class opposition and to organise liberation movements against colonial power and imperialism. Thanks to Marx's theory, we are in a better position to build a bridge between the past and the future. Let us use an illustration of this too, or, even better, let me give you two motivations for this. The first is an interpretation of Volume Two of *Capital*, where, through a critical analysis of the circulation of commodities and the socialisation of the exploitation of labour, Marx foreshadows a concept of the common. The second motivation is to discuss some examples of early developments in struggles for the common.

Let us start with Volume Two of *Capital*. Here, Marx develops an analysis of the conditions of the 'real subsumption' of society under capital, showing how socialised labour can be subsumed by capital not only 'formally' (in the concatenation of structures that maintain their individual specificity) but also 'really' (in the cooperation of a multitude of singular structures that have become unable to reproduce themselves separately). Now, assuming that society has been 'really' subsumed under capital – entirely, and in a manner that does not only change its external form but also the forms of production and reproduction of society itself – these transformations cannot be understood as forms of 'fetishism', as if they were only external, automated and meaningless. We must regard the subsumption of society under capital as real – we must assume that capital functions at the level of the social, and at this level we must identify the forms of production of value, extortion and extraction of surplus; at this level, and on this terrain, we must understand the modes of struggles of labour power against capital.

Forgive me for being a bit pedantic, but it is in order to affirm the *reality* of subsumption that Marx recovers the theories of the economic cycle in *Capital*, Volume Two, so as to make manifest – as cyclical formulae do – the social character of the process of capitalist production. In the formula C'-C' (which is that of individual and collective social consumption), Marx notes that under real subsumption, 'the transformation is not the result of a merely formal change of position belonging to the circulation process, but rather the real transformation which the use form and the value of the commodity components of the productive capital have undergone in the production process.'[3] On this same point, Marx insists that the constitution of total social capital represents an actual 'revolution in value', and that the outcome of this movement affects the constitutive parts of the value of the social product both in terms of exchange and in terms of use. 'Those who consider the autonomisation [*Verselbststündigung*] of value as a mere abstraction forget that the movement of industrial capital is this abstraction in action'[4] – where by abstraction Marx means the ability of social capital to recompose every revolution in value, each of its violent metamorphoses, and, even more so, all of the attempts of a fraction or part of capital to make itself autonomous. So essential is this shift to enable his analysis of capital to refer the relation between circulation and production back to the matrix of valorisation that Marx claims:

> The way in which the various components of the total social capital, of which the individual capitals are only independently functioning components, alternately replace one another in the circulation process – both with respect to capital and to surplus-value – is thus not the result of the simple intertwining of the metamorphoses that occurs in commodity circulation, and which the acts of capital circulation have in common with all other processes of commodity circulation, but rather requires a different mode of investigation.[5]

That is to say, one must consider the analytical categories no longer in their genesis but as a function of antagonism in the social totality. Only at this point does theory become a weapon of class struggle. What immediately follows is that social capital can no longer be regarded as the outcome of a process of 'competition' that would determine it, as if the laws sustaining it resulted from the war that small businessmen wage against one another – no, indeed: the laws that govern the total social capital are only those emerging from antagonism, from class struggle. The shift from the 'formal subsumption' to the 'real subsumption' of the society of the collective capitalist thus entails, as a first and fundamental consequence, that the capitalist 'despotism' over the working class in the factory extend over the whole of society, eliminating that 'anarchy' that had initially appeared to be hegemonic in the game of the market.

It follows from this that the social labour power internal to this metamorphosis presents itself as an abstraction that extends over the whole realm of subsumption, that is, the whole of society. Our theory is that there is a 'common' that, inside the capitalisation of social valorisation, fights against every cage that would be predisposed to enclose it. Why do we regard this abstraction as a common power? Because it is realised and embodied by workers' cooperation in the productive process, a cooperation that becomes ever more *extensive* and *intensive* as the productive development of capital advances.

More *extensive* because, as we have seen, the capitalist response to the struggles of the 1960s and 1970s was to flee the factory, or, when the factory was preserved, to empty it of workers. However, for capital, fleeing the factory meant investing in the whole of society with productive services, and putting this to work for the production of commodities. For workers, spatial mobility and time flexibility were forms wherein the *relative independence* of the worker was expressed in new forms of cooperation at the level of society – always *subordinated* but often *independent* from the direct command of capital. Capital managed to constrain this independence in the *precarisation* of wage labour.

More *intensive* because the second capitalist response to the great cycle of workers' struggles was, beyond the spatial and social extension of working processes, a massive introduction of automation, and the digitalisation / informatisation of labour. The subsumption of realms of social cooperation was thus matched by a subsumption – in the *general intellect* – of new intellectual and linguistic energies (of a newly educated labour power). The general productivity of labour made a huge leap forward, but above all it intensified the social cooperation of productive subjects, because cognitive work thrives thanks to linguistic cooperation, the knowledge that makes it what it is, and of the singular innovation it produces. Thus, the *independence* of living labour grows in the face of the dead labour that wishes to organise it. Thus is imposed *the common* of cooperation.

This radical transformation of living labour creates great problems for capital in controlling labour power. Capital can only succeed in subordinating that relative independence of social and cognitive living labour by means of management from above. The extraction, on the part of finance, of social value by means of an increasingly rigid *governance* of the social labour process thus comes to replace the direct exploitation of individual labour that was typical of the old management techniques, and so the traditional differentiation between the realm of 'real' production and the monetary management of production no longer applies. This differentiation is now impossible to hold onto, not only politically, but also practically from a standpoint internal to the economic process in general. At this level, capitalism supports itself on *rent*. The great industrialists, instead of reinvesting profit, recycle it in the mechanisms of rent. The circuit, the blood of capital, is now rent; rent plays an essential role in the circulation of capital and the maintenance of the capitalist system: it maintains social hierarchies and the command of capital.

Money also turns into the only measure of social production. Thus, we come to a definition of money as form, blood, inner circulation, where the value that is created socially is consolidated in the economic system as a whole. Here we find the total subordination of society under capital. Labour power, the activity of society, is subsumed under this money that is at once measure, control and command. Even the political class is internal to this process, and politics dances on this tightrope. Given the situation, it is logical that rupture – any rupture – takes place within this framework. I say this provocatively, but not merely so: we need to imagine what it would be like to build a *Soviet*, to bring struggle, power, the multitude, the common, into this new reality and the new totalitarian organisations of money and finance. The multitude is exploited, but it is exploited socially, exactly as the worker used to be exploited in the factory. *Mutatis mutandis*, the struggle over wages is confirmed at the level of the social (and in money). Capital is always a relation (between those in command and the workers), within which the subsumption of labour power under money is established. However, if the capital relation stays unchanged, it is within it that any rupture is determined.

The crisis of 2007, which is unending, can be interpreted starting from these premises. The crisis stems from a need to keep order by multiplying money (*subprimes,* with the completely horrendous mechanism to which they gave rise, served the purpose of a banking system in the process of seizing global command to pay for the social reproduction of a riotous labour power). We need to get our hands on *this thing* in order to destroy its ability to command. Make no mistake about it. Contrary to interpretations of the crisis that see its cause in a detachment of finance from real production, our conviction is that financialisation is not an unproductive and parasitical deviation of growing quotas of surplus value and collective savings. This is no deviation: it is a new form of capital accumulation within new processes of social and cognitive production of value. The financial crisis developing before our eyes is to be interpreted as a response to a blockage in the accumulation of capital produced by living labour on the global stage; and as the ensuing implosive result of capital accumulation, as the difficulty this process encountered in establishing an order for its new forms of accumulation.

How does one exit a crisis of this kind? Only through a social revolution. Today, any New Deal could only amount to new rights to the social ownership of common goods – a right that is evidently opposed to private property. In other words, if up to now all access to a 'common good' has taken the form of a 'private debt', from now on it is legitimate to reclaim the same right in the form of a 'social income'.

I promised earlier to give you a second motivation for the third reason, the theoretical reason, why we should start from Marx again – a practical motivation drawn from struggles. The most recent struggles lead to this realm, the *realm of the common*, and its reappropriation on behalf of workers and citizens. I want to remind you that these struggles concern *common goods of nature*, struggles for the reappropriation of water in metropolitan communities, for air quality, for a defence from the chemical and destructive invasion of the *bios* of the earth, struggles for the reappropriation of life, and environmental struggles in general. Then, there are struggles opposing the capitalist appropriation of the *social production of the common*, the exploitation of knowledge, and capitalist domination over communication and the logistical infrastructures of social production; struggles against the appropriation of intellectual production, against copyright, against the expropriation of patents and for the transparent and democratic use of algorithms. Finally, there are struggles opposing the financial extraction of social surplus value, in defence of an unconditional citizen's income, and struggles that, opposing private property, now identify themselves as fighting for a democracy of collective appropriation of all the products of social cooperation.

Capitalist *governance* has already understood this shift in the forms of struggles. One example is the ZAD of Notre-Dame-des-Landes (an occupation of hundreds of hectares of land to prevent the building of a useless airport). Following the victory of the occupiers, and withdrawal of the project, the State proposed contracts to legalise collective enterprises that had taken shape and consolidated in the ZAD through the occupation of land and active resistance against projects of speculation. What is the condition of these contracts? That those who agree to sign them do so as individuals, as private persons; in this way, the State refused to legitimise the enterprises that, through a common experience, had collectively emerged and generated a COMMON.

### Translated by Arianna Bove

Antonio Negri was a founder of Potere Operaio in 1969. He is author of a series of books with Michael Hardt including *Empire* (2000), *Multitude* (2004), *Commonwealth* (2009) and *Assembly* (2017).

**Notes**

1. Karl Marx, *Capital, Volume 1*, trans. Ben Fowkes (London: Penguin, 1976), 344.
2. Karl Marx, *Capital, Volume 3*, trans. David Fernbach (London: Penguin, 1991), 486.
3. Karl Marx, *Capital, Volume 2*, trans. David Fernbach (London: Penguin, 1992), 175.
4. Ibid., 185
5. Ibid., 194

# Theory Redux from polity

politybooks.com

### Xenofeminism

**Helen Hester**

How should gender politics be reconfigured in a world being transformed by automation, globalization and the digital revolution? This visionary book is the essential guide to one of the most exciting intellectual trends in contemporary feminism.

March 2018 | PB 9781509520633 | £9.99

### The Playstation Dreamworld

**Alfie Bown**

"An instant classic, a book that everyone who seeks to find a way in our confused social life will have to read. The Playstation Dreamworld is unputdownable, once you start reading it you will get addicted to it... as in a good video game!"
**Slavoj Žižek**

October 2017 | PB 9781509518036 | £9.99

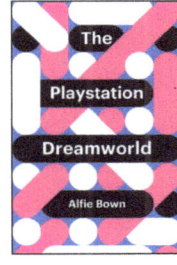

### Narcocapitalism
Life in the Age of Anaesthesia

**Laurent de Sutter**

"This fascinating book can be read in many ways: as a short history of modern psycho-pharmacology, as a theory of contemporary politics as anaesthesia of the social body, as a philosophical breakthrough on the ontological dimension of depression."
**Franco Berardi, author of *The Uprising and Heroes***

November 2017 | PB 9781509506842 | £9.99

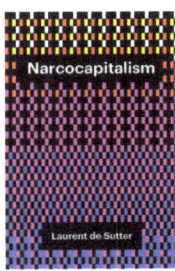

### Platform Capitalism

**Nick Srnicek**

What unites Google and Facebook, Apple and Microsoft, Uber and Airbnb? These firms are transforming themselves into platforms, signalling a major shift in how capitalist firms operate and how they interact with the rest of the economy: the emergence of 'platform capitalism'.

November 2016 | PB 9781509504879 | £9.99

To order, freephone John Wiley & Sons Ltd on **0800 243407**
politybooks.com

# The Palestinian Museum

Hanan Toukan

How are we to think about a museum that represents a people who not only do not exist on conventional maps but who are also in the process of resisting obliteration by one of the most brutal military complexes in the world? What is, and what can be, the role of a museum in a violent colonial context compounded by the twin effects of imperialism and capitalism? Whom does the museum speak for in such a context? And what can or should it say to a transterritorial nation while physically located in a supposed state-to-be, that has no real prospect of gaining control over its land, water or skies through current international diplomatic channels?

Four interrelated phenomena are central to thinking through these questions in relation to the recently opened Palestinian Museum in the university town of Birzeit in the West Bank, on a hill that offers a breathtaking view of farms, terraced hillsides and the Mediterranean Sea.[1] First, the convoluted, bureaucratic and deceptive nature of the Oslo Peace Process and the new phase of colonisation that it inaugurated in 1993.[2] This predicament, which has been described as one of living in a 'postcolonial colony'[3] is largely defined by the paradox of living in a state without sovereignty in the West Bank and Gaza under the guise of a diplomatic process leading toward a two-state solution. Under this regime, the Palestinian National Authority (PNA), established in 1994 as an outcome of the now unpopular Oslo Peace Accords, did not gain full sovereignty for itself or the Palestinian people it 'represents'. Rather, it became the middleman of the Israeli Occupation, managing security and repressing Palestinian dissent on behalf of Israel through its own internal military and intelligence apparatus, helping to intensify Israeli colonial strategies of spatial segregation and economic control. At the same time, despite its increasing unpopularity the PNA has continued to act as the internationally recognised representative of a state-to-be in international diplomacy. This role has necessitated its participation in cultural diplomacy and top-down identity formation in an attempt to rebrand the image of Palestinians as non-violent and modern global citizens residing within the 1967 borders – processes that are key to understanding how and why the Palestinian Museum has, from its inception, had to think about representing the story of the Palestinian people outside the limits of the diplomatically sanctioned, yet now probably defunct, two-state solution.[4]

Second, one must take account of ongoing Israeli colonial practices of cultural exclusion and military domination. Supported by an architecture of bureaucratic hurdles and procedures, the Israeli occupation uses a carefully designed system of legalised, institutionalised and normalised racial discrimination to debilitate the freedom of movement of objects, people and ideas that a museum or any institution of knowledge production requires in order to function. As I demonstrate, the Palestinian Museum has had to manoeuvre around this in order to materialise.

Third, the Palestinian Museum has indirectly interrogated the European museum's western-centric yet universalising mission of acquiring, conserving and displaying aesthetic objects as part of the project of constructing nation-states and indeed modernity itself. It is precisely because of the Museum's restricted spatial reality that it is able to intervene in a global discussion concerned with the role of the museum in our world. This conversation centres on the question of how to make the museum – an institution historically bound up with the emergence of the nation state and the notion of the public in eighteenth-century

Europe – relevant to the global realities that shape its direction today.⁵ The Palestinian Museum can be read as proposing answers to this question, first, through its mission of being 'a museum without borders',⁶ and second, in the very process of its construction by drawing on the land's historically terraced-landscapes to create a structure embedded in the communities and histories it seeks to speak to and for. Through this process, the Museum arguably rethinks the 'postcolonial museum'⁷ as an unstable yet dynamic memory-making institution in flux, as much a living archive of violence as an affective encounter with the weight of the land and history. In doing so, it intervenes in a global conversation about the sensorial dimensions of exhibition and collecting practices in violent settings on the margins of the global South.

The final aspect that informs my reading of the Palestinian Museum is the wave of state-supported building and renovation of museums and other art institutions underway largely in the Arab Gulf states but also in Lebanon, Egypt, Kuwait and to a lesser extent Jordan, from which the Palestinian Museum is arguably set apart by virtue of its status as an institution representing a transterritorial and stateless nation. Unlike the regional museum projects surrounding it that offer clear instances of top-down globally-attuned national identity formation, state-led societal development, and soft power and public diplomacy,⁸ the Palestinian Museum prompts a rethinking and reworking of the vexed relationship between local Palestinian non-citizens and transterritorial Palestinian publics and their supporters, on the one hand, and the aesthetic form of an exhibition and the tastes of its varied global audiences, on the other.

On the surface, it is easy to dismiss the beautifully landscaped, bunker-like, low and uneven $24 million building that has become known as the Palestinian Museum, as the vanity project of one organisation and possibly even one person. The Welfare Association, better known by its Arabic name Taawon meaning 'cooperation', Palestine's largest humanitarian and development non-governmental organisation founded in 1983 by a group of Palestinian business and intellectual figures, has spearheaded the project in its various iterations since its inception in 1997. Headed by Omar Al-Qattan, former Chairman and acting Director of the Palestinian Museum project, board member of Taawon, chairman of the Al-Qattan Foundation⁹ and son of one of Palestine and the Arab World's most beloved businessmen and philanthropists (the late Abdel Mohsen Al Qattan), Taawon played a highly visible role in the making of the museum. Taawon, which is highly respected regionally and locally in Palestine for its financial independence, especially from western funders, and for its humanitarian work, is well known for how seriously it takes its self-proclaimed mission to 'preserve the heritage of the Palestinians, supporting their living culture and building civil society'.¹⁰ The Museum, one of Taawon's flagship projects, became a crucial site for the implementation of its heritage mandate. As with most of its humanitarian projects, Taawon relied heavily on private money donated by Palestinian business entities on the association's board such as Arab Tech Jardaneh (a private practice of consulting engineers), Consolidated Contractors Company (one of the first established Arab Construction Companies), Al-Hani Construction and Trading based in Kuwait, Projacs International (the largest Pan-Arab project management firm), as well as the Bank of Palestine.

Yet as is always the case with the building of art institutions with private sector funds, questions concerning transnational financial ties, corporate ethics and relationships with local cultural elites arise. The role of Taawon prompted those working closely with the project and others observing from afar to ponder how much the project was about global capitalist elite collusion with the local NGO sector rather than a response to the needs of the Palestinian people. In this regard, people I interviewed or conversed with as part of my research raised a number of provocative questions: first, about the manner in which Taawon disbursed funds earmarked for the cultural sector to one museum as opposed to a wider range of cultural projects, arts organisations and other activist initiatives already underway in Palestine; second, about how Taawon was seen to run the museum as if it were one of its mainstream NGO socio-economic development projects, without the curatorial insight needed to get a Museum of this kind off the ground; third, in the eyes of some, especially those not working directly within the museum or in the art world, the opening of an empty museum in May 2016 made clear just how much it had been compromised by mismanagement; and finally, and perhaps most ominously, was the allegation that Taawon board members were getting returns on their in-kind donations to the Museum in a context that has allowed big businesses to set the terms of cooperation for smaller and more local businesses.

Sentiments like these gathered from discussions about the Museum are a reminder that even the most brilliantly conceived projects encounter friction when they leave the space of conception to become transformed into concrete projects. Specifically, the process by which museums located at the nexus of the colonial/postcolonial divide reinvent their spaces and visual narrations in contexts in which the divisions between public and private are opaque, and access to landscapes and architectures necessary for the movement of objects restricted, is fundamentally a question of the political economy of cultural production. Even if the Museum has been able to propose innovative museum practices (which it has), its ability to survive its near impossible predicament of belonging to a 'state' that is not in a position to defend itself, will ultimately depend on the extent to which the transnational networks, including the financial ones, that it draws upon will allow it to experiment freely with different forms of knowledge production, narrations of memory and cultural heritage preservation.

## An empty museum?

If there is a blotch on the Museum's image that metaphorically and visually represented some of the misgivings expressed about it, it was at its official opening on 18 May 2016, when there were no art objects in the building on display. The opening took place soon after the firing of Jack Persekian, the Museum's Chief Curator and Director since 2008, and one of the Arab region's most recognised contemporary arts curators, over 'planning and management issues'.[11]

The Museum was supposed to have opened with Persekian's curated project 'Never Part', which was to have featured illustrative material objects from the lives of Palestinian refugees all over the world. The 'Never Part' team envisioned and worked towards an empty museum for the opening, but they wanted interventions from artists contemplating the emptiness of the building vis-à-vis Palestine's experience of having had its material culture confiscated, destroyed or disappeared to accompany this emptiness. The point was to reflect on Palestine's predicament – its lack of control over borders, waters and skies – and to question the meaning of a museum, the artefacts and collecting practices that supposedly define it, in the case of a people violently dispersed all over the globe and prevented from accessing their past and material present. In *Art Is Not What You Think It Is*, Claire Farago and Donald Preziosi demonstrate how the architecture of contemporary museums inspires active relationships between exhibitions and visitors, thereby provoking the potential that germinates in the built structure of the museum.[12] Accordingly, when artists and curators are invited to converse with the spaces of museums rather than contexts of art-in-architecture, unexpected capacities may be set in motion which go beyond the ordinary encounters of exhibitions and spectatorship, works and visitors. Persekian and his team, conversant in global art theory and practice, were working within a genealogy of modern and contemporary art that conceptualised and theorised the museum space as an artwork and a statement in and of itself.[13]

But having the museum empty for the official opening, which was scheduled to coincide with Nakba Day,[14] did not go down well with the Museum Task Force set up by Taawon to take charge of the museum project. Less interested in the language of conceptual art and the contemporary global artscape's often experimental approach to engaging with the political, and more concerned with the Museum's role as a local cultural institution that speaks to the transterritorial Palestinian reality of displacement, solidarity networks and grassroots initiatives, Taawon might have seen in the proposed opening a shift in the role of the Museum from borderless centre for Palestinian culture and heritage to what they perceived as an overly abstract and theorised project conversing more with the global art sphere than the local cultural scene.[15] Being a grassroots organisation, Taawon may also have been attuned to the fact that Palestinians, who lack sufficient access to their own artefacts but who value whatever material culture they are still in possession of as a means of historical narration, needed to see a museum that carried their name with objects in it if only as a symbolic affirmation of their existence. Hence, even if the tradition of the empty museum (whether empty of audiences or artefacts) may have been an apt framework for highlighting the Palestinian condition in conceptual terms, in the Palestinian context, it takes on a different meaning.

When the Jewish Museum first opened without objects in Berlin in 1999 it was to highlight the eerily claustrophobic and uneven architecture of the zinc-clad building that was meant to evoke feelings of fear, disorientation and paranoia, even though the point of the museum was to celebrate Jewish contributions to the history of the city.[16] The initial emptiness of the Museum corresponded to the message being conveyed. In the case of the Palestinians, history has put them in the absurd position of perpetually having to convince the rest of the world of their very existence. In response, scholars, artists and filmmakers working in and on Palestine, interested in countering orientalist tropes representing the Palestinian as terrorist, victim or romantic revolutionary, are slowly building a formidable archive of the historical fact and experience of ongoing dispossession and displacement, but also continued survival on the land. By recording and proactively re-organising existing oral and visual testaments of surviving witnesses they are reassembling the story of the Palestinian struggle into a coherent and introspective counternarrative that rejects the central tenets underscoring the media and public discourse on Islam, Arabs and the Palestinians. Even if it is difficult to access, cultural heritage and specifically material culture is the site where this reclamation of narrative is fought for most fiercely.

Ironically, notwithstanding Taawon's misgivings about the curatorial conceptualisation of emptiness, the Museum ended up being empty on the day of its opening thanks to a series of internal developments that culminated in the dismissal of Persekian, officially attributed to differences over 'planning and management'.[17] Despite viewing the Museum as incomplete, Taawon decided to move ahead with its opening to honour the promise they had made to open it on Nakba day.[18]

It was difficult to ignore the ironies implicit in the opening of the empty Museum in 2016 by the ever-unpopular Mahmoud Abbas, president of the PNA. This was especially true of mainstream Western media coverage. Headlines such as 'Palestinian Museum Opens Without Exhibits', 'The Palestinian Museum Set to Open, Empty of Art', or, more provocatively, 'Palestinian museum opening without exhibits, but creators say that's no big deal' were predictably unkind.[19] Cynically hinting at a people with neither the capacity nor the cultural history required to fill such an expensive and well-designed building, the media latched on to the fact that the Museum was empty. Conveniently, these same media outlets almost entirely ignored the reality of Palestinian existence as a dispossessed people with histories, memories and material cultures scattered all over the world or stolen by their colonisers through the cultural appropriation of music, books, art and food, or the seizure of objects and especially archives.[20] This reality, in addition to the lack of control over the movement necessary for the travel of art objects – normally central to a museum's practice – makes compiling, acquiring and exhibiting works an almost impossible feat.

In artist Khaled Hourani's 2009 art project 'Picasso in Palestine', Pablo Picasso's 1943 portrait of his lover Françoise Gilot, *Buste de femme*, was exhibited on the grounds of the International Art Academy of Palestine in Ramallah. The bringing of Picasso's *Buste* to Ramallah, a collaborative effort between the International Academy of Art Palestine (IAAP) and the Van Abbemuseum in the Netherlands which began at the Middle East Summit held at the museum in 2008, was nearly three years in the making. In Hourani's project, the process of bringing one of Picasso's most famous works to Palestine included wrestling with the thorny politics of Oslo, international protocols defining museum loan traditions that normally deal only with sovereign states, the bureaucratic measures implementing so-called peace agreements, and Israel's control over checkpoints, airports and international insurance requirements. The point of the intriguing, even if overly elaborate and expensive, project was to highlight just how difficult it would be to bring artworks to Palestine.

## On the political economy of museums

Only a few months after the tumultuous official opening of the Museum without art objects in it, in a much discussed public speech as part of the Young Artists of the Year Award (YAYA), hosted annually by the Abdel Mohsen Qattan Foundation,[21] Al-Qattan reproached the failure of the Palestinian cultural and artistic milieu in the era of Oslo to produce any meaningful dialogue or questions about the demise of the Palestinian national project.[22] Having just returned from a trip to Gaza, Al-Qattan – also the director of the Al-Qattan Foundation, one of Ramallah's most prominent cultural institutions – seemed to be lashing out at the entire cultural scene. In fact, Al-Qattan expressed the discomfort that many, if not most members of the public, including writers, intellectuals and artists, feel in the West Bank and Gaza about the extent to which cultural work and especially the visual arts have been able to engage with the collective Palestinian experience of oppression. In his words, he wanted to use the opportunity of the YAYA to address what he described as a 'quickness, superficiality and general disengagement with historical and political subjects'.[23]

Much has already been written about the debilitating and depoliticising effects of the NGO-isation process sponsored by international aid to the region – a process that has led to what is described by Palestinians as the collapse of the national liberation project. With globalisation and transnational cultural markets becoming the norm as elsewhere, artists and their institutions have not only been forced to readdress their role in the politics of the region and the transnational networks they need in order to survive, but also to present Palestine's plight and contributions to critical global conversations in the arts and activism more broadly. In Palestinian artist Khaled Hourani's words, 'Artists started to reconsider the perception of arts, portraits, borders, artistic values, relations of artworks and exhibits, audience and arts dealers.'[24] Whether, as a generation of artists, they were in fact able to do so without compromising on the core values of cultural resistance and the role of contemporary art in it, is today a central and uncomfortable discussion in Palestinian cultural circles.

Interestingly, on the day of the official inauguration of the museum in 2016, the building was empty of artefacts but not of objects such as the materials needed for the construction of the museum like shovels, barrels and piles of cement. As some critics of the museum quipped, the fact that the museum was not emptied of its construction materials was a visual reminder of precisely how tied up it was in global capital circulation and real-estate development, a marker of Post-Oslo Palestine *par excellence*, rather than a representation of the dispossessed and oppressed people it supposedly represented.[25] This observation, which directly references the landscape dotted with cranes used to build the five-star hotels, restaurants and upmarket housing that have come to define the 'elite-driven production of space' in Ramallah in particular, prods us to think about the tensions between the provenance of the museum's capital and what it symbolises.[26]

It is a fact that most of the investors in the Palestinian Museum were businessmen who made their money in the Arab Gulf. It is also believed that donations included in-kind contributions, revenue from which was channelled back into the construction, management and development firms of some of the board's members. Adam Hanieh has shown how the internationalisation of Gulf capital throughout the economies of the Middle East has been a central feature of regional capitalist development over the last two decades.[27] Palestinian class formation since Oslo has gone hand in hand with the internationalisation of capital, a process that sits at the heart of the economic doctrine of neoliberalism. Hanieh posits that Palestinian class formation cannot be understood solely through the prism of Palestine's subordination to Israel. Important businesses based in the Gulf have played a critical role in restructuring society in ways that make it highly reliant and dependent on transnational capital in order to survive. Along these lines, Sherene Seikaly provides a fascinating account of a dynamic class of Palestinian capitalist entrepreneurs involved in both local and regional trade, enabling us to historicise today's class of Museum investors.[28] Contemporary businesses are part of a longer genealogy of capital accumulation and investment in Palestine and the region at large. At the same time, they are only one component in a contingently linked cluster of people, technology, objects and knowledge which circulate through the social and economic fields that museums inhabit.[29] This raises a question: even if the site of construction material and workers visually symbolise Ramallah's role in the normalisation of the Occupation, and provoked the ambivalent feelings that some felt toward the opening of an empty museum, might it still be possible to separate the function of the Museum as resistant praxis from the context of its provenance?

## Landscape and architecture

Taking up a mere 3000 square metres of the 40,000 square metre plot on which it stands, the landscape in which the Museum is set is as aesthetically and politically significant as the building and its artefacts. The visual and sensorial experience of standing in the foyer of the building is one of an affective encounter with the weight of history, the land and continued presence on it. Indeed the topography of the land on which the Museum is built and its terraced gardens designed, were as significant to the conceptualisation of the Museum as the building itself. According to Lara Zureikat, the landscape architect based in neighbouring Amman, understanding traditional practices of horticulture and working with the site's slopes and its existing plants were central to the Museum's mission to respect the cultural and natural heritage of the landscape and its determination not to disrupt it yet again.[30] This is in reference, and contrast, to the Israeli Occupation's practice of intercepting and intervening in the harmony of the landscape for settlement construction, surveillance and wall building purposes which sever Palestinians' access to cultivable land.[31] Predictably, Zureikat, who is a Jordanian national, was prevented by Israel from visiting the site of the project. She and her team resorted to the use of satellite imagery and internet communication to finalise the project. This reveals how, from the beginning, the process of turning the Museum into a material reality from an idea was imbricated with the Museum's objective of building on the transterritorial reality of Palestinians by thinking imaginatively about modes of delivery.

The building is therefore physically and conceptually responsive to its landscape and built environment. In the words of Conor Sreenan, chief architect of the project from the Dublin-based architecture firm Heneghan Peng, 'It was the physical that introduced us to the geopolitical. We literally traced the existing topography and looked at the way that the landscape had been inhabited for 2000 plus years'.[32] The idea, he explained, was not to be defined by the Occupation but rather to take back control of the landscape.

The hills of the West Bank, on which sit illegal Jewish settlements, visually embody what settler colonialism entails and the consequences it has had. Some of these include moving communities into territories acquired in war – a Zionist practice that predates the establishment of the Israeli State – in addition to settler violence against local Palestinian communities and the imposition of new demographic realities on the ground that will not only threaten the form but the very possibility of a future Palestinian State. The planting on the grounds of the Museum of groves of apricot, pomegranate, mulberry, cypress, olive, walnut and fig trees, lemons and oranges, herbs like zaatar, mint and other plants that Israel has appropriated as part of a policy of erasing the memory and identity of Palestinian people, are a step towards reclaiming what has been taken away.

But standing inside the small Museum and looking out of the floor-to-ceiling windows that adorn an entire wall that overlooks the hills and the Mediterranean Sea in the distance that Palestinians are barred from reaching, thanks to Israeli imposed restrictions on movement, the foundation on which Zionism stands is usurped, even mocked, if only momentarily. In other words, instead of directly confronting politics as such, the Museum may in fact be aiming to create a platform from which to expand the meaning of the political to include not only critical thought and the collection and exhibition of dispersed art, but also to link the lived and built environments and peoples' relationships to each of these. With this in mind, even the sight of the unpopular Mahmoud Abbas cutting the ribbon on the opening day becomes more palatable.

## The art institution, the state and decolonisation

The PNA complained about the Museum's apparent appropriation of what it saw as the state's role of cultural patronage, most visibly in the name the museum chose for itself: 'The Palestinian Museum'. Despite this point of contention, Taawon felt the need to be courteous and to invite the President because in the end, as Al-Qattan explained, 'we need to work with the existing bureaucratic structure and engage it, regardless of who is in power. We cannot function in isolation'.[33] Al Qattan's reasoning might sit uncomfortably with activists who see resisting colonial violence as a fundamentally confrontational act that requires tackling head-on the PNA's role as middleman of the Occupation. Yet it is perhaps the only way in which to get a grand project of this kind off the ground in colonised Palestine today. The question that this reality begs is whether a museum of this kind was needed and whether Taawon would have done better to distribute its millions to the multitude of artists, writers, film-makers, collectives, activists and smaller-scale arts organisations that are working laboriously to collect and document Palestine's history and cultural heritage – a question I heard on numerous occasions in the field.

Rasha Salti and Kristine Khouri's *Past Disquiet: Narratives and Ghosts from the International Art Exhibition for Palestine, 1978* revisits the making of The International Art Exhibition for Palestine which opened in Beirut in the spring of 1978 and which comprised some 200 works donated by artists in solidarity with Palestine from nearly 30 countries. Following its inauguration in Beirut, and after parts of it had travelled to Japan, Norway and then Iran some years later, the Israeli Army invaded Beirut in the summer of 1982 with the aim of flushing out the PLO. The building where the collection was stored was bombed, along with the offices of the PLO's Office of Unified Information where most of the archive of the exhibition would have been stored. Salti and Khouri's painstakingly curated exhibition traces the sheer challenge of locating the works, archives, stories and memories scattered today all over the globe, but which were intended as a seed collection for a museum in exile until the moment it could 'return' to a free Palestine.[34]

Palestinian artist Nasser Soumi has been working since the mid-1990s to recover some of this lost cultural history by navigating the labyrinth of facts, urban legends, hints, clues and social tensions that cluster around some of the disappeared paintings that featured in the show. When I recently asked him about his evident personal need to do so in the face of challenges he has faced from colleagues as well as the PNA that point to the impossibility of such collecting practices, he replied that Palestinians need some semblance of an art institution especially as their so-called state refuses to look for the story of resistance in places where it is not in control.[35] For him, finding these works and knowing their story is a way for Palestinians to reclaim part of their lost archive.

These histories and artistic initiatives point to the importance of a site around which an oppressed people fighting for liberation may gather to (re)present their narratives, (re)negotiate their strategies of protest in the face of oppression and reflect on their colonial pasts and presents by referencing objects and ideas that are accessible to them in physical or virtual form. From plans to set up a virtual museum and online archival platforms to the construction of satellite museums (in Chile, the US, UK, Jordan and Lebanon) and the novel incorporation of landscape and topography into its programmatic definition and practices, the Palestinian Museum has committed itself in both concept and practice to ongoing anticolonial and decolonisation processes.[36] Its space is, then, equally a potential launch pad for interventions into discourses on, and practices of, 'decolonisation', and specifically the 'de-westernising' of knowledge production in a changing postcolonial world, by calling into question the principles that sustain the current dominant knowledge production system, particularly in respect of art and museums in this case.[37]

To appreciate what a significant institution the Museum is, despite its precariousness, we need to revisit Palestinian historian Beshara Doumani's original conception of the project and the strategic plan he envisioned for it. Doumani was invited by Taawon in 2010 to submit a proposal for a museum to the organisation's Palestinian Museum Task Force. To this day, the Museum continues to use his original proposal as the blueprint for ongoing development of the project, even if it has been modified somewhat along the way. Doumani envisioned the museum as 'post-territorial' (in its need to encompass Palestinians who are scattered transterritorially and unable to access their homeland) and as 'a mobilising and interactive cultural project that can stitch together the fragmented Palestinian body politic by presenting a wide variety of narratives about the relationships of Palestinians to the land, to each other and to the wider world'.[38] His starting point wasn't the geographical locale of the West Bank and Gaza – even if the museum building would be situated near Ramallah, the purported capital of a future Palestinian State – but rather the dispersed and divided Palestinian population brought together through online technology.[39] This population is composed of Gazans under siege, Jerusalemite Palestinians walled off from the rest of their people, Palestinians living in the West Bank who are intercepted, harassed, enclosed and surrounded by a complex of Israeli checkpoints, as well the Palestinian citizens of Israel and all those living as refugees in neighbouring Arab countries and as exiles in the rest of the world.

Doumani, like Soumi and others who witnessed or remember Israel's destruction of the Palestine Information Department, sees the importance of investing in the materiality of cultural practices, even if they will always be under existential threat and part and parcel of global capital circuits. In reality, the multi-million dollar investment project that is the Museum can neither be defended nor easily rebuilt, should Israel decide to destroy it at any point. The Museum, like other initiatives in Palestine, whether 'state'- or civil society-led, is vulnerable to the closures, looting and destruction to which all Palestinian cultural heritage has always been subject. This destruction is a possibility that financial investors have had to contend with. Sreenan describes the stoic perseverance of financial and other investors in the project during the dark days of the Gaza slaughter by Israel in 2014 as 'possibly one of the most graceful acts of resistance one could ever witness'.[40]

Hence the question of the museum's role vis-à-vis the power structures it has to counter in the case of Israel and contend with in the case of the PNA was never one about whether its construction would in and of itself be a compromise with the post-Oslo configuration of power. Rather, it was always about how it would negotiate with these power structures in order to position itself as a space of critique, resistance and decoloniality in the convoluted colonial context of Post-Oslo Palestine. As Doumani puts it, complicating the issue, 'How this is done, of course, is of utmost importance'.[41]

## In the company of other museums

The Palestinian Museum was first envisioned as a commemorative structure built around a single chronological narrative that begins in 1948. As it developed, it became clear to all those involved that in distancing itself from 1948 as the starting point of a chronological historical narrative, it would reject the standard Zionist line that the notion of a Palestinian people was an idea constructed only after the establishment of the state of Israel in 1948. By beginning in the 18th century, it was agreed, the museum would better reflect the reality of the Palestinians as a dispersed people with urban, rural and intellectual histories who were in existence well before Zionists began to arrive in Palestine and violently established their state. In this, the Museum positions itself as a counternarrative not only to Israeli self-deception about the persecuted Jews of Europe having arrived to a land without a people, but also to the PNA's framing of the Palestinians as a people whose existence is articulated solely in opposition to Israel as is evident in the museum projects in which it is involved.[42]

In both the Al-Birweh Park/Mahmoud Darwish Museum and the Yasser Arafat Museum in Ramallah (opened in 2014 and 2016 respectively), the PNA wrests control over narration from the people it governs in the name of figures who were dominant players (and narrators) in the Palestinian resistance movement and, in the case of Arafat, the Palestinian state formation project in the aftermath of the Oslo Accords. In other words, unlike the Palestinian Museum, the emphasis in the PNA's new multimillion-dollar museum projects is more on state power and state building than on agency, peoplehood and transterritoriality. More crucially, by focusing on Arafat and Darwish as the main characters in a story about the Palestinian struggle, the resistance is reified and commodified in ways that are both fathomable on the international stage and productive of nostalgia for the local public. What is insinuated through the aesthetics and narratives of the museums is that these figures are part of the struggle for independence from Israel that has supposedly been achieved with the signing of Oslo. They are stories from a glorious past, relics from a bygone era, what Svetlana Boym has termed a 'dictatorship of nostalgia' that reigns at the supposed 'end' of a conflict.[43] Or alternatively, they are a chance to critique the past in order to imagine the future, as the director of the Yasser Arafat Museum suggested when I proposed my cynical reading to him.[44] Ultimately, the differing temporal orientations of the Darwish and Arafat Museums dedicated to the past as a way of thinking about the future, on the one hand, and the Palestinian Museum focused on the continuing reality of colonisation, on the other, are reflected in the way one affectively experiences each of the museums.

Both the PNA's museum projects are exercises in formal and institutional design that evoke the state's legitimacy. By commissioning the late Ja'afar Tuqan, one of the Arab World's most renowned modernist architects – known for his functionalism, simplicity and minimalism expressed in major institutional buildings such as mosques, government offices, banks and schools throughout the Levant and the Arab Gulf over the past forty years – the PNA was asserting its role as the neutral state apparatus representing the public interest. In the case of the Mahmoud Darwish Museum, which is also the 'temporary' mausoleum of Palestine's most loved poet, the small and darkened space that sits atop a mountain of stairs, and which holds most of Darwish's personal writings and belongings, could be an exhibition space visualising state grandeur anywhere in the world.[45] Unlike the Palestinian Museum, there is nothing inside save for the writings and book covers of Darwish's publications encased on the walls that tells visitors where they are. Formally, this could be a minimalist exhibition anywhere. Yet like the Palestinian Museum, the Darwish Museum also deploys indigenous plants and the terraced gardening typical of the landscape to emphasise Palestinian claims over the land.

The role of museums in contributing to visualising national identity is clearly identified in postcolonial literature.[46] How political actors make use of these institutions as tools for the conduct of diplomacy or to claim a symbolic significance for the nation-state through the collections that are held within them are matters that relate to the political function of museums and the emotions they conjure up for the communities they represent.[47] Yet the building of Palestine's museums, whether by civil society and private capital or by the state, cannot be fully understood outside of the tide of museum building in the region. Focusing on national identity, societal development and international understanding, museums in the Arab Gulf states of Qatar and the UAE have taken it upon themselves in recent years to redraw Arab and Muslim identity on the global map as part of a larger process of diversifying their oil-based economies by investing in other areas.[48] Despite replicating the tools, modes and ideas of western museum construction and maintenance, Gulf states have been credited with taking the initiative to de-westernise and decolonise Arab representations by delinking them from their original source: the western museum and its historic relationship to the nation state in the time of Empire.

In the words of the decolonial theorist Walter Mignolo, writing about the Qatari Museum of Islamic Art in Doha: 'What is happening is not merely an imitation of westernisation, but an enactment of de-westernisation in that western cultural standards are being appropriated and adapted to local or regional sensibilities, needs and visions. In the sphere of civilisations and museums, this is a significant departure.'[49] The suggestion that he and others have made is that prosperous and stable Arab capitals like Doha, Dubai, Abu Dhabi and Muscat have the capability to redraw the global cultural map by redefining the Arab capital in a manner that is neither 'Eurocentric nor Europhobic; neither retrograde nativist nor rootless cosmopolitan'.[50]

While there is something to these celebratory and hopeful takes on art infrastructure in the Gulf, what seems to be missing is an examination of how tied up these spaces are in regional geo-politics, economic diversification strategies and military alliances with western powers (evidenced not least by the location of military bases such as those of France in the UAE or the US in Qatar), even if they are seemingly de-westernising art discourses and collecting practices by re-routing the direction of travel and sales of each.

Decolonial claims do not seem to factor in the corporate power that often shapes the conversations that take place in and about museums, even if these museums – especially as in the case of the Gulf museums – are able to reverse art market trends by paying more for artworks than traditional western art patrons, such as the British Museum, are able to today. I would argue that this process by itself is not proof that a decolonial epistemic shift is occurring in the absence of evidence of the production of one's own knowledge on one's own terms, outside of market constraints.

My reference to other museums in Palestine and the Arab region more generally is not intended to suggest that the Palestinian Museum is somehow more resistant or more worthy as a museum 'for the people by the people'. Instead, my point concerns the need to start a conversation about the content and form of museums in the region that do not fit the emerging Gulf museum format of massive, powerful symbols of capital defined by aesthetically minimalist, white cube styles that are a means to exhume global relevance and centrality. I want to ask how smaller 'postcolonial' museums, like the Palestinian Museum, that are not commissioned as part of a larger national strategic plan, intervene in the space of 'decoloniality' that the Gulf is ironically now celebrated as spearheading.

It is no coincidence that the financial patrons of the Palestinian Museum have made their money in the Gulf. It is also possible that future links between the Palestinian Museum and Gulf museums will be solidified through staff training and other professional and infrastructural development that will be needed as the Palestinian Museum grows. What these links will signify, and how they will shape the direction that the Museum will take, warrant continuing scrutiny and discussion.

The Palestinian Museum's mission of wresting back the narratives, material culture and memories that have been so crudely taken away from the Palestinian people is a reminder of an integral element of decolonisation. If we think of decolonisation in the realm of museum curation as entailing not simply a decentring of the art market and the flows of art sales as suggested in the decolonial claims of Mignolo and others,[51] but also a forestalling of the violence of amnesia and narrative erasure that accompanies colonialism in Palestine, a new emancipatory definition of the term may be enunciated. For all its faults and the criticism it might incur in the future, the Palestinian Museum is ultimately striving to seize control over its destiny not only from its oppressor Israel but also from hegemonic understandings and practices of statehood, peoplehood, space, time and architecture. For that, it should be celebrated not only as a triumphant moment in the cultural history of the Palestinian people, but also as a genuinely emancipatory moment in the grand project of epistemic decolonisation, for Palestinians and for other colonised peoples everywhere.

*Hanan Toukan is Visiting Professor of Cultural Studies of the Middle East at Bamberg University. She is currently working on a book manuscript entitled* A Global Political: Art, Dissent and Diplomacy in the Arab World, *under contract with Stanford University Press.*

**Notes**

1. It is not my intention in this article to deal with the programmatic direction, thematic focus and evolving organisational structure of the Museum. Nor do I tackle the Museum's early exhibitions, 'Jerusalem Lives' and 'Labour of Love: New Approaches to Palestinian Embroidery', even though they are part of the larger research project from which this article stems. Here, I am interested in the conceptual underpinnings of the museum and how they relate to more general questions about the political economy of art institutions in violent and marginal contexts.
2. Adam Hanieh, 'The Oslo Illusion,' *Jacobin* (April 2013), jacobinmag.com/2013/04/the-oslo-illusion
3. Joseph Massad, 'The "Post-colonial" Colony: Time, Space, and Bodies in Palestine/Israel', in *The Pre-occupation of Postcolonial Studies*, eds. Fawzia Afzal-Khan and Kalpana Seshadri-Crooks (Durham, NC: Duke University Press 2000), 311–46.
4. As I write these words, Palestinians are attempting to come to terms with President Trump's declaration of Jerusalem as Israel's capital in December 2017, in effect putting an end to the two-state solution and the long discredited Oslo Peace Process.
5. See Eilean Hooper-Greenhill, *Museums and the Interpretation of Culture* (London and New York: Routledge, 2000).
6. See the Museum's website on this concept: palmuseum.org/about/the-building-2.
7. On the 'postcolonial museum', see Alessandra De Angelis, Celeste Ianniciello, Mariangela Orabona and Iain Chambers, eds., *The Postcolonial Museum: The Arts of Memory and the Pressures of History* (Abingdon: Routledge, 2016); Sonja

Mejcher-Atassi and John Pedro Schwartz, eds., *Archives, Museums and Collecting Practices in the Modern Arab World* (Abingdon: Routledge, 2016), which have paved the way for a reconceptualisation of objects and collections as 'processes or practices and not just things'; see also Elizabeth Edwards, Chris Gosden and Ruth B. Phillips, eds., *Sensible Objects: Colonialism, Museums and Material Culture* (Oxford: Berg, 2006).

8. See for instance Pamela Erskine-Loftus, Victoria Penziner Hightower and Mariam Ibrahim Al-Mulla, eds., *Representing the Nation: Heritage, museums, national narratives and identity in the Arab Gulf States* (Abingdon: Routledge, 2016); Hayfa Matar 'Museums as Signifiers in the Gulf', in *Cities, Museums and Soft Power*, eds. Gail Dexter Lord and Ngaire Blankenberg (Washington, DC: The AAM Press, 2015). Peggy Levitt, *Artifacts and Allegiances: How Museums Put the Nation and the World on Display* (Oakland, CA: University of California Press, 2015) offers a dynamic approach to understanding museums' roles as sites of cosmopolitanism in an increasingly transnationalised and global world.

9. The A. M. Qattan Foundation (AMQF) is an independent, not-for-profit developmental organisation working in the fields of culture and education, with a particular focus on children, teachers and young artists.

10. Taawon, accessed 13 March 2018, taawon.org.

11. *Artforum*, 'Jack Persekian, Director of Palestinian Museum, resigns', accessed 19 October 2017, artforum.com/news/jack-persekian-director-of-palestinian-museum-resigns-56674.

12. Donald Preziosi and Claire Farago, *Art Is Not What You Think It Is* (Oxford: Wiley-Blackwell, 2012).

13. See for instance Steven Conn, *Do Museums Still Need Objects?* (Philadelphia: University of Pennsylvania Press, 2010); Edwards et al., eds., *Sensible Objects*.

14. Nakba is the Arabic word for catastrophe and Nakba Day (May 15) was officially designated by Yasser Arafat in 1998 as the official day of mourning to coincide with Israel's official celebration of its establishment in 1948.

15. For Al-Qattan's criticisms of the global artworld's approach to cultural production which he sees as 'far too restricted, abstract, filled with jargon, falsely academic', see Shany Littman, 'Even Empty, the new Palestinian Museum Is Making History', *Haaretz*, 26 May 2016, haaretz.com/israel-news/culture/.premium-1.721510

16. Esra Akcan, 'Apology and Triumph: Memory Transference, Erasure, and a Rereading of the Berlin Jewish Museum', *New German Critique* 37:2 (2010), 153–179.

17. *Artforum*, 'Jack Persekian'; James Glanz and Rami Nazzal, 'Palestinian Museum Prepares to Open, Minus Exhibitions', *The New York Times*, 16 May 2016, nytimes.com/2016/05/17/world/middleeast/palestinian-museum-birzeit-west-bank.html

18. Zina Jardaneh, chair of the Board of the Palestinian Museum, interview with author, 17 December 2017.

19. 'New Palestinian museum opens without exhibits', BBC News, 18 May 2016, bbc.com/news/world-middle-east-36322756; William Booth, 'Palestinian museum opening without exhibits, but creators say that's no big deal', *The Washington Post*, 18 May 2016; 'Palestinian history museum opens without any exhibits', *Associated Press*, 19 May 2016, ynetnews.com/articles/0,7340,L-4805141,00.html

20. See for instance Hannah Mermelstein, 'Overdue Books: Returning Palestine's "Abandoned Property" of 1948', *Jerusalem Quarterly* 47 (2011); Gish Amit, 'Owner-less Objects? The story of the books Palestinians left behind in 1948', *Jerusalem Quarterly* 36 (2009); Sarah Irving, '"Endangered Archives" program opens up priceless Palestinian heritage', *The Electronic Intifada*, 13 May 2014, electronicintifada.net/blogs/sarah-irving/endangered-archives-program-opens-pricless-palestinian-heritage

21. The Young Artist Award, named after the late artist Hassan Hourani, is one of the most important events in the visual arts calendar of Palestine and has been organised on a biannual basis by the A.M. Qattan Foundation since 2000.

22. For some who were present at the YAYA ceremony, Al Qattan's words were harsh generalisations that overlooked the real achievement in getting Palestine on to the world cultural map. For others, Al-Qattan was pushing his audience to think honestly and critically about the global political economy of arts production that Palestinian artists, like artists elsewhere, have had to negotiate with, often at the expense of effacing local historical and ongoing processes of resistance. See Tarek Hamdan, 'Omar Al-Qattan: Bakae'ya Muta'akhira ... Walakin' ('Omar Al-Qattan: A Belated Jeremiad ... or Not'). *Al Akhbar*, 26 October 2016. Al-Qattan offered a detailed response to the *Al-Akhbar* piece, which he saw as wrongfully representing his statement: '(Cultural) Palestine Will not Die', A.M. Qattan Foundation, accessed 19 February 2018, qattanfoundation.org/en/qattan/media/news/omar-al-qattan-cultural-palestine-will-not-die.

23. Interview with author, 20 December 2017.

24. Khaled Hourani, 'Globalisation Questions and Contemporary Art's Answers: Art in Palestine', in *Globalisation and Contemporary Art*, ed. Jonathan Harris (Oxford: Wiley-Blackwell, 2009), 301.

25. Lara Khalidi, independent curator from Palestine takes up this point in her paper 'The Museum Before the Museum', presented at Harvard Graduate School Quincy School of Design, 6 November 2017.

26. Nasser Abourahme, 'The Bantustan Sublime: Reframing the Colonial in Ramallah', *City* 13:4 (2009), 499–509.

27. Adam Hanieh, *Capitalism and Class in the Gulf Arab States* (New York: Palgrave Macmillan, 2011).

28. Sherene Seikaly, *Men of Capital: Scarcity and Economy in Mandate Palestine* (Stanford, CA: Stanford University Press, 2016).

29. Levitt, *Artifacts and Allegiances*, 8.

30. Lara Zureikat, phone interview with author, 23 November 2017.

31. Eyal Weizman, *Hollow Land: Israel's Architecture of Occupation* (London: Verso, 2012), 120.

32. Conor Sreenan, phone interview with author, 5 December 2017.

33. Omar Al-Kattan, phone interview with author, 17 December 2017.

34. For the curators' description of the project and its content, see Kristine Khouri and Rasha Salti, 'Past Disquiet: From Research to Exhibition', *Artl@s Bulletin* 5:1 (2016), Article 8.

35. This conversation was part of an exchange I had with Soumi and others on a panel titled 'Before the Museum', for which I was invited to be the discussant, as part of the symposium *Shifting Ground: The Underground Is Not the Past* held at the Khalil Sakakini Cultural Centre as part of the Sharjah Biennial 13: Tamawuj chapter held in Ramallah between 10-14 August 2017.

36. For instance, the Museum is currently running two projects, 'Palestinian Journeys' and the 'Palestinian Museum Digital Archive', that constitute a large part of the open access digital platform that will collect, organise and archive Palestinian history in Palestine. See, palmuseum.org/projects/e-platforms-1.

37. For an earlier take on the changing scope and content of the decolonisation process, see Jan Nederveen Pieterse and Bhikhu Parekh, eds., *The Decolonisation of Imagination: Culture, Knowledge and Power* (London: Zed Books, 1995).

38. Ursula Biemman, 'A Post-Territorial Museum: Interview with Beshara Doumani', *ArteEast Quarterly*, 1 February 2010, arteeast.org/quarterly/a-post-territorial-museum/?issues_season=spring&issues_year=2010.

39. I am not suggesting that this approach is the Palestinian Museum's alone. Since the late 1990s many museums have invested in an online presence by incorporating a wide range of web-based formats into their programmes and exhibits to enable access by a global public.

40. Conor Sreenan, skype interview with author, 5 December 2017.

41. Beshara Doumani, informal discussion with author, Providence, RI, 4 December 2017.

42. I want to stress here that this counternarrative is extremely important and necessary insofar as it responds to Israel's military and Zionist discursive narrative that attempts to erase the Palestinian people. However, there is a need to go beyond the defensive. As Doumani puts it, 'how can Palestinians take control of and shape their own narratives, but not in a defensive mechanical way that simply responds to how they are represented by others?'(Biemman, 'A Post-Territorial Museum'.)

43. Svetlana Boym, *The Future of Nostalgia* (New York: Basic Books, 2002), 354.

44. Mohammad Halayka, interview with author, Ramallah, 23 May 2018.

45. Both the mausoleums of Yasser Arafat and Mahmoud Darwish are generally regarded as temporary in anticipation of the day when they can be transplanted to Jerusalem, the occupied capital city that Palestinians, like Israelis, perceive as theirs.

46. Rodney Harrison and Lotte Hughes, 'Heritage, Colonialism and Postcolonialism', in *Understanding the Politics of Heritage*, ed. Rodney Harrison (Manchester: Manchester University Press, 2010).

47. Clive Gray, *The Politics of Museums* (Basingstoke: Palgrave Macmillan, 2015); Melissa Nisbett, 'New perspectives on instrumentalism: an empirical study of cultural diplomacy', *International Journal of Cultural Policy* 19:5 (2013), 557–575. It is also interesting to take note of a roundtable discussion conducted between Jack Persekian, the former director of the Palestinian Museum, curator Lara Khalidi and artist Yazan Khalil, on the nature of a museum in the context of a state that does not exist. Khalidi questions whether Palestinians are able to creatively take advantage of their non-state status to interrogate other forms of political existence that the museum could experiment with. The one point that Persekian goes back to is that the museum is a civil society project that does not intend to represent the state but rather, works in parallel to it. See *Muqaddima fi al Mathaf al Falastinya* (Welfare Association and the Palestinian Museum, 2014), 10–14.

48. Suzi Mirgani, 'Introduction: Art and Cultural Production in the GCC', *Journal of Arabian Studies* 7:1 (2017).

49. Walter Mignolo, 'Enacting the Archives, Decentering the Muses: The Museum of Islamic Art in Doha and the Asian Civilisations Museum in Singapore', *Ibraaz* Platform 006 (2013), 11–12, ibraaz.org/usr/library/documents/main/enacting-the-archives.pdf.

50. Hamid Dabashi, 'Rethinking the Arab capital through art', *Al Jazeera*, 10 April 2017, aljazeera.com/indepth/opinion/2017/04/rethinking-arab-capital-art-170409105111270.html and 'What are the Saudis afraid of?', *Al Jazeera*, 17 December 2017, www.aljazeera.com/indepth/opinion/saudis-afraid-171217082544270.html

51. Mignolo's understanding of decoloniality (as opposed to decolonisation) is closely linked to the process of 'delinking' as he expounds it in 'Delinking: The rhetoric of modernity, the logic of coloniality and the grammar of de-coloniality', *Cultural Studies* 21:2-3 (2007): 449–514. Here he refers to a process that leads to decolonial epistemic shifts that propose alternative universalities or what he terms 'pluriversality' as a universal project (453).

*Dossier: Economies and Times of Deportation*

# The deportation power

Nicholas De Genova

When we contemplate deportation,* it is revealing, in the spirit of Michel Foucault, to excavate a genealogy of the actual practices. 'We have to analyse [power]', as Foucault remarks concisely, 'by beginning with the techniques and tactics of domination.'[1] Elsewhere, Foucault credits Marx with having provided him with 'the fundamental elements of an analysis' concerned with 'not just the representation of power, but of the real functioning of power ... power in its positive mechanisms.'[2] Deportation must be approached precisely as a technique or tactic of domination, a 'positive mechanism' of 'the real functioning of power.' So how, we may ask, has deportation emerged as an actual 'mechanism' of power, and what is its genealogy?

Various forms of expulsion long predated deportation as we know it today, as William Walters has so insightfully demonstrated,[3] and the targets of such tactics were often citizens. As a specific, juridically inscribed, and ordinarily individualised mode of immigration enforcement, deportation really only comes about in the latter part of the nineteenth century. Prior to that, migration had been largely unregulated and state borders were relatively open for the transnational mobility of labour. In the United States, for instance, provisions for the deportation of 'undesirable' migrants were only enacted as a means of enforcing the explicitly racist Page Act of 1875, specifically targeting Chinese migrants, whereupon the denial of admission at a US port of entry would trigger a deportation. Then, with the subsequent Chinese Exclusion Act of 1882, the purview of deportation was broadened to become a penalty for lacking a certificate of legal residence, and thus a form of interior immigration enforcement rather than just a pragmatic remedy to the inadmissibility of a migrant interdicted at a border.[4] Immigration law itself was virtually non-existent until this era, which introduced a panoply of racial, religious, moral, criminological, public health and political exclusions, prominently distinguished by the sorts of overtly racist laws, enacted across the Americas and beyond, which specifically sought to bar the migration of Chinese labour. In this regard, it is instructive that deportation was first enacted not against *all* non-citizens and therefore not primarily as a way to enact a partition between citizenship and non-citizenship, but rather as a technique for the exclusion of a particular, expressly racialised, and racially denigrated category of transnational human mobility. In a sense, the primacy of this racial obsession preceded and importantly prefigured what were still relatively inchoate notions of national identity and even citizenship. The service that deportation thereby did for hardening and clarifying the boundaries of nation-state space and citizenship is evident, but perhaps becomes much more stark only in retrospect. Maybe the 'deportation creep' that eventually comes to contaminate the presumptive security of citizenship can thus be seen to have started even sooner, beginning with a rather specific and circumscribed

---

\* Earlier versions of the pieces by Nicholas De Genova, Clara Lecadet and William Walters included in this Dossier first appeared as a conversation in French, 'Expulsion, Pouvoir, Mobilisation', in the journal *Vacarme* 83, 15–21, https://vacarme.org/article3133.html. We are grateful to the editors for permission to reproduce this material here.

target among the full spectrum of non-citizen 'foreigners' and advancing inexorably to encompass them all – to the point that now, on an effectively global scale, there is virtually no non-citizen (including the ostensibly 'legal' 'permanent resident') who is not potentially deportable, given the right combination of circumstances and triggering contingencies.[5] Daniel Kanstroom demonstrates how the mounting use of deportation law as a form of 'extended border control' also came to serve the ends of 'post-entry social control.'[6] Little surprise, then, that deportation increasingly sweeps up into its purview putatively 'suspect' categories of citizens, again prominently featuring those who are racially affiliated with 'foreignness'.[7]

If today we have come customarily to understand the susceptibility to deportation as a principal and defining distinction that separates citizenship and non-citizenship,[8] we need to remain vigilant against ever imagining that citizenship can be assumed to be somehow equated with any presumable 'safety' from various forms of coercive expulsion. After all, the other conventional association with the term 'deportation' – especially in many European contexts – is Nazism's herding of Jews and other 'enemies' into prison labour camps, which of course were eventually converted into death camps. So, it seems perilous to become complacent about the idea that deportation could ever be exclusively reserved only for non-citizens. If nothing else, the meticulously legalistic proclivities of the Nazis demonstrate precisely that citizens can always be stripped of their legal personhood and subjected to any and every atrocity otherwise more routinely reserved for non-citizens. Indeed, over recent years, and still today, we have witnessed reactionary statist campaigns against the spectral threat of 'migration' even in contexts where those who are made to stand in as the 'foreign' object of nativist contempt and suspicion are not in fact migrants or refugees at all. In particular, there have been an escalation of nativist convulsions against 'illegal immigrants' targeting native-born (racialised 'minority') fellow citizens. In the eastern borderlands of the Democratic Republic of the Congo, native-born Congolese citizens who are the descendants of Hutu and Tutsi people resident for generations on the Congolese side of the border have been derisively labeled 'Rwandans' and targeted for expulsion.[9] Similarly, in the Dominican Republic, the native-born descendants of migrant workers who were recruited generations earlier from neighbouring Haiti have been recast as 'Haitians', legally stripped of their birthright citizenship, and rendered stateless, denigrated as 'illegal immigrants' in the only land where they have ever lived.[10] Meanwhile, in Myanmar (Burma), Rohingya Muslim native-born citizens have similarly been legally stripped of their citizenship, castigated as 'illegal immigrants' from Bangladesh, and subjected to vicious pogroms, confined in virtual concentration camps, massacred and driven across the border in the hundreds of thousands.[11] Indeed, these examples are but a few of the more extraordinary among a proliferation on a global scale of new formations of nativism directed not merely at migrant 'foreigners' but towards minoritised fellow citizens who may be repurposed as virtual or de facto 'foreigners' – indeed, often as outright 'enemies' – *within* the space of the nation-state.

None of this is to deny or dispute the basic truth that deportation today pervasively serves as a defining feature of the sociopolitical difference between citizenship and non-citizenship, which is to say, in other words, the functionality of deportation in our contemporary sociopolitical scene for enacting in a very blunt and deeply consequential way the divide between the 'inside' and 'outside' of the space of the state. But, as I have often argued,[12] while deportation is obviously devastating for many people who are actually deported as well as for their loved ones and so many others directly connected to them, the most productive power of deportation operates for the great majority of people who are susceptible to deportation but who do *not* get deported. This is how deportation contributes to the precaritisation of migrants. Importantly, this means that deportation, perhaps more than anything else, does a crucial work of subordination on the 'inside' of the space of the state. And then, on the 'other' side of the border, 'outside' the space of the deporting state – as Nathalie Peutz, Clara Lecadet, Tanya Golash-Boza, Shahram Khosravi and other contributors to the growing ethnographic literature on the aftermaths of deportation have shown[13] – there is life after deportation even if the deporting state imagines deportation to be a kind of closure, a seemingly conclusive act of dumping 'undesirable' migrants onto the ordinarily poor countries to which they are juridically affiliated by their (sometimes only apparent) citizenship. Furthermore, life after deportation frequently involves the re-mobilisation of the deported migrants, the re-initiation of their migratory projects, often against all odds and under circumstances that may look more than ever like the flight of refugees from conditions in which life is truly inviable. But this reminds us that even under the worst of circumstances, and within the very asphyxiating constraints of various regimes for governing human mobility, there are persistent manifestations of autonomy, which I have called the 'autonomy of deportation'.[14]

The moral economies of 'deservingness' that are often invoked to defend some migrants against deportation frequently become complicit with upholding the supposed appropriateness of deportation for others. Meanwhile, the internationalisation of an effectively global regime of deportation depends ever more comprehensively on the infrastructures that undergird and facilitate it. What partly fascinates me is how these two concerns may be linked – how the infrastructures and apparatuses and other technologies of power that allow for people to be disposed of (the *dispositifs*, if you will) are inseparable from the discourses and logics and rationalities that render something as appalling and violent as deportation into something so apparently mundane, so seemingly 'normal'. This has much to do with the ways that bureaucracy is implicated with the proverbial 'banality of evil', as Arendt called it, but, more specifically, it is centrally concerned with the configuration of migration as a purely and merely 'administrative' affair, generally constructed so as to be 'outside' of the purview of politics proper.[15] This is why every question

Image: Shahram Khosravi, Elliniko (2017)

of migration and borders has to be rescued from the normalisations of technocratic discourses and rationalities, and rendered apprehensible as a question of struggle.

The observation that there are always those who demand more deportation rather than less is crucial. It recalls to mind that the larger economy of deportation – by which I mean its economy of power, and specifically the uneven distribution of deportation – tends to operate in a context where there are always many more illegalised and deportable migrants than the number who are actually deported. And those who are hostile to migrants know this perfectly well, because the social fact of 'illegal' migration is a more or less public secret. It is also in this respect that the highly visible spectacles of migrant illegality not only stage border enforcement as a grand act of ostensible exclusion but also tend simultaneously to expose such border policing efforts as always inherently beleaguered and insufficient. In this way, they serve to authorise the incessant demand for *more* control, more enforcement, more border reinforcement, and thus serve nonetheless as reminders of the permanent presence of still more 'illegal' migrants and the incorrigible versatility of 'irregular' or 'unauthorised' migrations. The border spectacle, which presents itself as a scene of exclusion, in fact also reveals its own obscene underbelly of subordinate inclusion.[16]

Here, we must recognise the remarkable systematicity with which deportation ever increasingly supplies capital with the ever-renewable resource of routinely disposable labour, in the exquisite form of illegalised (hence, deportable) migrant labour. As I have long argued, even in the face of escalating deportations (in the United States and across the world), it is usually still the case that only a minority are actually deported while the great majority of those who are susceptible to deportation remain in a protracted condition of vulnerability to this profoundly punitive repercussion of the law. What emerges then, in a still more stark way, is the pivotal role of deportation in producing the conditions of possibility for sustaining the casual and callous disposability not only of migrant labour *per se*, but also the outright and abject *disposability of human life*. Whole categories of people are simply treated as superfluous and, although their illegalised (hence, 'cheap' and tractable) labour is plainly in great demand and truly desirable to many employers, their (racialised) bodies, their persons, their lives and the wider communities in which they participate are branded as 'undesirable' and rendered virtual 'waste', human 'garbage' to be simply disposed of. It is in this sense, perhaps, that deportation has assumed a paradigmatic quality in our era of neoliberal global capitalism.[17]

*Nicholas De Genova is Professor and Chair of the Department of Comparative Cultural Studies at the University of Houston. He is co-editor of* The Deportation Regime: Sovereignty, Space, and the Freedom of Movement *(2010).*

**Notes**

1. Michel Foucault, *'Society Must be Defended': Lectures at the Collège de France, 1975-1976* (New York: Picador, 2003), 34; cf. Michel Foucault, 'The Subject and Power', *Critical Inquiry* 8 (1982), 788.
2. Michel Foucault, 'The Meshes of Power', in *Space, Knowledge and Power: Foucault and Geography*, eds. Jeremy W. Crampton and Stuart Elden (Aldershot: Ashgate, 2007), 156.
3. William Walters,'Deportation, Expulsion and the International Police of Aliens', *Citizenship Studies* 6:3 (2002), 265–292; reprinted in *The Deportation Regime: Sovereignty, Space, and the Freedom of Movement*, eds. Nicholas De Genova and Nathalie Peutz (Durham, NC: Duke University Press, 2010), 69–100.
4. Angelo N. Ancheta, *Race, Rights, and the Asian American Experience* (New Brunswick, NJ: Rutgers University Press, 1998); Robert S. Chang, *Disoriented: Asian Americans, Law, and the Nation-State* (New York: New York University Press, 1999); Bill Ong Hing, *Making and Remaking Asian America Through Immigration Policy, 1850-1990* (Stanford, CA: Stanford University Press, 1993); Hyung-chan Kim, *A Legal History of Asian Americans, 1790-1990* (Westport, CN: Greenwood Press, 1994); Adam M. McKeown, *Melancholy Order: Asian Migration and the Globalisation of Borders* (New York: Columbia University Press, 2008); Lucy E. Salyer, *Laws Harsh as Tigers: Chinese Immigrants and the Shaping of Modern Immigration Law* (Chapel Hill, NC: University of North Carolina Press,1995); Alexander Saxton, *The Indispensable Enemy: Labour and the Anti-Chinese Movement in California* (Berkeley, CA: University of California Press, 1971); cf. Kitty Calavita, *U.S. Immigration Law and the Control of Labour, 1820-1924* (New York: Harcourt Brace Jovanovich, 1984); Daniel Kanstroom, *Deportation Nation: Outsiders in American History* (Cambridge, MA: Harvard University Press, 2007).
5. See, for example, Julie A. Dowling and Jonathan Xavier Inda, eds., *Governing Immigration Through Crime: A Reader*

(Stanford, CA: Stanford University Press, 2013); Melanie B. Griffiths, 'The Convergence of the Criminal and the Foreigner in the Production of Citizenship', in *Citizenship and its Others*, eds. Bridget Anderson and Vanessa Hughes (Basingstoke: Palgrave Macmillan, 2015), 72–88; Ines Hasselberg, *Enduring Uncertainty: Deportation, Punishment and Everyday Life* (Oxford: Berghahn Books, 2016); Daniel Kanstroom, *Aftermath: Deportation Law and the New American Diaspora* (New York and Oxford: Oxford University Press, 2012); Nathalie M. Peutz, 'Embarking on an Anthropology of Removal', *Current Anthropology* 47:2 (April 2006), 217–241; Juliet P. Stumpf, 'The Crimmigration Crisis: Immigrants, Crime, and Sovereign Power', *American University Law Review* 56 (December 2006), 367–419.

6. Kanstroom, *Deportation Nation*, 92.

7. Jacqueline Stevens, 'U.S. Government Unlawfully Detaining and Deporting U.S. Citizens as Aliens', *Virginia Journal of Social Policy & the Law* 18:3 (2011); cf. Kanstroom, *Aftermath*.

8. Bridget Anderson, Matthew Gibney and Emanuela Paoletti, eds., *The Social, Political and Historical Contours of Deportation* (New York and London: Springer, 2013).

9. Stephen Jackson, 'Sons of Which Soil? The Language and Politics of Autochthony in Eastern D.R. Congo', *African Studies Review* 49:2 (September 2006), 95–123; Stephen Jackson, 'Congolité: Elections and the Politics of Autochthony in the Democratic Republic of the Congo', in *Rhetorics of Insecurity: Belonging and Violence in the Neoliberal Era*, eds. Zeynep Gambetti and Marcial Godoy-Anativia (New York: Social Science Research Council and New York University Press, 2013), 63–92; Lars-Christopher Huening, 'Making Use of the Past: The Rwandophone Question and the 'Balkanisation of the Congo', *Review of African Political Economy* 40:135 (2013), 13–31.

10. Eve Hayes de Kalaf, 'Dominican Republic Has Taken Citizenship from up to 200,000 and Is Getting Away with It', *The Conversation*, 19 June 2015, https://theconversation.com/dominican-republic-has-taken-citizenship-from-up-to-200-000-and-is-getting-away-with-it-43161; Eve Hayes de Kalaf, 'How a Group of Dominicans Were Stripped of Their Nationality and Now Face Expulsion to Haiti', *The Conversation*, 8 April 2015, https://theconversation.com/how-a-group-of-dominicans-were-stripped-of-their-nationality-and-now-face-expulsion-to-haiti-39658; cf. Stacie Kosinski, 'State of Uncertainty: Citizenship, Statelessness and Discrimination in the Dominican Republic', *Boston College International and Comparative Law Review* 32:2, (2009) 377–398; Edward Paulino, 'Anti-Haitianism, Historical Memory, and the Potential for Genocidal Violence in the Dominican Republic', *Genocide Studies and Prevention* 1:3 (2006), 265–288.

11. Chris Lewa, 'North Arakan: An Open Prison for the Rohingya in Burma', *Forced Migration Review* 32 (2009), 11–13; Cresa L. Pugh, 'Is Citizenship the Answer? Constructions of Belonging and Exclusion for the Stateless Rohingya of Burma', Working Paper #76 (October 2013), International Migration Institute (IMI), Department of International Development, University of Oxford. Also Working Paper #107 (October 2013), Centre on Migration, Policy and Society (COMPAS), University of Oxford, accessed 20 October 2018, https://www.compas.ox.ac.uk/media/WP-2013-107-Pugh_Stateless_Rohingya_Burma.pdf

12. Nicholas De Genova, 'Migrant "Illegality" and Deportability in Everyday Life', *Annual Review of Anthropology* 31 (2002), 419–477; Nicholas De Genova, *Working the Boundaries: Race, Space, and 'Illegality' in Mexican Chicago* (Durham, NC: Duke University Press, 2005); Nicholas De Genova, 'The Deportation Regime: Sovereignty, Space, and the Freedom of Movement: Theoretical Overview', in *The Deportation Regime*, eds. De Genova and Peutz, 33–65.

13. Nathalie Peutz, 'Embarking on an Anthropology of Removal', *Current Anthropology* 47:2, (2006), 217–41; revised version reprinted as 'Criminal Alien' Deportees in Somaliland: An Ethnography of Removal,' in *The Deportation Regime*, eds. De Genova and Peutz, 371–411; Clara Lecadet, 'From Migrant Destitution to Self-Organisation into Transitory National Communities: The Revival of Citizenship in Post-Deportation Experience in Mali', in *The Social, Political and Historical Contours of Deportation*, eds. Bridget Anderson, Matthew Gibney and Emanuela Paoletti (New York and London: Springer, 2013), 143–58; Clara Lecadet, 'Europe Confronted by its Expelled Migrants: The Politics of Expelled Migrants' Associations in Africa', in *The Borders of 'Europe': Autonomy of Migration, Tactics of Bordering*, ed. Nicholas De Genova (Durham, NC: Duke University Press, 2017), 141–64; Tanya Golash-Boza, *Deported: Immigrant Policing, Disposable Labour, and Global Capitalism* (New York: New York University Press, 2015); Shahram Khosravi, 'Deportation as a Way of Life for Young Afghan Men', in *Detaining the Immigrant Other: Global and Transnational Issues*, eds. Rich Furman, Douglas Epps and Greg Lamphear (Oxford: Oxford University Press, 2016), 169–81; Shahram Khosravi, ed., *After Deportation: Ethnographic Perspectives* (Basingstoke: Palgrave Macmillan, 2017)

14. Nicholas De Genova, 'The Autonomy of Deportation', *lo Squaderno* 44 (2017), accessed 20 October 2018, http://www.losquaderno.professionaldreamers.net/wp-content/uploads/2017/05/losquaderno44.pdf; Nicholas De Genova, 'Deportation: The Last Word?', in *After Deportation*, ed. Khosravi, 253–66; cf. Nicholas De Genova, Glenda Garelli and Martina Tazzioli, 'Autonomy of Asylum? The Autonomy of Migration Undoing the Refugee Crisis Script', *South Atlantic Quarterly* 117:2 (2018), 239–65.

15. Nicholas De Genova, 'Deportation', in *Migration: A COMPAS Anthology*, eds. Bridget Anderson and Michael Keith (Oxford: Oxford University Press, 2014), accessed 20 October 2018, http://compasanthology.co.uk http://compasanthology.co.uk/deportation-2/

16. Nicholas De Genova, 'Spectacles of Migrant "Illegality": The Scene of Exclusion, the Obscene of Inclusion', *Ethnic and Racial Studies* 36:7 (2013), 1180–98.

17. Nicholas De Genova, 'The Deportation Regime'; Nathalie Peutz and Nicholas De Genova, 'Introduction', in *The Deportation Regime*, 1–29.

# Deportation, nation state, capital
## Between legitimisation and violence
Clara Lecadet

As Abdelmalek Sayad has written: 'To think about immigration (or emigration) is to think about the state.'[1] Attempting to question both the political structure of the state and its resonances for the individual, he adds that the risk of expulsion is what weighs on the mind of every immigrant and leads to a life of uncertainty and insecurity. It does not take an extreme political context, but simple, legislative changes and political decisions to tip foreigners into, or maintain them in, an illegal status which could lead to expulsion.

The political context in which Sayad made this comment was certainly marked by the 1974 suspension of legal access routes to migration for work in France and by the closing of other European countries to foreigners from former colonies. As public policies for the return of immigrants were put in place in the 1970s, they aroused the opposition of the Spanish, Portuguese and Algerian governments to the expulsion of their citizens.[2] From the 1990s, the return of immigrants, traditionally organised at a national level, became the cornerstone of European policy. The reinforcement of control measures at the external borders of Europe and of the expulsion of 'illegal' immigrants was concomitant with the creation of an area of free movement within the European Union. If this paradigm of return seems central to the current migration regime that has been imposed by a network of agencies including individual countries, intergovernmental organisations and certain NGOs, it is important to trace its origin, and to measure how deep-rooted it is in relation to the construction of political power in nation states.

The work of Mae Ngai and Daniel Kanstroom in the United States, and of Gérard Noiriel in Europe, together with the critical genealogy of deportation established by William Walters, have shown the central role played by the expulsion of foreigners and its progressive institutionalisation in the building of nation states. Its divisive function has certainly contributed to their internal and external construction. Initially barely regulated, expulsion measures have come to precede, accompany and contribute to the establishing of definitions, categories and statuses produced by the state apparatus. Expulsion becomes part of the internal structure of the state by becoming the final arbiter in separating citizens from non-citizens. It makes concrete those legal distinctions which would otherwise remain simple legal fictions.

The bureaucratic nightmare involved in obtaining papers and their associated rights finds its radical expression in expulsion. This in-between situation which leaves so many foreigners in a 'legal limbo',[3] but which also leaves room for individual and often discretionary measures for legalisation, allows the state to express and reaffirm its absolute power over the status – illegal or otherwise – of foreigners in its territory. Expulsion also shapes the outside appearance of the nation state in various respects. It creates a sort of blind spot to the extent that expelled migrants are consigned to invisibility, both actual and symbolic. The fact that foreigners are a central consideration in thinking about the state contrasts all the more sharply with the fact that once they are expelled, they are never again mentioned in public debate. They disappear after expulsion, and are often deprived of any means of legally appealing and annulling the decision that has been made. 'Expelled migrant' is not a recognised legal term. This is the point of the 'Declaration on the rights of expelled and deported persons' by Daniel Kanstroom and Jessica Chicco of Boston College Law School, a project which seeks to articulate full rights for expellees.

While expulsion may appear inconsequential and apolitical from a state-centred point of view, one only needs to cross borders and to strip oneself of the methodological nationalism which conditions a great part of our research and our viewpoints, to realise that expulsion means that expelled migrants are condemned to violence, destitution, rootlessness, and even death. At the same time, this realisation may also be an opportunity for social and political reorganisation. We must therefore deal with the policies and practices of expelling countries together with the social and political effects of expulsion in the countries where migrants are deported. In this way, we can achieve a more accurate mapping of the power relationships which allow such measures to be put in place, as well as an increased concern for the fate of people thus caught up in the implacable logic of the state.

While expulsion is a form of social destitution and radical political exclusion, it nonetheless generates mobilisation and new forms of collective subjectivity on the part of expelled migrants, who organise themselves on the basis of this denial of their political existence. The Association Malienne des Expulsés [Malian Association of Expelled Migrants] created in Bamako in 1996, the Association Togolaise des Expulsés [Togolese Association of Expelled Migrants] created in Sokodé in 2008, the association Welcome Back Cameroon[4] founded in Yaoundé in 2006, and the Network of Ex-Asylum Seekers in Sierra Leone, which began in Freetown in 2011, are all initiatives which prove that expellees can use their ordeal as a source of collective action to claim public visibility and recognition. Their drive to self-organisation leads these people, considered second-class citizens, to become political subjects. Central to this is their claim that their participation in public debate takes its legitimacy, above all, from what they have experienced, and that they are therefore, more than anyone else, entitled to speak about it. The presence of the Malian Association of Expelled Migrants in public debate in Mali for more than 20 years, and the slogans of the Network of Ex-Asylum Seekers in Sierra Leone, such as 'Make us feel we belong' or 'Don't stigmatise us', show the involvement of these movements in the fight against the hardening of expulsion measures and citizenship claims in their countries of origin.

But the visibility created by expulsion is also significant if we look at it from the point of view of the relations between nation states, where countries of origin or of transit to which expelled migrants are returned are politically subordinate. Expulsion reveals relations on a global level, which are based on political power. It is part of the renewal of forms of political hegemony resulting from the colonial period, as is demonstrated by the pressure brought to bear on African countries by the European Union and the International Organisation for Migration (IOM) on the issue of the externalisation of European borders, and also in relation to the adoption of legal instruments in migration policy that conform to, and are usually dictated by, European interests.

Expulsion is not only an instrument distinguishing the status of a citizen from that of a foreigner and a factor in the political subordination of countries. To understand expulsion as part of the structure of nation states, we must include a reflection on the economic dimension of its use. The implications of expulsion for the organisation of work and the conflicts which it involves would complement an analysis of expulsion in terms of political rights and power struggles. Long before migration policies became a clear and visible part of the construction of individual countries, expulsion was an *ad hoc* way of treating foreign workers, for reasons rooted in both economic utilitarianism and nationalism, of which migrant workers have always been the main target. Thus, Gérard Noiriel considers that the French law of 1893 on the 'protection nationale du travail' [protection of national workers] was a milestone in the history of legislation and policy on residence permits.[5] It is also pertinent to consider questions of political rights and their underlying economic dynamic. From the nineteenth century on, expulsion has been a powerful means not only of excluding foreign workers, but also of creating divisions within the workforce. In her analysis of the struggles of the Popular Front in France in the 1930s, the philosopher Simone Weil demonstrates that the participation of foreign workers in the struggles which brought about major social reforms was not only not recognised, but the existence of these workers was marginalised within the movement, leaving them in a precarious position and liable to expulsion, as well as lacking any political rights. She denounces the denial of colonialism by the left-wing government of that period, and sees foreign workers as internal colonial subjects.[6]

Such mechanisms for the subordination of a foreign workforce, possibly leading to expulsion, became even more marked and visible with the circulation of workers connected to globalisation, and because of policies of selection and rejection based on usefulness to the economy of the host country. Emmanuel Terray has coined the term 'délocalisation sur place' [on-site relocation] to refer to the use of a low-paid, foreign workforce, whose cheap labour is in competition with 'national' labour and is easily expelled.[7] But it is not enough to say that workers can be expelled when they are not, or are no longer, useful to the economy of the host country; they are expellable and expelled even when they are 'useful', in order to maintain a constant pressure on the labour market and wages and to put a stop to any possibility of organisation or claims for workers' rights. The same thinking is also at work in a brutal way in the global South and enables us to understand the long-standing process of the expulsion of foreign workers between different African countries.[8] While the externalisation of European borders and its resulting imperialism undoubtedly play a leading role in the current reconfiguration of borders and migration policies in Africa, it is nonetheless the case that expulsion retains a 'local' dimension as a tool to increase the turnover of manpower which can be exploited at will. Equatorial Guinea and other oil-producing countries brutally and regularly expel migrant workers. If we look at the brutality of these measures for expelling foreign workers at different levels, and try to understand how they work together, we can then comprehend the importance of expulsion in the global functioning of neo-liberal capitalism.

Since expulsion is presented as a guarantee of national order and a pragmatic means of subduing the workforce, we must therefore think beyond the national framework, both in terms of the economic organisation of labour and the political means for the control, detention and expulsion of foreigners, in order to appreciate the current reconfigurations of expulsion measures. There is, in fact, a whole web of interrelated actions in various disguised forms, as can be seen in the 'transfer' of asylum seekers in Europe under the Dublin III Regulation, and the 'evacuation' or 'humanitarian repatriation' carried out by the IOM from Libya or Niger, which sends migrants back to their country of origin as part of the political trend towards fixing populations and preventing them from migrating and/or enabling their return. The enumeration of these various levels, labels and kinds of legitimisation poses the question of whether the global discourse on 'governing migration' and on the need to return migrants simply redeploys what nation states have historically set up in relation to inclusion and territoriality at a wider scale.

Movements trying to challenge these policies are also established at various scales – local, national and transnational – but their mode of operation remains by and large fragmented. In their radical form, they aim to challenge the systemic framework of inclusion and exclusion established in the political structure of the nation state, as is the case with the No Borders Network which defends the principle of freedom of circulation and demands the abolition of borders, or with the current rallying cry 'Abolish ICE' [Immigration and Customs Enforcement] in the United States. This is also the case with the English network End Deportations, which asks for the abolition of the detention and deportation of migrants, or the French *sans-papiers* movement in the 1990s and for certain groups of undocumented migrants all over Europe which defend the principle of global legalisation and freedom of circulation. At the same time, we should not minimise the impact of the increasingly individualised forms of power predicted by Foucault on movements that are often organised around specific issues: protecting schools, preventing expulsion to countries where deportees' lives are at risk, and so on. The resources of the law are used to demand protection for individuals belonging to specific categories or coming from countries at war and thereby considered unsafe according to international conventions, thereby fuelling a policy of 'case by case' treatment.

As such, the struggle against the principle of expulsion itself is generally not at the heart of these movements. Instead, at their centre there are a number of motives which may seem similar, but are based on very different relations to the state: the claim for freedom of circulation, based on a radical critique of the state, is at quite some distance in its assumptions from demands for reception centres or pleas for hospitality, which make the state and its citizens legitimate actors in their duty of openness towards foreigners, but which do not radically question these structural roles. Despite criticism and opposition, strategies of resistance and occasional public outrage caused by certain deportations, the virtual consensus on expulsion across the political board seems, at least in liberal democracies, to rely upon the degree of acceptability of this measure. There is a strong tendency in the moral economy of the United States and Europe to link expulsion with an offence having been committed. Such legitimising positions make it difficult to develop a radical political critique of expulsion.

The intensely normalising process of these measures aims to neutralise criticism and make it inoperable. Governments, helped by international institutions like IOM or UNHCR, work to make expulsion publicly acceptable by incorporating it into a whole framework of 'migration governance'. In the twentieth century, there was a major shift from expulsions that played a key role in statelessness, violence and mass crimes in the interwar period and during the Second World War, and the expulsion of undocumented foreigners as part of current migration policies. This does not mean that from the nineteenth century on there were no expulsions of foreign workers, as there certainly were in France. But the change brought about by the Second World War and its role in raising a European consciousness and in building a unified, peaceful European area, seems to have implicitly moulded the discourse and views on 'return' policies developed from the 1970s in various European countries. Care has been taken to dispel any idea of continuity between the treatment of non-European foreigners and the violence of the first half of the twentieth century. A number of texts and legal instruments adopted after 1945 aimed to limit expulsions and to bring about forms of protection for those who had been displaced by the wars and/or stripped of their national rights. But as Arendt indignantly noted in relation to measures taken by the United States to strip communists of their nationality, countries considered to be democratic have adopted practices which had been considered the reserve of totalitarian states.[9] In the case cited by Arendt, expulsion could be aimed at citizens born in the country as a result of their loss of nationality. But it would apply above all to foreigners, in the light of their precarious administrative situation, and would be the central issue in the growing process of legitimisation and normalisation.

How could such measures be developed whilst also remaining acceptable? They had to be inserted into a political framework that made belonging to one's country of origin – even if this 'belonging' was purely formal or went totally against generations of residence in a different country – the ultimate justification of all the measures taken in regard to foreigners. This had to be based on a political and legal rhetoric which minimised its coercive dimension. Thus the Return Directive adopted by the European Parliament in 2008 contained such references as: respect for the rights and the dignity of expelled persons, recourse to a 'reasonable' use of force against resistance, development aid to third countries to promote the lasting resettlement of returnees, etc.[10]

The historical weight and the symbolic burden of expulsion remain, however. The very use of the term 'return' is symptomatic of what Sayad would call an 'alibi term'. As a political artefact, it is a euphemism for the violence inherent in expulsion; it erases the complexity of migration journeys in which expulsion is rarely synonymous with return, and it 'naturalises' return as an inherent part of migration. This effort at normalisation by both international institutions such as IOM and national governments combines discourse and practice: the rationalisation of coercion in manuals handed out to escorts, the creation of economic and policing partnerships with countries of origin, etc. There exists in expulsion a constant tension between norms and violence. And it is not by chance that activists in France insist on using the term 'deportation', which is immediately associated in French with the deportation of the Jews, a tactic which raises problems but which refuses normalisation. It is particularly difficult to fight a policy which is both unilateral and fragmented in its implementation.

What distinguishes individual expulsion on commercial flights and the expulsion of groups on specific flights set up by liberal democracies from mass expulsion campaigns in an authoritarian context? Do these demarcation lines have any meaning? What are the criteria: the brutality of the methods, the number of people sent back, the respect for the rules of law or their suspension?

Numerous examples show the extent to which the lines are blurred: did not the European Council consider, in September 2015, collective expulsion programmes as a means of dealing with what was considered to be an influx of refugees unprecedented since the Second World War? Is not the attempt to circumvent the rules of readmission by printing a European pass a sort of legal coup? Does not the use of force in a democratic context create victims in exactly the same way as in an authoritarian one? Long-winded procedures and the careful use of words try to cover up the reality of practices, but they cannot eradicate the violence, the destitution to which expelled migrants are condemned or the issue of their treatment in their country of origin.

When Saudi Arabia carries out expulsion campaigns again and again (with up to a million foreigners expelled in a year), there might be reports on the intensity of the xenophobic violence involved in these campaigns or on the appalling number of those targeted by such measures,[11] but they never generate the degree of scandal that is aroused for political conflicts such as war, civil war or political repression. Thus, even when expulsion is carried out on a grand scale and without the resources and deferments that are possible in a state subject to the rule of law, the principle of sovereignty is so powerful that there is no international reaction other than in the form of humanitarian aid financed by governments via IOM, which further contributes to the depoliticisation of the issues raised by expulsion campaigns. There is an international political consensus on expulsion to the extent that, given the hypocrisy and political structures involved, the proportions and the methods of expulsion become almost irrelevant.

*Clara Lecadet is a researcher at the National committee of scientific research (France). She is the author of* Le manifeste des expulsés. Errance, survie et politique au Mali *(2016), and co-editor with Michel Agier of* Un monde de camps *(2014) and* Après les camps. Traces, mémoires et mutations des camps de réfugiés *with Jean-Frédéric de Hasque (forthcoming).*

**Notes**

1. Abelmalek Sayad, *L'immigration et les paradoxes de l'altérité 1. L'illusion du provisoire* (Paris, Raisons d'agir, 1991[2006]), 161; translation author's own.
2. Patrick Weil, *La France et ses étrangers. L'aventure d'une politique de l'immigration de 1938 à nos jours* (Paris: Gallimard, 2005).
3. See Emmanuela Paoletti, 'Deportation, Non-deportability and Ideas of Membership', Working Paper Series 65, Refugee Studies Centre, Oxford Department of International Development, University of Oxford, 2010, https://www.rsc.ox.ac.uk/files/files-1/wp65-deportation-non-deportability-ideas-membership-2010.pdf
4. Oscar Francis Eyezo'o, its founder and president, is also a Unionist and as such is very aware of the economic issues underlying the deportation process and of the necessity to defend migrant workers' rights. He is the author of the book *Et je fus expulsé* [And I Was Expelled] (CreateSpace Independent Publishing Platform, 2018).
5. Gérard Noiriel, *Une histoire populaire de la France* (Paris: Agone, 2018).
6. Simone Weil, *Contre le colonialisme* (Paris: Editions Payot & Rivages, 2018).
7. Emmanuel Terray, 'Le travail des étrangers en situation irrégulière ou la délocalisation sur place', in *Sans-papiers: l'archaïsme fatal*, eds. Etienne Balibar, Monique Chemillier-Gendreau, Jacqueline Costa-Lascoux and Emmanuel Terray (Paris: La Découverte, 1999), 9–34.
8. Sylvie Bredeloup, 'Tableau synoptique: *Expulsions des ressortissants ouest-africains au sein du continent africain (1954–1995)*', *Mondes en développement* 23:91 (1995), 117–121.
9. Hannah Arendt, *The Origins of Totalitarianism* (New York: Meridian Books, 1986).
10. Directive 2008/115/EC of the European Parliament and of the Council of 16 December 2008 on common standards and procedures in Member States for returning illegally staying third-country nationals, https://eur-lex.europa.eu/legal-content/EN/TXT/?uri=CELEX%3A32008L0115
11. Human Rights Watch, *Saudi Arabia: Mass Expulsions of Migrant Workers. Abuses During Detention, Deportation*, 2015, https://www.hrw.org/news/2015/05/09/saudi-arabia-mass-expulsions-migrant-workers

# Expulsion, power, mobilisation
William Walters

Questions of sovereign power, socioeconomic precarity, racialisation, citizenship and exclusion converge and clash around deportation.[1] In this short intervention I propose to reflect on certain aspects of the power of deportation in three areas. The first is citizenship and belonging, and more specifically what we can learn about the instability of citizenship under liberal democracy by looking at deportation. Second, I make a point about what we could call the infrastructure of deportation. Finally, I reflect on how deportation, citizenship and infrastructure are, in turn, related to a particular politics of visibility.

Clara Lecadet is right to insist in her contribution to this issue of *Radical Philosophy* that the various categories that differentiate hierarchically between citizens and non-citizens would be rather meaningless were there no weapon of deportation that stands available to carry out the ultimate division between these statuses. By way of extending her point, I think we should not overlook the frequent situations in which this line gets blurred. For example, Jacqueline Stevens has identified numerous cases in recent years where US authorities have detained or deported US citizens, sometimes because the latter could not prove their citizenship.[2] With the Windrush scandal we are currently witnessing a not dissimilar violence in Britain. Many people who migrated to Britain from the Caribbean in the post-WWII years – typically within a framework combining Commonwealth citizenship and labour recruitment – have found themselves threatened with (and in some cases subjected to) deportation procedures. This has happened when they fail to meet the ever more complex and exacting requirements that immigration authorities have in recent years established for proving long-term residence and legal citizenship.[3] Turning hospitals, landlords and universities into immigration authorities, 'weaponising paperwork',[4] and channeling as well as fostering racialised antagonisms and hierarchies, the hostile environment policy that Theresa May initiated as Home Secretary turned these citizens into 'illegal immigrants'.[5] It showed that far from being a mere instrument dedicated to border control, deportation operates as a system that draws and redraws boundaries and identities of us and them, citizenship and belonging, and much else.

This unsettling of the citizen/non-citizen line through deportation happens from other directions as well. In an age when combatting Islamicised terrorism has become one of the most privileged justifications for muscular state action, we are witnessing a version of the deportation machine that is at once old and new. Here I am thinking of recent moves in countries like Britain and Canada to denationalise and deport certain people in the name of national security, a move that has sparked scholarly debate about the return of banishment. As Audrey Macklin has put it:

> From antiquity to the late 20th century, denationalisation was a tool used by states to rid themselves of political dissidents, convicted criminals and ethnic, religious or racial minorities. The latest target of denationalisation is the convicted terrorist, or the suspected terrorist, or the potential terrorist, or maybe the associate of a terrorist. He is virtually always Muslim and male. [6]

In these and perhaps other contexts it is tempting to speak of a *deportation creep* whereby this practice, while formally reserved for (and indeed legitimated as a power restricted to the governance of) the *non-citizen*, in fact exceeds those boundaries and sometimes gathers citizens in its net as well. But from a more historical perspective it is not so much a deportation creep that is at issue. For such a notion implies that deportation is meant for non-citizens, so that when it touches upon – or more aptly, *seizes* – the citizen, this is the exception rather than the norm. We should not forget that in other times and places, as Macklin's remark suggests, deportation was routinely and lawfully used on citizens and domestic populations as well. As Kanstroom has argued, 'the direct link between citizenship status and the "right to remain" is a modern one'.[7] In other words, we have seen a long-term shift from practices of banishment, ostracism and transportation which could target elites as well as masses, foreigners but also subjects and citizens, to today's policies which legitimate deportation by associating it almost exclusively with non-citizens.[8] Yet the shift is not total or absolute. Citizenship is by no means an iron-clad guarantee against one's deportation.

If deportation has gradually become formalised and legitimated as a measure confined to the non-citizen, and if conversely citizenship has become associated with the right to remain, this shift has much to do with the inter-nationalisation of the world; it correlates with the historical-political process that has seen the world's population divided, distributed and governed according to a logic of nation states, of national territories and populations, rather than formal empires and colonies.[9] With the globalisation of the nation-state form there are, in principle, no 'outside' or 'empty' places, no colonies, penal or otherwise, where you can banish your citizens or unwanted subjects. (Deeply inscribed in colonial history, the US Naval base at Guantanamo Bay is a notable exception here.) Modern deportation could be considered postcolonial in this precise and quite limited sense.

Today there exist virtually no colonies to which you can transport your unwanted people. But what does exist is development aid, trade agreements and various other sticks and carrots by which you can cajole other states to play the game of 'readmission'.[10] This is, I think, what Lecadet alludes to in recognising that deportation today enacts power relations not just on the scale of citizens and others, but between states, and operates as a significant way in which a hierarchy of states is staged at the world level. Perhaps one could talk about deportation creep on two levels then: a practice that rubs up against the norm that it is only non-citizens who can be expelled, and a practice that calls into question what we understand by sovereignty; that is, which political authority controls what borders and decides what persons can cross those borders.

This theme of sovereignty brings me to a second theme that Clara Lecadet has highlighted. It has to do with the external dimension of deportation, namely the relations between states. Kanstroom has also foregrounded this theme, suggesting that we should shift from seeing deportation in purely state-centric terms toward recognising that an international deportation system exists which now has its own consistency, its own irreducibility.[11] Within this system it is not just people who are moved around. Practices move as well, as is the case when immigration authorities adopt control techniques from agencies and experts in other countries. Sometimes this is done within formal regulatory frameworks, such as the EU's return policy; at other times through *ad hoc* expert panels that investigate 'best practices' of 'assisted' as well as 'forced' removals. Put differently, one can say there are in fact many mobilities at play within this international system of deportation – not only deportees, but escorts, goods, buses and planes, diplomats, identity papers, medical inspectors, development funds, and so on.

To this discussion concerning deportation as an international system I want to add a point about infrastructure. After all, the possibility of forcibly moving people great distances, this power on which deportation depends, is at some level a matter of material capability. In addition to the international relations between states, and between states and international agencies, we need to reckon with the material geographies of deportation. We need to think about deportation in terms of its routes, corridors and networks, a system of passages which not only crosses political borders, but which negotiates land, sea and air. Why do we only seem to talk about routes when they are associated with smugglers, or with migrants seeking to circumvent border controls? What about the routes of deportation which states have crafted? We know historically how banishments and transportations involved terrible ship voyages that turned distant (and not so distant) islands and even whole continents into places of punishment, exile and confinement. Similarly, we learn from the work of Ethan Blue how America's railway network was repurposed and appropriated, how it became a quasi-carceral geography in the deportations that began in the 1920s.[12] What interests me especially is global aviation and the channels and corridors of deportation it has made possible in the last 30 or 40 years.[13] If deportation has become truly internationalised – meaning a practice that can in principle obtain between any two countries irrespective of their geographical relationship – then the power of global aviation is a significant yet largely unacknowledged factor in such a development.

Finally, I would like to make a point here about how we understand the normalisation of deportation, and the question of what an analytics of visibility might offer. Certainly, we can speak of the modes of legitimation that frame deportation. In this dossier, we have considered binaries of citizen versus noncitizen, and we have talked about racialisation and foreignness as elements that have historically served to make deportation seem not at all extraordinary, despite the violence it entails, but on the contrary quite acceptable to significant sections of the public. And we have also highlighted important transformations in the post-WWII years wherein deportation undergoes a kind of softening – which is not a softening at all – whereby the operational procedures acquire new terms like 'reasonable force', 'dignity' and 'return', and new practices like psychological counselling.[14] I agree that many of these elements, practices and terms are connected to a paradigm of legitimation.

That said, I think it is possible to supplement what we understand by legitimation by thinking also of visibility. Power is legitimate when it is embedded in normative frameworks and enjoys a certain degree of consent from the governed. When we say that deportation is legitimated by specific measures, we mean: it is rendered acceptable, normal, moral even, by being embedded in particular discourses, and associated with particular kinds of justification. What I would add to this is that we should also think about deportation in terms of regimes of visibility; of what Rancière, in a well-known formulation, might call its 'distribution of the sensible'.[15] The forms of resistance which have been mobilised against deportation practices and programmes in recent years are a good place to start such an analysis.[16] And here I have in mind Foucault's point that forms of resistance can offer a promising entry point for the analysis of different forms of power.[17] Let us start with practices that campaigns to stall or prevent particular deportations employ.

When the UK government moved to deport Yashika Bagheerathi to Mauritius in 2014, a very visible and in many ways influential campaign was mobilised. It brought to the public's attention various facts: she was a schoolgirl, she was taking A levels, she had a promising career ahead of her. Now, this move might reinforce the problematic logic Clara Lecadet has identified with anti-deportation mobilisations, namely that it entrenches the dichotomy of the deserving and non-deserving, and directs public debate to the merits and demerits of particular cases and perhaps away from the discussion of the very principles of deportation. At the same time, and more positively, does it not also entail the production of a kind of counter-visibility? In the absence of such campaigns there would only be numbers, targets, cases, statistics. But in the public space generated by petitions, demonstrations, tweets, etc., the deportee becomes a person, a face, a human life. Or take the practice of last resort that many people, along with their supporters, facing situations of deportation have employed. Surrounded by security escorts, waiting in the departure lounge, or while being shepherded onto the plane, they refuse to depart in silence. They alert fellow passengers that they are being deported against their will, or they protest to the captain and crew that this is not right. In that act of appeal is there not a making visible? And not just making themselves visible as deportees. After all, despite the policies and practices designed to neutralise their presence, they may be in key respects quite visible already. They are also making visible the relations of complicity, the regime of silence which can otherwise allow deportations to proceed in full view of a public. It is as though they are saying: are you fellow passengers comfortable to sit there while this happens? Infrastructure brings deportees into contact with passengers who can always be transformed into witnessing publics. Moreover, those publics can be multiplied when, as recently was the case with Elin Ersson's refusal to take her seat on a plane until a man being sent to Afghanistan was removed, the smartphone-YouTube nexus relays such practices to a much wider audience. As I noted at the outset, infrastructure, citizenship and visibility are entangled in new power relations of deportation.

Consider the practice of disrupting charter flights. One reason governments have made charter flights a tool of expulsion is precisely because they channel the activity of deportation away from crowded airport lounges and away from other passengers. Charters often fly from small airports, or the least conspicuous areas and times of the large terminals. They board people in secrecy. When activists disrupt these flights – as was the case with the Stansted 15 in March 2017 – they don't just frustrate a particular operation.[18] They challenge these lines of visibility and invisibility: they publicise the charter flight as a *secret* flight, mobilising around it the negative connotations that otherwise attach to the clandestine movement of people.

So, visibility and invisibility are really important features of the government of deportation. And yet, we cannot buy into what I would call the logic of exposure here. By a logic of exposure I mean the idea that injustices exist and that by exposing and publicising them a public will become outraged and demand a stop to the practice. Of course, there is some truth to this logic. At the same time, we know enough about the logics of what Nicolas De Genova has called 'border spectacles' to recognise that, far from negating particular policies, their publicisation can often reinforce the practice, becoming an integral element in the process.[19] You only have to read the comments in any online news story about a particular deportation to see this. Campaigners expose the horrors of a particular detention centre, or the mistreatment of a particular case, and the comments that append the story will say: Why are we so concerned about these people? Let's deport more not less!

Ultimately, we have to recognise that deportation entails multiple forms of visibility and invisibility, sometimes very contradictorily. Here I concur with Nicholas Fischer's argument that we do not get far if we approach the study of the politics of migration control in terms of fixed notions of secrecy and publicity. Instead, we need to understand that the field of migration politics is structured by a specific 'dialectics' of secrecy and publicity, hiding and detection.[20]

Governments publicise some aspects while making others, such as the operational side, as secret as possible. Migrants and their allies employ visibility strategically. Without wanting to diminish or underestimate how difficult it is to publicise a wrong, making particular practices or policies visible will not be enough. Given the power of the spectacle to absorb such counter-measures, to redeploy them, as it were, there has to be also the question of the forms and the mediators of visibility: the question of how, by what means, in what form deportation is made – or not made – public.

Images: Collectif La Chapelle Debout / Brigade Anti Deportation (photos: Michelle Weitzel, 2018; Williams Walters, 2018).

*William Walters is Professor of Political Sociology at Carleton University, Canada. He is author of* Governmentality: Critical Encounters *(2012), and is currently working on three projects: a book on the uses of secrecy, a co-edited volume on vehicles and migration, and a collaborative research project on the aerial geography of deportation.*

**Notes**

1. See such key works as Nicholas De Genova and Nathalie Peutz, eds., *The Deportation Regime: Sovereignty, Space, and the Freedom of Movement* (Durham NC: Duke University Press, 2010); Daniel Kanstroom, *Deportation Nation: Outsiders in American History* (Cambridge MA: Harvard University Press, 2007); Liz Fekete, 'The Deportation Machine: Europe, Asylum, and Human Rights', *Race and Class* 47:1 (2005), 64–91.

2. Peralta, Eyder, 'You Say You Are American, but What if You Had to Prove It or Be Deported', *National Public Radio*, 22 December 2016, https://www.npr.org/sections/thetwo-way/2016/12/22/504031635/you-say-you-re-an-american-but-what-if-you-had-to-prove-it-or-be-deported

3. Luke De Noronha, 'The "Windrush Generation" and "Illegal Immigrants" are Both our Kin', *OpenDemocracy*, 1 May 2018, https://www.opendemocracy.net/uk/luke-de-noronha/windrush-generation-and-illegal-immigrants-are-both-our-kin

4. William Davies, 'Weaponising Paperwork: The Windrush Scandal', *London Review of Books* 40:9, 10 May 2018, https://www.lrb.co.uk/v40/n09/william-davies/weaponising-paperwork

5. Imogen Tyler argues convincingly that the hostile environment policy centred upon the drive to increase 'voluntary returns' within the overall composition of the deported; an end it sought through coercive administrative measures coupled with a widespread propaganda campaign whose brand was 'Go Home'! That the latter was a dog whistle bringing the hate speech of the far right into official governmental discourse was, she avers, no accident. See Tyler, 'Deportation Nation: Theresa May's Hostile Environment', *Journal for the Study of British Cultures* (2018) (forthcoming).

6. Audrey Macklin, 'Kick Off Contribution', in *The Return of Banishment: Do the New Denationalisation Policies Weaken Citizenship?*, eds. Audrey Macklin and Rainer Bauböck, EUI Working Paper RSCAS 2015/14, 1–6.

7. Kanstroom, *Deportation Nation*, 26.

8. See William Walters, 'Deportation, Expulsion, and the International Police of Aliens', *Citizenship Studies* 6:3 (2002), 265–292.

9. Barry Hindess, 'Citizenship in the International Management of Population', *American Behavioral Scientist* 43:9 (2000), 1486–97.

10. See Jean-Pierre Cassarino, ed., *Unbalanced Reciprocities: Cooperation on Readmission in the Euro-Mediterranean Area* (Washington: Middle East Institute, 2011).

11. Daniel Kanstroom, 'The "Right to Remain Here" as an Evolving Component of Global Refugee Protection: Current Initiatives and Critical Questions', *Journal on Migration and Human Security* 5:3 (2017), 614–44.

12. Ethan Blue, 'Strange Passages: Carceral Mobility and the Liminal in the Catastrophic History of American Deportation', *National Identities* 17:2 (2015), 175–94.

13. William Walters, 'Aviation as Deportation Infrastructure: Airports, Planes, and Expulsion', *Journal of Ethnic and Migration Studies* (2017), DOI: 10.1080/1369183X.2017.1401517; see also Biao Xiang and Johan Lindquist, 'Migration Infrastructure', *International Migration Review* 48:S1 (2014), S122–S148.

14. On 'soft deportation', see Barak Kalir, 'Between "Voluntary" Return Programs and Soft Deportation: Sending Vulnerable Migrants in Spain Back "Home"', in *Return Migration and Psychosocial Wellbeing: Discourses, Policy- Making and Outcomes for Migrants and Their Families*, eds. Zana Vathi and Russell King (Abingdon: Routledge, 2017), 56–71.

15. Jacques Rancière, *Disagreement: Politics and Philosophy*, trans. Julie Rose, (Minneapolis: University of Minnesota Press, 1999).

16. For an important work showing the relevance of Rancière's thinking on the perceptible to the politics of anti-deportation, see Peter Nyers, 'Abject Cosmopolitanism: The Politics of Protection in the Anti-Deportation Movement', *Third World Quarterly* 24:6 (2003), 1069–93. For a more recent examination of struggles over deportation that is exemplary in examining the role of TV news, public relations and other aesthetic practices in mediating the production of deportable people, see Imogen Tyler, 'Deportation Nation'.

17. Michel Foucault, 'The Subject and Power', in *Michel Foucault: Power. Essential Works of Foucault 1954-84*, ed. James Faubion (New York: Free Press, 2000).

18. Graeme Hayes, Steven Cammiss and Brian Doherty, 'Deportation and Direct Action in Britain: The "Terrorist Trial" of the Stansted 15', OpenDemocracy, 16 March 2018, https://www.opendemocracy.net/graeme-hayes-steven-cammiss-brian-doherty/deportation-and-direct-action-in-britain-terrorist-trial-o

19. Nicolas De Genova, 'Spectacles of Migrant "Illegality": The Scene of Exclusion, The Obscene of Inclusion', *Ethnic and Racial Studies* 36:7 (2013), 1180–98.

20. See Nicholas Fischer, 'Clandestins au secret: Contrôle et circulation de l'information dans les centres de rétention administrative français', *Cultures & Conflits* 57 (2005), 91–118.

# Stolen time
Shahram Khosravi

The most remarkable reason for deportation I have seen is from 1914, when a Russian Jew was deported from Sweden after six years. A short sentence in the police report, explaining why he should be deported, reads: 'He was a bad shoemaker.' It was not enough to be a labourer; one had to be a good labourer. In the same year, two other Russian Jews were deported because one lacked 'a sense of rightness' and the other one had 'venereal diseases'.[1] The religious undertones concerning chastity, virtue and the Protestant work ethic that were used to justify deportation of these three men are obvious. Almost a century later I witnessed how the Protestant ethic was also used to rationalise rejection of an asylum seeker. In 2007 I accompanied a young man who had been living in Sweden without a residence permit for a period of several months to a meeting with a lawyer to formulate an asylum claim. I helped with translation. The lawyer asked what he would say if the authorities asked why he had not sought asylum when he had arrived in Sweden several months earlier. The young man said he would lie and say that he just arrived. The lawyer got upset and said: 'We in this country are Protestant, and we do not lie.' The man was later deported.

Following Carl Schmitt's idea that 'all significant concepts of the modern theory of the state are secularised theological concepts', I would say that the current deportation regime has an inherently religious dimension.[2] The introduction of 'crime involving moral turpitude' (CIMT) in US deportation law demonstrates very well the link between the notions of sin and deportation. The term CIMT is vague and lacks definiteness and clarity. Deeply rooted in religion and loaded with religious overtones, CIMT is a grey zone in which the distinction between the unlawful and the sinful has disappeared; subsequently, legal conceptions of crime and religious conceptions of sin become indistinguishable. Sin is thus a violation not only of divine rule but also of society's well-being, and a non-citizen sinner is subjected to criminal law. The lack of precision means that the application of the law regarding what is 'contrary to the rules of morality' is left to the discretion of the judges, who can deport non-citizens not only for criminal offences but also for sinful acts.[3]

There is a fundamental sinfulness in being a foreigner: the unforgivable sin of being on this side of the border with a 'foreign' skin colour, language, name, face or religion. Foreigners are undesired ones who never stop being seen as foreigners, no matter how long they have lived in the country, no matter how integrated they are in the society, no matter whether or not they were born in the country. A long-term, sometimes lifelong, re-entry ban for deportees discloses the fact that foreigners' sins are imprescriptible: never forgotten; never forgiven.

Even now people are deported because they are bad crafts(wo)men, or face denial of admission at the border because of disease, or simply because of the sin of lying in a Protestant land. In 2017 Norwegian immigration authorities started a deportation process of a whole family of twelve people, a couple who received asylum in Norway in 1990, their children (only four and nine years old when they came to Norway) and grandchildren (born in Norway). Their Norwegian citizenship was withdrawn, and they were ordered to leave the country after 27 years. The couple are accused of having lied about their nationality when they sought asylum in 1990. The authorities claim that they are Jordanian nationals and not Palestinians. The sin of lying to the state results in collective punishments of denaturalisation and deportation almost three decades after the alleged sin of lying. Expulsion of what is believed to be foreign and harmful is, in this way, part of nation building, part of a secularised state with an inherently religious nature.

Deportation is also part of the border regime that aims to keep people in their places within the class hierarchy. As Nicholas De Genova argues, the condition of deportability renders migrant workers a distinctly disposable commodity and creates a flexible and docile labour force. Deportation as a way of controlling the mobility of workers is crucial for maintaining the wage gap between citizens and non-citizens and also between the global North and the global South. There is a direct link between outsourcing to countries with low wages and the restrictions placed upon the mobility of the people of those countries. Recently a number of US academics have been exploring the relationship between mass deportation and outsourcing and offshoring. Mass deportation provides a flexible and culturally suitable labour force that is bilingual and has the 'right' cultural capital for transnational corporations; for example, in the Dominican Republic and El Salvador. Deportation preserves and reproduces social inequalities and global injustices. Deportation aims to maintain the unequal access to resources, and upholds unequal distribution of wealth.

For instance, keeping Afghans in Iran 'deportable' has been a strategy to allocate them to specific regions of the country with need of a cheap labour force and also to specific occupations. Through the discriminatory policies of the Iranian authorities, the Afghan presence in the labour market is so firmly established that many Iranians use the word Afghani synonymously with 'unskilled worker'. Depriving non-citizens' chances to improve their socioeconomic conditions is a global trend. In July 2018 a new law in Sweden gave a second chance to 9,000 unaccompanied asylum-seeking children (the majority of them Afghans) with a deportation decision allowing them to stay to attend upper secondary school. After they finish school, however, they have to leave the country, unless they have a job. That means these youngsters should forget their dreams of a higher education. Many young Afghans, who were born in the condition of undocumentedness in Iran and never had a chance for higher education, face the same barrier in Sweden. They are destined to remain 'unskilled workers' wherever they go. Deportability at the global level generates a removable underclass of workers in both the country that one escapes from and the country in which one seeks refuge. Deportation has been added to neoliberal policies of social abandonment, which expose vulnerable groups to multiple expulsions from communities, the labour market, the housing market, the spheres of security, the health care system, the education system and state protection.

Moreover, deportable Afghans in Iran are used to trigger divisions within the working class by engendering a circuit of paranoia among Iranian workers who believe that the real threat against their class interest is migrant workers and not the widespread un(der)employment, political oppression, institutionalised corruption, regularly unpaid salaries and financial insecurities. When Iranian workers got permission to celebrate May Day in 2015, thousands of them demanded expulsion of the Afghan labour force from the country. I cannot agree more with Günther Anders, the German Jewish philosopher, who in another deportation context put it this way: 'to have a faithful slave, give him an under-slave.'[4]

Deportation is not only a spatial expulsion, but also a temporal one. Deportability is a statement of a spatial as well as a temporal dis-belonging. The deportee's *tomorrow* belongs elsewhere. Expulsion is nothing less than robbing an individual of the viabilities of life. It wipes out the vision of a better future. To unfold the brutality embedded in the deportation regime, we should examine the deportee's time. Similar to the case of human trafficking, deportation is forced and coercive. There are explicit elements of exploitation in deportation. As part of the global apartheid of the right to mobility, removal of migrants is part of a brutal neoliberal political system that is also inextricably intertwined with an exploitative economic system. Both human trafficking and deportation lead to accumulation of wealth through the stealing of time. In modern societies, time is associated with success and money. It has become a form of capital that, similar to money, can be invested, saved or wasted. Capital grows through stealing of time. When people are spatially removed, they are automatically robbed of an amount of time.[5] People, particularly long-term residents, have worked, built networks, paid taxes, spent time learning the local language and becoming accustomed to the culture, fallen in love, and maybe had children, before being sent to countries to which they may have little connection. The time people have *invested* to achieve these goals is lost by deportation. The time people have *spent* to accumulate social and cultural capital is thwarted by deportation.

Sudden arrest and deportation means having no chance to prepare for the journey, to sell accumulated property, to claim wages owed or to collect one's belongings. Being deportable usually means that one has lived an informal life, with a job that was not registered, with no insurance and with belongings that were not documented. An illegalised life (time) is unreclaimable, since it is not considered to have existed at all.

A not unusual consequence of deportation is losing money in the form of unpaid wages. The deportees' worked time is stolen. Many deportees believe that their employers reported them to the police to save the money they owed them in the form of unpaid wages. Lacking the right to have a bank account, many undocumented migrants ask others to save their money. Undocumented people buy cars and properties registered in the names of documented people and citizens. Deportation makes it difficult if not impossible to regain all these. What about taxes and social security contributions people may have paid before being removed? What about unused holiday? How many working hours are stolen? How much money did their employers save in the form of unpaid wages? How much money does the state save in the form of unpaid pensions? How much surplus value has been produced for capitalists through deportation globally?

We live in the age of mass deportation. Almost three million people were deported from the United States between 2009 and 2016, and several million more are scheduled to be deported in coming years. Europe is organising the deportation of almost a hundred thousand people to Afghanistan alone. Agreements with states, like Turkey, are signed; huge amounts of money have been paid to alleviate removals. Likewise mass deportation is growing outside the global North. Saudi Arabia has deported hundreds of thousands of migrants every year in recent years. Since 2016 more than a million Afghans have been forcibly sent to Afghanistan from Iran and Pakistan. How much time has been stolen?

In some deportation regimes the link between deportation by states and accumulation of wealth by private actors is explicit. The Iranian and Pakistani authorities force Afghans to pay the cost of their own deportation. The travel costs across the border to Afghanistan for a large family, all the bribes they have to pay and the initial resettlement costs push deportees to turn to moneylenders, who demand high interest rates. The cost of debts results in long-term exploitation. In 2016 a large family were deported from Pakistan to Afghanistan. An Afghan moneylender paid all the costs of their journey, that is, deportation. Since their deportation, all the members of the family – from the grandmother to the youngest child, only eight years old – have been working on the moneylender's farm for free. This is an example of how deportation and human trafficking knit together.

Besides the time invested economically, what about all the time spent on building networks, friendships, emotional relationships? For long-term residents, deportation means leaving their youth and childhood behind, and all the memories they formed in the places they called home. What about all the years deported parents are separated from their children, and their partners? The Windrush scandal is one example of the brutality of the theft of time: long-term residents are denied benefits, access to healthcare, education or housing, and are threatened with deportation after several decades spent in the UK working, paying taxes and building communities.

Another devastating consequence of stealing time is keeping people in a condition of circulation. A common experience of deportees is being sent back in time, expressed as being sent 'back to square one'. The sense of going back to square one illustrates how deportation deprives people of their time invested in building a life in the host country. Keeping people in circulation is a way to slow down, to defer, to deny future plans and to create disruption in the stages of the life cycle. A life in circulation is an indefinite position of *not becoming* in what is supposed to a 'normal life course.' In the condition of circulation one never gets the chance to finish anything. This is a way to keep people as permanent 'unskilled labourers' (as in the case of Afghans in Iran and Sweden), and removable when they are not good ones (as in the case of the bad shoemaker). Unlike the Foucauldian surveillance and disciplinary society that operated by confinement, this regime of circulating people is more similar to a Deleuzian control society that operates by keeping people continuously on the move.[6] This is a controlled movement of people sent back and forth between undocumentedness and deportability: between countries, between laws, between institutions. To keep people in circulation so that their experience is usually one of 'not arriving', an experience of temporariness, being constantly on the move, is a control mechanism that propels them back towards square one. As Clara Lecadet argues, the circulation of manpower is a means of subjugating workers.

The threat of being pushed towards square one hangs not only over the heads of non-citizens but, as William Walters highlights, increasingly also over the heads of racialised citizens. Mahad Abib Mahmud was only 14 years old when he arrived in Norway as an unaccompanied asylum seeker in 2000. He received asylum and later on gained Norwegian citizenship. In 2017, after 17 years, he was stripped of his Norwegian citizenship and had to leave the country. Norwegian authorities claimed that Mahmud was originally from Djibouti and not from Somalia, as he had said on arrival. He has a science degree and worked in a public hospital in Oslo; he had bought a house and had an extended social network. He was forced to leave Norway to seek asylum in Iceland. Earlier this year his application was rejected. In 2018 he is back to the same square he was on 18 years earlier, and his time has been stolen.

As Marx showed, surplus value is generated from time that capitalists do not pay for, the time they steal from labourers. The extra value added to commodities comes from stolen time. Like people who have been trafficked, deportees' time is actively stolen. Using the term *stealing* emphasises how deportation is part of the accumulation of wealth in the hands of a few by dispossessing the migrants of their *saved*, *spent* and *invested* time. Demonstrating how deportees' time is stolen repoliticises in this way the concepts of borders and deportations that have been naturalised and depoliticised by the ideology of the nation state.

Image: Shahram Khosravi, Idomeni railway station (2018).

*Shahram Khosravi is Professor of Social Anthropology at Stockholm University and author of several books including* Precarious Lives: Waiting and Hope in Iran *(2017). He is also editor of the collection* After Deportation: Ethnographic Perspectives *(2017).*

**Notes**

1. Tomas Hammar, *Sverige åt svenskarna* (Stockholm: Caslon, 1964), 343.
2. Carl Schmitt, *Political Ecology: Four Chapters on the Concept of Sovereignty*, trans. George Schwab (Cambridge, MA: MIT Press, 1985).
3. Mary P. Holper, 'Deportation for a Sin: Why Moral Turpitude Is Void for Vagueness', *Nebraska Law Review* 90:3 (2013), 647–702.
4. Günther Anders, *Et si je suis désespéré que voulez-vous que j'y fasse* (Paris: Editions Allia, 2016), 8.
5. Lauren, Martin, 'Deportation and the dispossession of time', *Darkmatter* (2015), accessed 20 October 2018, http://www.darkmatter101.org/site/2015/10/05/deportation-and-the-dispossession-of-time/
6. Gilles Deleuze, 'Postscript on the Societies of Control', *October* 59 (Winter 1992), 3–7.

# Centre for Research in Modern European Philosophy

## public lectures on philosophy, politics and culture

**2019**

In collaboration with the Institute for Modern and Contemporary Culture **IMCC**

| Date | Speaker(s) | Title |
|---|---|---|
| **17 January** | Catherine Malabou CRMEP | Is Science the Subject of Philosophy? Miller, Badiou and Derrida |
| **24 January** | Lucy Bond IMCC<br>Howard Caygill CRMEP | Is Memory the Basis of History (after Trump)? |
| **7 February** | Stella Sandford CRMEP | Reason in Reverse: Kant, Freud & Faults |
| **28 February** | Radha D'Souza WLS<br>Peter Hallward CRMEP | What's Wrong with Human Rights? |
| **14 March** | Étienne Balibar CRMEP | Towards a Socialist Cosmopolitanism |
| **28 March** | David Cunningham IMCC<br>Peter Osborne CRMEP | Poetics of Contemporary Art |

**Thursdays 6.00 pm** — University of Westminster, 309 Regent Street, London W1B 2HW

Free but booking via Eventbrite is essential

**www.kingston.ac.uk/crmep**

Kingston University London

UNIVERSITY OF WESTMINSTER

# Fallen angel
## Guy Lardreau's later voluntarism
Peter Hallward

The French philosopher and erstwhile Maoist militant Guy Lardreau (1947-2008) was the first to admit that much of his work was haunted by a single problem, one posed by the revolutionary political history of the twentieth century.[1] The great revolutions in Russia and China, and several other places inspired by their example, pursued radical change in the literal sense. They had dug down to the root of things, and tried to uproot them. They had sought to break patterns of injustice and inequality so entrenched that they had been suffered, for centuries, as part of the immutable order of things. More than a mere break with historical tendencies, the great revolutions thus aspired to change human nature itself, to shake it to its most apparently 'unchangeable' foundations.[2] They did not hesitate to take up Rousseau's famous challenge, to 'denature' humanity and make the world anew – and it's no accident that in Lardreau's early work, alongside Mao and Lenin, the key source of inspiration is Rousseau, and a sharply anti-Kantian version of Rousseau at that.[3] The most sincere revolutionaries vehemently rejected the sort of critical limitations Kant insisted on, limitations that, for Lardreau as for Marx and so many other Marxists, position him first and foremost as an anti-revolutionary thinker: they had sought precisely to force both history and nature into line with the ideal and uncompromising principles of reason.

To invoke the metaphor first adopted in Lardreau's most famous book, *L'Ange*, co-written with Christian Jambet in 1976, and which endures as the central figure of his last published writings, the modern revolutions can thus be understood as essentially *angelic* projects. The term 'Angel', to cite what is perhaps Lardreau's clearest explanation of his usage, 'is the name of the possibility that human nature, for so long established in a certain way, might change from top to bottom.' For a particular historical period this possibility took on a 'political face' – the period of *la Grande Politique*, between the French and Cambodian revolutions (FD, 83).

After enthusiastically embracing the apparent consequences of China's Great Proletarian Cultural Revolution in the late 1960s and early 1970s, however, Lardreau soon came to the conclusion that any genuinely radical revolution could in actuality lead only to catastrophe. Actual revolutions led to the guillotine, the gulag, and the killing fields of Cambodia. The more ardent a revolution's desire to build heaven on earth, the more hellish its worldly consequences. By the end of his life, the only difference Lardreau recognised between 'legitimate' French revolutionary figures like Robespierre and Chaumette, on the one hand, and reviled war criminals like Goebbels or Pol Pot, on the other, is that, at least over the longer historical term, 'the former succeeded whereas the latter failed. *Vae victis* ...' (FD, 24). Ever since its true visage was exposed in Cambodia, the 'political face' of the Angel has vanished without trace, and without any prospect of return (even if angelic hope as such always persists, as an eternal yearning or possibility) (FD, 83).

Something about the very desire or will to 'bend political power to the highest ends of reason', as Lardreau suggests in several late texts, seemed doomed to 'result in the necessary reversal of best into worst.'[4] The real source of this necessity, he eventually decides, lies in the quality of such a will itself – revolutionary political will, in other words, seems to operate as a sort of malevolent inversion of Kant's conception of a morally 'good will'. Where the latter figured as the only thing 'in the world, or indeed even beyond it, that could be considered good without limitation',[5] there is likewise no limit to the evil of the former. Lardreau's great problem, then, is to understood how political projects undertaken with the very best of intentions invariably turn bad, and 'not because the will behind this undertaking became lazy or forgetful, but on account of this will itself.'[6]

Lardreau's chief concern, early and late, is with the nature of such political will. I addressed Lardreau's early voluntarism – in particular as developed in his first book *Le Singe d'or* [*The Golden Monkey*, 1973] – in an article published in an earlier issue of this journal (*RP* 190). What is unusual about Lardreau's subsequent turn away from revolutionary zeal in the mid to late 1970s is that, unlike some of his comrades in French Maoist political circles, he did not simply reverse course, and fling himself with equal enthusiasm into the arms of neo-liberal reaction.[7] Instead he sought to combine a version of his original revolutionary intransigence, while restoring a strict, broadly Kantian demarcation of rational and moral ideals, on the one hand, and historical reality or actuality, on the other. Only unconditional affirmation is worthy of the ideal, but any attempt to actualise or implement it is itself criminal. In his final, posthumously published book, *Faces de l'Ange déchu*, Lardreau puts it in increasingly strident if not openly 'inquisitorial' terms: the only 'perversion that cannot be forgiven, the only irremissible misdeed or sin …, is the bad will to realise the Idea' (FD, 170).

Affirmation of the ideal, in short, becomes a more and more emphatically spiritual exercise, purged of all worldly contamination. As a political figure, the angel can now appear only as 'fallen [*déchu*]', as a figure of renunciation and withdrawal. In the end, this logic will allow him to affirm both the enduring reason of the Maoist slogan '*on a raison de se révolter*' – it is right or reasonable to rebel – while embracing the most reactionary (in the literal sense) aspects of French counter-revolutionary thought: the ultra-conservative Catholic restoration urged by thinkers like Joseph de Maistre and Louis Bonald. Like these bitter enemies of the Enlightenment and of all ideas of historical 'progress', Lardreau concludes that the French Revolution found its essence and 'its highest truth in the guillotine'. If 'with respect to the Revolution, all that matters to thought has come from the Counter-Revolution' (FD, 101n.6), this is because only the counter-revolutionary thinkers were equipped to grasp both the material and the 'Sublime' aspects of the Terror (FD, 24). Bonald had it right: 'only religion can understand politics' (FD, 133).

If his Maoist work of the early 1970s was entirely oriented by 'an act of faith' in the masses and the profoundly rational 'rightness' of their revolt,[8] we can analyse Lardreau's subsequent attempt to separate the domains of faith and actuality across three distinct through overlapping moments, in a sequence that for the sake of simplicity might be summed up as a retreat from Rousseau's politics to Kant's morality. In *L'Ange* (1976) he still affirms the will to revolt against the evils of the world, while acknowledging that so long as it commits to an actual emancipatory political project then revolt may always be deluded, co-opted and harnessed to new forms of oppression. In *Le Monde* (1978) he withdraws revolt from any political engagement with the world at all, in order to take refuge in an uncompromising 'moral attitude', one that upholds our duty to respect the imprescriptible rights that should apply to every individual in all situations. In *La Véracité* (1993), the explicitly Kantian framework for this moral attitude is re-affirmed but reframed along still more strictly 'negative' lines, in keeping with the purely 'supersensible' and supra-actual quality of our freedom to posit an unconditional moral law.[9]

# I

Co-written with Lardreau's long-time comrade Christian Jambet (who shared both Lardreau's political convictions and his erudite fascination with ascetic spirituality and esoteric religion), and long considered a sort of 'cult classic' on the experimental fringes of recent French philosophy, *L'Ange* (1976) retains the same basic political orientation as *Singe d'or* (1973), framed by an archetypal scenario that pits the 'rebel' (the insurgent, the dissident, the heretic …) against the 'master' (the boss, the Party, the state ...).[10] In the Lacanian terms that Lardreau now begins to adopt, what defines any master is the command '*cède sur ton désir*' (LM, 85) – 'give up on your desire' – whereas every rebel rejects precisely this imperative. Across both *Singe* and *L'Ange*, 'what I've been constantly saying is that a world without master must be possible',[11] i.e. a *world* of absolute justice. The fundamental issue remains a matter of making a stark choice, between the 'side of the people' or that of their oppressors (LA, 42). Popular revolt or submissive resignation: these alternatives continue to define the political spectrum.

In this sense there is no retreat here from the earlier commitment to Maoism,[12] and far from renegation what Lardreau seeks is to 'go still further in my imperfect conversion ...; I still don't claim to be doing anything else than pursuing a Maoist philosophy.'[13] Like *Singe*, *L'Ange* continues to reject the idea that a world without mastery or oppression might ever come about through some immanent form of necessity or progress, some development of the existing conditions of oppression, on the model of socialism as emerging out from capitalist industrialisation. Genuine, i.e. 'cultural' revolution, in the Maoist sense, remains the contrary of progress or maturation, and of the anticipatory knowledge induced from the logic of progress. To engage in revolution is here to plunge into a project that thwarts all anticipation of what is to come, and all 'planning' for the future. Cultural revolution does not complete or accelerate what is established but breaks abruptly with it, on the model of an apocalypse. To revolt is to resist the temptation to 'know what is to come', to avoid 'predicting the new', and 'the first principle of cultural revolution' remains one of humility in the face of its imminent future. 'I can never say what should come, since if what comes is new then this must exceed what I had foreseen', as a matter of course.[14]

Like all of Lardreau's subsequent work, *L'Ange* also continues to affirm forms of an ascetic, self-sacrificing discipline and commitment, at the furthest remove of any *anarcho-désirant* call to 'go with the flow'. As with *Singe*, as far as desire and the body are concerned what is at stake in *L'Ange* remains 'not the liberation but the abolition of the body'.[15] Angel and monkey might thus seem to have more in common than these titles imply. Unlike *Singe*, however, *L'Ange* is newly concerned with the way that even the purest and most well-intentioned forms of such dedication may nonetheless be accommodated within, or usurped by, mechanisms of domination. A couple of years on from its dissolution, Lardreau is ready to admit that 'the Gauche Prolétarienne might have been one of the discourses that the Master made use of it, and that he will continue to make use of, as a mechanism for enabling his own metamorphosis.'[16] In *L'Ange*, the issue is most starkly posed in the sections of the book that evoke the exemplary experience of those early Christian ascetics (Saint Jerome, Chrysostomos and various others) who both lived and declared an especially intransigent form of 'absolute revolt' against the prevailing way of the world (LA, 93–99). What is primary, in this sequence, is the moment of absolute zeal that inspired these Red Guards of Christ in the decades that followed his crucifixion, 'this surreal crowd that swarms in the deserts of the Orient, these monks with wasted bellies, their bodies lacerated with chains, these ruined figures whipped by wind and rain, these worm-eaten but radiant stylites, these voluntary madmen' (LA, 101). The early monastic thinkers, inspired by a resolutely Manichean conception of reality, propose their own version of cultural revolution *avant la lettre*. They invert every accepted form of value, renounce all inheritance, refuse any loyalty to family and familiarity, deny the body, reject sexual difference and desire, affirm the all-or-nothing simplicity of redemption, pursue a heroic anonymity, adopt a permanent posture of self-criticism, embrace the most severe forms of frugality and discipline. They accept that 'the path of saintliness is a path of struggle *alone*' (LA, 148).

But how then could it happen, ask Lardreau and Jambet, that this uncompromising posture of revolt was so easily and so quickly accommodated within a new configuration of mastery? How could a discourse of pure revolt, directed against the figure of mastery as such, directed against the very survival of society, in turn become the witless 'instrument of the Master,' and allow itself to be used, as a sort of safely marginalised lunatic fringe, in ways that help consolidate the social and institutional mainstream? How, in short, was the uncompromising discourse of *saints* bent to

the base needs of an emergent *church*?

The answer, which applies both to early Christianity and to the revolutionary projects of the twentieth century, relies on conversion of cultural revolution into a merely 'ideological' revolution. An ideological revolution is that 'miracle' which succeeds in reducing the most subversive of ideals and practices to a 'docile instrument' of order, by isolating their most dedicated proponents (now invested with a special 'vocation' or 'profession') from their fellows and putting them back *to work*, in cloistered obedience to the will of a new master (LA, 115). Whereas cultural revolution rejects every form of mastery in the unmediated dualism of oppression/revolt, ideological revolution mediates subjective responses to socio-historical 'causes' and economic conditions and integrates rebellion within a rational historical order or development – and in the process it transforms the critique of mastery into the mere substitution of one master for another (LA, 151–52). The quality of the *will* involved is thereby fundamentally changed. Determined through coordination with the apparent 'necessity' of its material base, 'ideological revolution is, subjectively, a mitigated will [*une volonté mitigée*], and objectively, a will to mitigation', whereas the sole 'law of cultural revolution' remains a 'will of absolute purity' (LA, 110; cf. LM, 19–20), a will to pursue 'the deliberate, systematic inversion of all the values of this world' (LA, 87).

Recognition of the means by which the zeal of the early Christian ascetics was harnessed to the needs of a new institutional order allows Lardreau to see how his own cultural revolution had been usurped, how 'we too have no doubt simply been a moment of an ideological revolution that made use of us, and which in a sense we completely failed to understand', leaving us as little more than obedient pawns of 'the will of the Master' (LA, 135). By 1976, Lardreau had already come to the conclusion that any attempt to change the world by political means, for instance by organising a political party on the Leninist model, could only lead to variations on a Stalinist outcome.[17]

A rejection of *all* mastery, Lardreau now argues, must also include a rejection of the very will, striving or desire for a world without mastery. This is because Lardreau now accepts, following Lacan, that desire *as such* is the domain of the master. 'We have a very elevated idea of the Master, an elevated idea of his history, and ... like Lacan, we think that nothing that relates to desire escapes him.'[18] (Following *L'Ange*, Lacan will figure above all in Lardreau's work as the prophet who spoke an uncomfortable but oft-cited truth to the young would-be revolutionaries of May 68: 'What you aspire to as revolutionaries is a master. You will get one.'[19]) Since political and sexual desire obey the same logic, the idea of 'sexual liberation' must thus be dismissed as an especially acute contradiction in terms – which accounts, parenthetically, for Lardreau's critiques of Sade, Deleuze and Lyotard. Genuine revolt must be a-sexual or extra-sexual, and the first reason why Lardreau and Jambet now conceive of the revolutionary as 'angelic' should be taken quite literally. 'This image of the Angel must be understood very simply ...: a body without sex.'[20] Or rather – as a body without body, a body purged of all flesh and material desire, one dedicated to nothing other than 'perpetual praise' of its transcendent creator (LA, 104).

The further and deeper reason why Lardreau admits that to wait for the angel's advent is the only way to preserve 'the hope of revolution' is that this serves to illustrate the actual 'conditions of possibility' of rebellion, i.e. to illustrate their necessary *non*-actuality (LA, 36, cf. 79). Not only is cultural revolution doomed to ideological recuperation in history but the alternative, the successful realisation of cultural revolution, would herald nothing less than the end of history and of humanity as we know it, and thus the end of all realisation too.

Pushed to its limit, Lardreau's position now culminates, in effect, in a double wager – first on rebellion rather than submission, and then on rebellion's necessary *failure* rather than possible success. The first wager is a matter of pure incantation, without reason or cause: 'The Angel must come', since the alternative is intolerable despair (LA, 36, 70). Even if mastery has always triumphed, so far, and even if revolt serves only to reinvigorate oppression, nevertheless 'once again, and come what may, we will make the mad wager: the Angel, whose annunciation it is our turn to declare, has always been defeated – but he will finally triumph in an unprecedented revolution' (LA, 152). Lardreau accepts that history has backed him into a corner, but not yet that he must yield; what remains is the logic of the gamble or wager as such, in its undecidability, demanding that between the two worlds, the world of what has been and the world of what might be, and their respective actors, 'one must choose [*il y a à choisir*]' (LA, 153). Lardreau now makes of this un-reasonable and discontinuous quality of revolt its highest virtue, an index of its unassimilatable resistance to integration in the rational progress of history. It is in the form of a pure leap that Lardreau and Jambet seek, 'against all forms of power and domination, and in spite of everything, to maintain the hope that another world is possible', by 'pushing right to the end, right to the point of paroxysm, the logic of rebellion' (LA, 10, 13). If *L'Ange* still retains an account of revolutionary will, it is already stretched close to the point where it becomes indistinguishable from a leap of faith.

The second wager, however, is now indissociable from the first, and becomes more urgently so over time. Every revolt runs the risk of barbaric inhumanity; revolutions can only prevail in a world geared to suppress them through recourse to violence on a massive scale. On this point, after Stalin, after the Gulag, and after the brutality of the Cultural Revolution, the Khmer revolution in Cambodia that began in 1975 marks the point of no return. The shift from cautious anticipation of this revolution to a definitive judgement of its actual consequences, furthermore, marks the stark dividing line between *L'Ange* and *Le Monde*, which Lardreau and Jambet published two years later. Lardreau will then be ready to bet that any and every revolutionary project, once it is put into practice, must always fail. If the practice of political will requires the direct conjunction of an intention or purpose and its execution or actualisation, Lardreau's recognition of the Cambodian catastrophe, shortly after the publication of *L'Ange*, marks the definitive end of his defence of such a practice, and confirms his re-orientation of the will from politics to morality (LM, 13).

## II

The concluding reference to the Khmer Rouge, in *L'Ange*, restates in a single phrase the basic argument of the book. 'If the Cambodians are right to revolt' (as a matter of course), the actual outcome of the Khmer Rouge project, whatever it might be, will not itself resolve or 'suppress our transcendental question, regarding the possible autonomy of revolt itself' (LA, 233). In other words, revolt in Cambodia, like any revolt anywhere else, can always be justified as an end in itself, as an immediate reaction to oppression – and a few years after *L'Ange* was published its authors readily admitted that 'it's true that the Lin-Biaoist sympathies we had at the time allowed us to hope that the Khmer revolution would be victorious, and to feel sympathetic towards it.'[21] The rapid accumulation of evidence of Khmer crimes, however, did not so much confound an earlier endorsement of their actual revolution, as cement Lardreau's answer to precisely that transcendental question which already accompanied it in *L'Ange*, and which now receives an unequivocal answer. Khmer atrocities provide clear proof that anyone who still seeks to rebel against or at least limit the violence of mastery and oppression must first deny any *actual* application of 'the possible autonomy of revolt itself', any worldly or political possibility of moving 'beyond the history of the master.'[22] From now on, Lardreau will tacitly accept that, as far as justice and morality are concerned, the only kingdom that matters is indeed 'not of this world'.

This conclusion only follows, of course, if we first accept the Khmer's own self-description more or less at face value, as Lardreau seems to do both before and after the revolution in Cambodia – as if they really were nothing more than ruthless idealists who sought to abolish rather than reinstitute mastery, as if they really were driven by a revolutionary pursuit of absolute justice and equality. Lardreau and Jambet interpret the Khmer sequence not as an exceptionally brutal engagement with some of the many constraints that characterise Cambodia's situation (and the situation of weakened peripheral states in the capitalist world system more generally), but exclusively as an illustration of what must always happen when a 'will to purity' fully resolves to purge society of oppression. Such an angelic will, they conclude, *must* ultimately encourage a barbaric 'will to create a community of *bodies without flesh* [de *corps sans chair*], bodies stripped of desire and self-regard, a community without social ties.'[23] In keeping with this new invocation of necessity and this newly inexorable logic of revolution, the revelation of Cambodia's killing fields marked for Lardreau, as for many of his contemporaries, a definitive break with the Marxian pursuit of political power as a means of realising freedom and overcoming poverty and injustice.[24] From now on there will be no better indication of one's relative 'maturity', Lardreau suggests following Kant, than the readiness with which one accepts that we can and must live 'without great hopes or expectations.'[25]

It should be stressed, however, that such readiness remains as much a wager as was the original revolutionary project itself, albeit now a wager on *failure* rather than success. From the mid 1970s, as Alberto Toscano notes, Lardreau's understanding of revolution in general comes to be shaped by a quite specific judgement of failure and disaster, the failure of Cultural Revolution in Lin Piao's China along with the various failures to imitate or radicalise it abroad.[26] Even if one were to agree that the narrow category of 'failure' might be the most economical way to characterise these projects, Lardreau makes no attempt to explain why these particular failures might warrant the extension of this characterisation to *all* revolutionary projects (for instance those undertaken in Cuba and other parts of Latin America). If Lardreau does not concern himself with such political judgements it is because by the late 1970s he has convinced himself that 'what we are living and experiencing today isn't simply the repeated failure of revolutions to fulfil their programme to bring happiness to the people (which justified them in the eyes of simple souls) but the failure of the very Idea of Revolution.' What has failed, and failed definitively, is the very idea that 'political struggle might radically transform people's lives' (LM, 13). This failure is something that has now *taken place*, irredeemably, and Lardreau's judgement stands without appeal (FD, 44, 146).

If the idea itself has failed, and failed irredeemably, then its every instance must no doubt fail as a matter of course, and we might say that for Lardreau what will be at issue from now on, strictly speaking, is not the relative successive or failure of this or that project, but the need for any project to retreat without reservation from the very dimension in which it might either succeed *or* fail, i.e. to retreat from its very existence and temporality as a project *tout court*. In *Le Monde*, even those fading traces of revolutionary political affirmation that had persisted in *L'Ange* are purged without remainder, so as to count only 'for nothing, strictly' (LM, 279). Long before he writes his last, explicitly counter-revolutionary texts, Lardreau had reached the conclusion that any prospect of 'rational politics' is dead and buried: 'in my view there is no longer any clear and distinct idea of politics – which means that politics is no more'; the 'concept of politics has died' and politics can no longer be thought by any philosophy worthy of the name (FD, 43, 58).

In other words, what is now at issue is the possibility of an alternative idea that might ground the eternal legitimacy of revolt, without running the risk of its actual success or failure. If the political question is inevitably consumed in the violence of social dissolution and re-constitution, from now on the philosophical question will ask whether there might be some wholly 'real' dimension beyond all such constitutional force, i.e. a dimension that might serve both as a secure basis for the determination of the will and as a foundation for the certainty that it is indeed still, always and everywhere, right to revolt.[27] Confronted with the world's reality and injustice, where might we find 'the point that resists' the whole way of the world, the point from which we might refuse all the compromises we make to accommodate ourselves to the 'reality' we inhabit? Where might we find 'the granite point from which a certain deduction will be possible', one unmediated by reality or compromise, 'a point of the eminently "real", therefore, in the sense of being irreducible, inescapable, imperative – but one, nonetheless, that "reality" never takes into account' (LM, 40)?

Lardreau finds this point or dimension – and with it the key to his later philosophy as a whole – in Kant's idea of transcendental or extra-worldly freedom, understood in practice as the freedom to posit an unconditionally binding moral law, such that 'freedom and unconditional practical law reciprocally imply each other.'[28] Like most of his readers, Lardreau acknowledges Kant as the first philosopher to posit an unbridgeable gap between (a) the hypothetical, goal-oriented and context-sensitive imperatives at issue in politics and history, and (b) the unconditionally and immediately binding categorical imperative of the moral law, the law that everywhere obliges us to act only on grounds that all other rational actors could affirm, and in ways that treat ourselves and 'all others never merely as means but always at the same time as ends in themselves.'[29] In Kant's moral law, which transcends all historical particularity and every 'chain' of causation, Lardreau finds that 'granite' foundation he had failed to find in political commitment. 'The moral law, as we know, holds absolutely – it is even the only absolute that Reason can *encounter*, by which I mean: that requires no hypothesis.'[30] The law's command is absolute both everywhere and always, for *all* subjects and for all times, and for each time, for each instance, for each subject as *a* subject or as any *one* subject (LM, 98).

Kant's moral law thus furnishes, *Le Monde* argues, a secure basis for universal human rights understood precisely as protections for dissident rebels who might oppose the imposition of any actually-coercive universal norms, and thus rights to safeguard all 'claims made on behalf of the singular, of the particular, against the despotic universal' (LM, 58). Kant proposes not one account of morality among others, but an epochal discovery. 'There is no *Kantian* morality', properly speaking, for Kant's philosophy prescribes nothing less than morality itself, morality in general: '"Kantianism" exists only as the enunciation of the conditions of possibility for morality as such' (LV, 149). In due course, Lardreau will come to recognise Kant's insistence on the disjunctive relation between politics and ethics as not only unprecedented but also

> insurpassable, for I judge that no philosophy managed to model the problem before him, and none fully confronted it after him. Certainly not Hegel, who dissolves it by making the state, i.e. the highest figure that philosophy could lend to politics, the realisation of the ethical idea; nor Marx, even more so, whose way of thinking obliges him to conceive of the moral problem merely as an accident of politics.[31]

Between upholding the 'moral attitude' that consists in recognising our duty to obey the law, and participation in any worldly or political project that might try to change society or the course of history, there is now an abyss without mediation. Every philosophy of history and every philosophical conception of the world ultimately seeks, one way or another, to reconcile us with the order of this world, or its projected future order, and thus serves to justify its unjustifiable injustices. To be 'philosophical', in one conventional sense of the word, is indeed to submit to the way of the world (LM, 27–29). The freedom to posit the moral law, by contrast, is precisely that – a pure *positing* that is entirely 'free', *gratuit*, free of any constituent link with nature or world. What then allows Lardreau to pit his unconditional 'moral attitude' against any merely 'moral conception of the world' (i.e. any project to improve the world) is precisely its foundation in a purely regulative idea. In Kantian terms,

> everything depends on the point that Freedom is an Idea, i.e. that it is impossible to decide between the statements by which it can be either affirmed or denied, if we approach it from the perspective of speculative Reason; forever undecidable for science, what is at stake is only illuminated if one has already made the ethical choice. That Freedom is a postulate means that, whatever rational legitimacy might subsequently be conferred upon it, this legitimacy will only be admissible and convincing for those who have already made the choice to live morally (LM, 30–31).

There is no saving those who might prefer to make the alternative choice, the 'barbaric choice' that commits them to the sole dimension of the world. But for those who choose freedom and morality, the essential question is no longer what can we *do* to improve the world, or 'what pure moral protestation is *capable* of, against the rising insistence of barbarism in our world.' It is a matter, instead, since duty commands capacity, of accepting the simplicity of the Kantian imperative. It is enough to ask 'what must I do?', and to disregard the doing itself as a secondary matter, trusting as a matter of course that 'we can do all that we must' (LM, 16–17). Following this line of thinking to its conclusion, 'we will not say that freedom is real, or that we can affirm things *about* freedom, but that we must simply affirm it, since it is only "*under the idea of freedom*" that we can conceive of a moral attitude' (LM, 40). The priority is now to dissociate freedom from its affirmation 'not merely from *this* world, but from *a world*', any world. It is enough, and necessary, simply to 'affirm that "there is freedom" [*il y a de la liberté*], but without affirming it of anything, neither of the world nor of man' (LM, 38).

Inverting the priorities of *Singe*, in *Le Monde* Lardreau stresses this difference between Kantian and Rousseauist conceptions of autonomy. Kant's formulation of a self-legislating law, unlike Rousseau's socialised or actualised version, cannot force anyone *else* to be free. The law 'cannot itself oppress anyone; it does not proceed before any tribunal, it does not shape any institution, it distributes no power; it is only ever expressed from the point of view of a [singular] subject, posed as such, and as irreducible to every other – and no one can express the moral law for someone else' (LM, 97). It is precisely the effort to actualise or apply the law that allows a dutiful moral attitude to relapse into a mere assertion of mastery. Kantian autonomy tumbles toward a proto-criminal 'Rousseauist autonomy' as soon as 'a subject comes to maintain that the universality of the law that he [*il*] prescribes for himself must, in actuality, be realised', and thereby concludes that 'it is no longer the law that lends form to his will, but his will that gives the law its content' (LM, 98). To ward against this danger, which Lardreau encounters in some of Kant's own texts – e.g. those which, like the essays on history, progress and perpetual peace, suggest that 'Kantian morality *wills* [*veut*] its own realisation' over the course of human affairs [LM, 35]), and which he might also have found more emphatically in Heidegger's insistence, reading Kant's moral philosophy, that 'what is genuinely law-giving for willing is the actual pure willing itself and nothing else'[32] – the solution is to retreat to the purely formal, extra-actual quality of 'the Kantian imperative, that the subject *can* always will that the maxim of his action be [universalisable], but that he never actually *wills* it thus' (LM, 99). The supersensible or noumenal domain must be respected as what it must remain, as *réel* in a roughly Lacanian sense, rather than embraced as the basis of a capacity that might be realised in practice.[33]

On this condition, by abandoning all reference to the will as practice or capacity in favour of the law as unconditional duty, Lardreau can preserve his old opposition between submission and revolt, precisely by abstracting the latter from its engagement with any actual target or obstacle. Read in this way (and thus against the voluntarist and indeed commanding or 'masterful' grain of so much of Kant's own moral theory), Lardreau's Kant offers a kind of 'autonomy that, because it is entirely cut off from the political conception of the world, does not demand mastery', while still reminding each and every individual, always as *an* individual, of one's categorical duty: '*do not give up on your desire*' (LM, 97). Do not conform to the way of the world. Precisely because it subtracts itself from the complex chain of causes and interests that shape the world, the Kantian moral attitude amounts to a 'pure gesture of retreat or withdrawal, of subtraction from obedience, through which, by stubbornly refusing to give up, a subject thereby affirms himself as autonomous. Kant with Lacan, in short.'[34]

The price Lardreau has to pay in order to sustain this new formulation of revolt over submission, however, is exorbitant. Since revolt is now indistinguishable from 'retreat' [*retrait*] it not only leaves the world of oppression untouched, it also resonates all too easily with a socio-economic world that is itself beginning, in its incipient neoliberal reconfiguration over the course of the 1970s, to privilege private interests and de-regulated market 'liberties' over any residual commitment to public goods and collective projects. It resonates in particular with the familiar liberal appeal to tolerance: you must not yield on your desire, so long as your desire does not infringe on the free pursuit of others' desires (cf. LM, 104–8). This is another consequence of privileging Kant over Rousseau: rather than seek to fortify and concentrate a common interest in the collective good, Lardreau's moral attitude aspires only to a gentle or 'soft autonomy', one that flaunts its harmless humility. 'It wants gentleness [*douceur*], the universal tolerance of those small differences in which everyone finds their small joys' (LM, 110; cf. 16), free from the temptation of any great expectations in political action or historical development.

What must remain excluded from consideration, in this as in every stage of Lardreau's work, is the sphere of history in a broadly Hegelian or Marxist sense, i.e. as a sphere in which cumulative strivings for collective emancipation might contribute to actual [*wirkliche*] transformations over time. Lardreau condemns such an understanding of history as one that effectively serves, like earlier forms of theodicy, to validate an immoral logic of instrumental expediency. Understood as a story of progress or liberation, one guided by its promises and ideals, History with a capital 'H' lends a *meaning* [*sens*], a direction and a justification to the meaningless and unjustifiable suffering caused by political violence, and thereby tries to render the intolerable tolerable (LM, 24–29). In *Le Monde*, Lardreau and Jambet conclude that *L'Ange* itself, far from abandoning politics for spirituality, had not gone far enough in the dissociation of morality from politics and history. Insofar as the figure of the angel might still hold out some redemptive promise, did it not collude in justifying a history marked by suffering and evil? 'Did not the Angel give us, in spite of our denials, a point of view on this particular history' – from a perspective outside it, yes, but nevertheless one that made it possible to recognise an 'intelligibility of History?' (LM, 280).

After losing the fight to subordinate it to political prescription in *Singe*, history figures after *L'Ange* only as a domain of exile and alienation. The paradigm for this, as for so much of Lardreau's later work, is established in the early Christian church, by the division that separates the spiritual, monarchist approach to redemption (guided by an immediate contempt for the flesh, desire, and for all that might align us with the ways of this world) and the rival 'historicist model', whereby the Church is established as an institution designed to lead its people through the trials and tribulations of this world, and to accept the world as the sole theatre of salvation.[35] History is consolidated as that dimension of social existence in which rebellion must always appear as essentially unreasonable, if not mad or *insensé* – the dimension in which it is, and always has been, wrong or unreasonable to revolt (cf. LA, 97). The manichean clarity of revolt prevails solely in the purity of the present, as an abrupt interruption of any dialectical coordination of structural conditions and subjective responses. 'Our most profound metaphysical thesis, our "esoteric" thesis', Lardreau argues, is quite simply that 'the past doesn't exist' (LA, 21; cf. 57). As Lardreau observes in his

*Dialogues* with the great historian of feudal society, Georges Duby, history as such, history in general, is always written by the victorious few, driven at all times by their fundamental 'fear of the people'.[36] History does not recall 'the way things were' but only the way the victors decide that they must have been, in order for them to have contributed to what has since become the established order of things. 'Historical memory is not Proustian …; memory is an instrument of mastery', and it 'retains only that which can be, properly speaking, mastered.'[37]

What is perhaps more unexpected is the way in which Lardreau's subsequent reflection on mastery itself comes to reframe his understanding of the antagonism between master and rebel. If every actual rebellion leads to a renewal of mastery and submission, could it also be that still more radical forms of submission, on the model of submission to an absolute law, might renew potential rebellion? Could unconditional submission to a *fully* absolute or extra-worldly master, a master beyond any relation 'with' rebels who are themselves confined to this world, open an alternative path to freedom from all worldly or historical constraints?

This is the question Lardreau tackles in his reading of the sixth-century Syriac ascetic Philoxenus of Mabbug, *Discours philosophique et discours spirituel* (1985). Once again he makes no secret of the Maoist roots of the essential choice that separates 'philosophical' from 'spiritual' discourse, the choice between reliance upon oneself, as the selfish subject of one's own petty mind, and the alienating-and-liberating 'subversion through which the subject of thought is affirmed as thought by the Other', i.e. as the thought and will of the creator or master who thinks through me. In the Maoist context, such subversion allows Mao to think of himself as thought by the masses, such that to follow Mao demanded the 'disappearance of all thought of one's own, all "selfish" thought, so as to allow the masses to think me, by thinking their thought in me. Hence that strange paramnesic feeling that seizes any reader who moves from the texts that express this Maoist subversion to our "spiritual" texts, or vice versa.'[38] The Maoist militants do not 'think for themselves'; they are a vehicle for the masses who think through them, and who alone determine what must be thought. As Lardreau will later point out, the Counter-Revolution grasped a version of precisely the same point (to opposite ends), when with Bonald it argued that the 'first law' of a revolution is that 'those who believe they are directing it are only its instruments' (FD, 135).

The Christian name for our absolute master, of course, is God, and what distinguishes its properly 'spiritual' mode of devotion is the individual's fully unconditional or absolute submission to the divine will. The Christian ascetic seeks to eliminate all that might block or filter his reception of divine instruction, in its simplicity and sufficiency, so as to be in a position to receive 'the word of God without judging or scrutinising it, without trying to verify it, accepting it with the same immediate self-evidence with which the child accepts the authority of the master'.[39] For the ascetic, the decisive question is not whether or not to believe *in* God, but simply that of believing God, believing what God says, and thus of obeying his commandments, without any need for evaluation or justification. If classical philosophy offers the progressive clarification of a *cogito*, an 'I think what I am thinking', this spiritual alternative offers the less reflexive, more abrupt and more brutal 'illumination of a *cogitor*, through which the subject experiences himself as that which is thought in thinking – in the thinking of the Other'.[40]

Spiritual insight thus begins where the subject's *own* thinking ends, through an ascetic dis-propriation of himself that is simultaneously a liberation in the infinite transcendence of the altogether Other, an 'silent illumination in which the Other seizes and captures him, enrols or enlists him, determines his place and name, and subjects him to the treasure he was seeking, and which found him'.[41] I am no longer, in short, the subject or author of my own thought, and

> it is not me who progresses, but God who makes me progress, insofar as I abolish myself as me …. The sole path that is open to me, that might allow me to render myself worthy of contemplation, is to empty myself of all thought of my own, all thought that is proper to myself [*me vider de toute pensée propre*]: in the absolute silence of the intellect which, by deserting itself, has finally regained, outside itself, its true nature, God can come to imprint, as he originally did, His contemplation.[42]

Spiritual contemplation is liberation from desire, finitude and mortality, and it proceeds through absolute submission to an infinite master. To rebel against the limits of this world, and against the grain of its historical development, may yet 'succeed', according to this logic, if it is willing to submit to the will of a master who transcends this world altogether.

## III

*La Véracité* (1993), no doubt Lardreau's most systematic and substantial philosophical work, is far from a simple abnegation of his earlier voluntarism. As one of its chapter titles confirms, the book adheres both to the old slogan '*on a raison de se révolter*', and to the old dualism: 'there are people who submit; there are people who revolt' (LV, 250).[43] It is now taken as self-evident that 'History, as the place where Reason waited for the highest good to be realised, has failed', but Lardreau insists that this should not be interpreted as renegation of revolt as such. 'Far from this meaning that we must renounce the revolt that was summoned by historical illusion, the only idea that is rendered invalid is the idea that revolt might one day find an end: my thesis does not serve to restrict rebellion, but to generalise it.'[44] In a late text Lardreau evokes with some sympathy the month-long '*insurrection des banlieues*' in France in the autumn of 2005 as an example of the sort of revolt he can still affirm – a revolt without specific demands to pursue or specific projects to implement, apart from a single insistence, an 'empty' claim made on a pure idea in the most Kantian sense: a demand for 'respect' as such (FD, 158).[45]

If in *La Véracité* the abiding question persists, 'is there freedom, or not?' (LV, 263n.10), what sets it apart, however, from *L'Ange* and *Singe* is the strictly negative configuration of its 'superaffirmative' answer. Lardreau's later philosophy is negative in the same sense as apophatic theology, which provides him with his paradigm. If truth is divine and transcends our finite means of expression, then 'we can say nothing true except the negative – or again: every affirmative proposition is a fantasy, is the truth can only ex-ist in relation to the soul as an event, i.e. as something purely unrepeatable'.[46] Or in more Lacanian terms, 'every form of intelligibility stumbles upon a remainder, a left-over, which interrupts its closure. This remainder is the real itself', which persists as 'that which can neither be said or understood.'[47] Forever lost behind the 'wall of words', this ungraspable real 'tolerates only oblique statements' that evoke its absence. In this context the proper function of fiction, for instance, is not to create imaginary realities that we might 'possess', but rather to indicate the cruel limit of all imagination, to dramatise the irreducible disjunction between discourse and world, and to allow for the experience of 'an object of which no image might form.'[48] The Greek origins of philosophy itself, Lardreau argues, suggest that it stems from a negative relation with the discourses that pre-existed it, those of the *physikoi*, and then of the sophists; philosophy will distinguish itself, then, by its *lack* of any distinctive object or concern, and thus its lack of any positive relation with 'truth' [*la vérité*].[49] In ways that are somewhat comparable with Adorno's later writings, a philosopher is mainly recognisable here on account of a critical opposition to a prevailing 'positive' dogma, e.g. to social convention, revealed religion, political expediency, the 'common sense' of self-preservation through adaptation to the status quo. The Dreyfusards, to evoke an example that Lardreau cites in 1998, did not stake their position so much on the demonstrable 'truth' of Dreyfus' innocence as on their quasi-instinctive opposition to the socio-military establishment that condemns him.[50]

A negative conception of liberty, along these lines, will be one that affirms a right to rebel against its every encroachment or oppression (and thereby one that implies the transcendental certainty of our freedom), but as far as actual practice is concerned, it will affirm only a freedom to rebel *against* oppression, and not one that might further become capable of taking the positive steps needed to overcome it, or to establish a more just social order, or to accomplish any particular political goal. Every time rebellions have acquired 'the opportunity to deploy their power, and actually annihilate the regime they objected to', so as then to undertake the task of remaking society, the result in each case has been 'a horror beyond words' (LV, 240). By thus severing the link between a wholly 'supersensible' freedom and any worldly practice of emancipation, Lardreau conflates will and wish while at the same time eliminating any practical basis for hope.

This conception of 'negative liberty' is itself part of a fully systematic or 'symphonic' negative philosophy, again organised along broadly Kantian lines. The alternative approach, which Lardreau rejects, would be one that (following Aristotle for instance) starts out from positively given objects or situations, such that our various interests are more or less directly determined by these objects, e.g. our interest in understanding the natural world, in organising our collective life, in caring for our soul, and so on. If a positive philosophy seeks to establish the truth [*vérité*] of what it can know or experience, a negative philosophy will privilege the '*véracité*' of a real beyond experience and beyond our capacity to represent or reconstruct the logic and tendencies that shape our experience. Here as everywhere, Lardreau's target is any 'philosophy of life, of fullness, of necessity',[51] including 'the party of Hegel and of Marx, the party which refuses that there might be, between what is and what should be, between the real and the rational, any gap at all.'[52] Between the negative assertion that 'nothing is all [*rien n'est tout*]' and the positive affirmation of an 'absolute immanence' that might sustain and reconcile all realities, there is only the stark opposition of a *prise de parti*.[53] Against his Aristotelian, Hegelian, Marxian, and also Deleuzian adversaries, the 'constitutional' approach that Lardreau adopts from Kant and Lacan is instead organised around what falls outside its grasp, and that is thus 'constitutionally' free from access or interference.

This remains a 'materialist' approach, Lardreau will insist, insofar as it rejects any spiritualist or vitalist alignment within some deeper form of reality, and transcends any enclosure within an immanent ontology. To be a negative materialist is to recognise that

> everything cannot be reduced to what we think, and matter signifies the limit or stumbling block that, whatever its progress, mind [*l'esprit*] cannot move beyond, for it does not amount merely to an ordinary insufficiency [of mind or thought] but rather informs the law of its activity…. A *materialist* philosophy will

be one that represents to thought, as the last instance or highest authority, the irrepresentable, that is, that which sides with the Real.[54]

The French Counter-Revolution of the 1790s, for instance, qualifies as eminently 'materialist' in this peculiar sense, insofar as its critique of the Terror, of its logic and its consequences, rests in the end, says Lardreau, on the 'brute sensory recognition' of spilt blood – the fact that '*this*, this that I see, and smell, *this* is blood …' (FD, 25) – an acknowledgement of blood as *réel*, compounded with reverence for its sacrificial quality. Inspired by Lady Macbeth, the late Lardreau maintains that 'no trace of blood can be erased' (FD, 105).

It also remains a *rationalist* approach, in keeping with the axiom that equates reason and revolt, insofar as it presumes that each distinct interest of reason constitutes or 'produces the reality it is interested in, while also letting fall away a real [*un réel*]' that eludes it (LV, 211): reason is always 'interested in something other than that which, since it institutes it, it can know' (LV, 220). Theoretical reason is concerned with understanding the laws that regulate the way things appear in the world we perceive and experience, but recognises that the world thus constituted is not 'whole' or not-all (the subject is never simply a part of the empirical world, and is unable to constitute every aspect of that world), and that there is a real or noumenal dimension that falls outside the domain of appearance.[55] Practical reason, by contrast, can access this noumenal freedom by indicating its own 'suprasensible' vocation, but only at the cost of neglecting the sensible, singular character of any particular individual (LV, 244).

More specifically, practical reason or freedom is here subject to at least three sorts of negative limitation. It is limited, first of all, to a strictly private or individual sphere. Collective power and sovereign force rely in the end on the more or less intelligent 'exercise of violence, be it that of the prince or the rebel.' Power remains a matter of positive capacity by definition, one that can make possible that which has hitherto seemed impossible (LV, 222). Whether it be long established or in the throes of revolutionary change, society privileges what it takes to be the collective good over individual dissent, and society as such always tends to 'stifle' the unique idiosyncrasies of an individual, in favour of a 'particular group' or class and its shared priorities. The more it affirms a generalised will, precisely, the more a social group tends toward what appears as the totalitarian horizon of every social formation, or what Lardreau derides here as 'society-without-toilets [la *société-sans-chiottes*], in which the subject will never find any *obscene* recess where surveillance ceases, and where he can enjoy his singular difference.'[56]

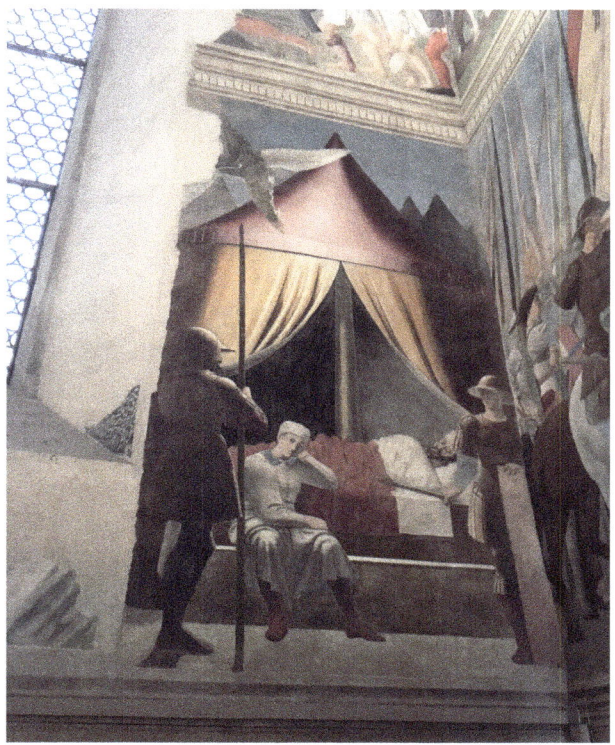

Against this logic of collective conformism, Lardreau concludes that the only subject who can affirm the principle '*on a toujours raison de se révolter*' must be the individual *sensu stricto*. On the one hand, individuals not only have no social power, they also have no social *reality*, since the abstract category of 'an individual' corresponds to no actual, social-determinate person. The individual as such falls out of the socially constituted world, and for that very reason may evoke the dimension of the *real* (LV, 220).[57] The individual is thus the only subject who can uphold the moral law, which itself testifies to the real or noumenal dimension *par excellence*, i.e. to a freedom that we can never positively experience or know. The moral law runs counter to established social interests or realities as a matter of course, precisely because it commands us to act in ways that might be affirmed, indifferently and universally, by *all* individuals, always and everywhere, regardless of their social position or capacity, as effectively 'interchangeable'.[58] Only a universal law or right can honour every individual assertion of singularity. On the other hand, the individual is also the only subject who is existentially concerned with his or her *own* happiness or suffering. Again inverting the priorities of *Singe*, Lardreau now affirms a properly 'pathological' duty, 'a duty to make *oneself* happy', in neo-Epicurean pursuit of a '*private* happiness [le bonheur *privé*]' (LV, 197, 202).

In this fully privatised domain our ethical choices, in short, can no longer be justified through reference to any actually-ongoing historical project or political goal, and must instead proceed 'in the absence of any project on a world scale', 'in the absence of any plan or intention that is not emphatically selfish [*égoïste*]' (LV, 201). It follows that rebellion is only as legitimate as its object is evanescent and its subject isolated, such that 'the most pure revolts will not at all be those that boast the most "sublime" ambitions, and that signal a radical will to "change the world", but on the contrary, those that lower themselves to the slightest objects, the most humble and most transparent things' (LV, 249).

Freedom is further limited, in the second place, by the fact that its exercise, or existence, can only be presupposed (in keeping with the argument of Kant's second *Critique*) through the experience of pure commandment or law. What sustains a 'negative politics' is solely its capacity to interrupt any proposal that might violate the moral law and the rights that follow from that law: human rights are only worthy of veneration since they condemn, without any concern for context or content, any project that might treat some individuals as means to a positive, socially determined end.[59] 'The notion of right' is precisely that 'pure idea of a form, without any empirical content' (LV, 213; cf. LM, 43) which forecloses any such project. Grounded solely in the 'pure universality of the law,' free from all natural or historical determination, human rights now 'represent, with regard to politics, what is ethically imprescriptible.'[60]

In defending this wholly formal conception of moral obligation, Lardreau's position is indeed, as he describes it, 'more Kantian than Kant's own' (LV, 150), and he rallies behind Kant at precisely that point where he has most often been attacked, by Hegel and so many of those who have followed Hegel. Lardreau's negative formalism allows him to respond to Hegel's critique of Kant's abstraction and universalism by interpreting indifference to pragmatic content and socio-historical actuality as a virtue rather than a defect. What sustains the moral law is precisely the fact that it must be postulated, in the most radically abstract sense, as a pure norm that can for that very reason apply to any individual and every situation.[61] Hegel is quite right to claim that Kant has no interest in social reality or actuality – but this is precisely because Kant's sole concern is with the supra-social and supra-sensible 'real' of absolute self-legislation, whose every commandment is immediately 'concrete' in the sense that it applies unequivocally to every individual, in every situation. From Lardreau's 'desiccated' Kantian perspective, it is rather Hegel's position that is abstract, and suspect, since it allows for the suspension of moral criteria in deference to an apparent 'meaning or direction of History' that Hegel presumes rather than proves. Hegel avoids the *real* of moral duty, in short, because he aligns himself with and acquiesces to an imaginary 'reality' of socio-historical progress, which is itself nothing more than the retrospective rationalisation of our actually-established order (LV, 169). If Hegel's subjects are situated according to time, place and the specific cultural resources of their 'ethical life', Lardreau's neo-Kantian 'subject is only practical on condition that he see himself *as if he was himself the law*', the law that transcends every situation. Strictly speaking, 'there is no other *subject* than the law as such' (LV, 183), whose commands apply in the same way across all situations.

In the third and most fundamental place, then, again in line with this affirmation of Kant over Hegel, freedom is both limited and absolutised here by its isolation from the dimension of actuality altogether. Lardreau's freedom is properly nothing other than a freedom to posit ourselves as free from reality or actuality *tout court*, in an affirmation that is absolute and unconditional as it is negative and empty. Of such a pure postulation, 'nothing can be predicated, since it can only be represented as the power to begin absolutely, as freedom' (LV, 153).[62] This neo-Kantian approach enables Lardreau to salvage his notion of freedom from both psychological and historical compromises. Understood as a *positive* or natural capacity, for instance as a primordial spontaneity or anarchic appetite, freedom can only be understood as in tension with itself, whereby (as with Plato, or Freud) one part of the psyche must strive to command the other. By contrast, if following Lardreau's Kant we conceive of freedom from the negative experience of commandment and obligation alone, then we can stabilise the ground of freedom in the sole dimension of practical reason – albeit at the cost of confining it to this one dimension.

The same logic allows Lardreau to retain a sublime or 'angelic' conception of politics, by confining it to the vanishing present of a pure refusal or rejection of what is actually established. The angel now figures what can be presented or embodied of our unpresentable, disembodied freedom, our 'real' noumenal freedom from all embodied desire, all difference, all inequalities, our 'death to the world' (LV, 240–41). As soon as we try to turn this 'real' into the basis of an actually-existing 'reality', however, the angel becomes a figure of death pure and simple, a barbarian figure of absolute lawlessness or crime. In keeping with the Lacanian distinction of *le réel* and *la réalité* (whereby the latter is an imaginary social construct, sustained through collective delusion and conformism), Lardreau classifies this barbarian angel as 'the Angel of imaginarisation': exemplified by Stalinist totalitarianism, it incarnates the pitiless determination to make an egalitarian mirage the basis of a new social reality. Through such 'imaginarisation of rebellion', 'rebellion abandons the negativity that lent it its power, and is impregnated with a full positivity, and grows into the wish to become, itself, the new state.'[63]

In a late twist to his angelic typology, Lardreau gives the name 'cannibal angel' to the figure that might seek, refusing all imaginary *réalisation*, to refer us back to the Lacano-Kantian dimension of a 'real beyond reality'. This cannibal angel of *réellisation* incarnates

*the will* to bring every world back to the chaos that is

its truth, to bring every community back to its essential dispersal, to dissolve every tie [*lien*], beginning with that tie by which a body is *a* body. The background against which this Angel detaches the liberation of the subject from any relation of authority is nothing other than the ruin of relation in general. Like the Terror as described by Hegel, its politics is a politics of absolute freedom, that is to say, of death. And since, when all is said and done, this Angel will associate only with these dismembered bodies, I will call it the *Cannibal Angel*.[64]

Whereas the barbaric imaginary relates the will to its realisation and deludes its subjects with the 'positivity of a *content*' (the promise of a new social order), the cannibal angel preserves the integrity of the real as such, precisely by absolving it from any sort of positivity, realisation, or relation. After initially associating the Khmer Rouge and the Cultural Revolution with the barbarian imaginary,[65] in his last political writings Lardreau classifies them instead under this other, more 'complicated' though no less destructive form of 'abjection', 'that by which negativity, far from renouncing itself, goes right to the very limit of itself.' The Khmer ultimately deserve to be recognised as a subject of *réellisation* rather than *réalisation* insofar as they were driven less by the ambition to constitute a new imaginary society than by the deathly determination simply to 'destroy their people, which is to say themselves.'[66] In less extreme forms, Lardreau suggests that the cannibal figure may at least be compatible with a minimal sense of self-preservation and indeed self-love. Thus understood in its most 'affirmative' sense, so to speak, 'the Cannibal Angel does not "delude" [*ne "leurre" pas*] ... it liberates negation from any determinacy to which it might be applied' and its mode of subjectivation offers no 'prognostic, therapeutic, or practical value', other than a recognition that what is thus liberated from relation and imaginary relations remains a *real individual*, an individual with the 'pathological duty' to look after itself.[67]

If we are to avoid social catastrophe, then, Lardreau insists that freedom must remain a pure end in itself, absolved of any means that might realise it and of any relation to an obstacle that might thwart it. The only way to uphold our unconditional duty to rebel against any and every infringement upon our freedom is to restrain our very desire to destroy the cause of such infringement (LV, 243). Revolt is only justified if it is *for* nothing, or next to nothing – '*for two pennies*' (LV, 249), or for a mere acknowledgement of 'respect' (FD, 158). Even a Christian restraint from confronting the injustices of this world is here not restrained enough, if it simply defers the advent of justice to *another* world (LV, 247). In Kantian terms, what Lardreau affirms is a conception of duty purged of any assurance – an assurance on which Kant himself so often insists – that we are actually capable of carrying it out. To the extent that will (as distinct from wish) is a matter of capacity and realisation, this is duty severed even from the will to follow it.[68] One and the same duty both commands us to continue in the old project of revolt, and to despair of ever carrying it out.

## IV

Lardreau's ultimate position doesn't simply equate an absolute but wholly abstracted conception of revolt with resigned acceptance of the status quo. In his last writings, he seeks to inject such acceptance with a sort of exaltation of its own, as if a sufficiently radical and unquestioning submission might now itself retain some of the ascetic self-denying and self-overcoming qualities he earlier associated with Maoism and Syriac discipline. Some of the main points of reference here might seem to be as far removed from his early invocations of Rousseau and Mao as can be imagined: the far-right nationalism of Charles Maurras and Action Française (albeit one qualified by a passing appreciation for Blanqui and the Communards of 1871), combined with a fascination for the ultra-Catholic and ultra-royalist partisans of the French Counter-Revolution.[69] The concision and syntactical contortions characteristic of Lardreau's later writing are even more extreme in his last fragments, but as always he strives to find continuity beneath apparent contraries. The anti-authoritarian inflection of his early Maoism, he now readily admits, was itself always compatible with unquestioning reverence for another conception of mastery, one in which reverential obedience and radical emancipation from oneself are opposite sides of the same coin.

In keeping with the whole philosophical tradition,

always, I have taken as my maxim the crude slogan of liberation: *sapere aude* – dare to give yourself a master! Everything else is feigned freedom, and real slavery: in my youth, to be anti-authoritarian meant being prepared to shout 'Long live President Mao! Only cretins saw in this a demand for submission (FD, 120).

And he adds, in his increasingly provocative style, that today 'I persevere in saying: long live comrade Stalin, long live President Mao, may they live, with the Virgin Mary, for ten thousand years!' (FD, 120). The path that began with the opposition of master and rebel has come full circle.

It's precisely the mass veneration that can surround a figure like Mary, or the saints, or a pope (FD, 71–76), that lends Catholicism its trans-historical 'grandeur', and allows it to persist as an enduring framework for popular unity, and to preserve the integrity of popular traditions. The greatness of Catholicism seems to rest precisely in the transcendent aura with which it invests the figures it reveres. The Reformation, by contrast, stands condemned precisely for its rejection of all aura, reverence and mastery, and for its reckless assertion of freedom from transcendent authority – a merely selfish and self-centred freedom that can only turn subjects against themselves, as they try to devise substitute forms of self-mastery or autonomy that divide body from mind, and desire from conscience. Catholicism engineers more or less 'blind' forms of mass unanimity, and the more instinctive or 'involuntary' its reflexes the more immediately they operate, and the more profoundly they resonate; Protestantism, by contrast, begins and ends with all too deliberate schisms. Lardreau is now perfectly ready to accept that 'the Inquisition is the truth of Catholicism', and seems willing to embrace it as an acceptable price to pay for maintaining a collective faith; on the other hand, 'this or that imbecile sect – Mormons, Christian Scientists, Pentecostals [etc…] – are the truth of Protestantism, which only exists in the form of sects' (FD, 121). As for the fading figure of revolution, it appears from a counter-revolutionary perspective as little more than a wilful, infantile defiance of genuinely ingrained authority – or citing Bonald, 'the revolution is "the badly raised child elevated to the highest level of power"' (FD, 136).

It's hard to imagine how Lardreau might have pushed his 'dialectic of the will' any further along the road of absolute negation. In the process, and leaving aside the intrinsic interest of such a properly idiosyncratic and intransigent philosophical project, Lardreau provides a striking and suitably negative lesson for anyone still interested in the concept and practice of political will. The more we absolutise the will, the more we isolate volition from the domain of actuality, the more we empty it of all those qualities and capacities that enable its exercise.

*Peter Hallward is Professor of Modern European Philosophy in the Centre for Research in Modern European Philosophy at Kingston University, and a member of the* Radical Philosophy *editorial collective.*

**Notes**

1. This article is a relatively direct continuation of a previous piece on Guy Lardreau, called 'Reason and Revolt: Guy Lardreau's Early Voluntarism and its Limits', published in *Radical Philosophy* 190 (March 2015), 13–24, https://www.radicalphilosophy.com/article/reason-and-revolt.
2. Guy Lardreau, *Faces de l'Ange déchu* (Paris: Le Centurion, 2018), 52, 182; unless otherwise indicated, all translations are the author's own. Subsequent references to *Faces de l'Ange déchu* are given in the text using the abbreviation FD.
3. 'Good social institutions', Rousseau argues, 'are those that best know how to denature man, … to transport the I into the common unity, with the result that each individual believes himself no longer one but a part of the unity' (Jean-Jacques Rousseau, *Emile*, in his *Œuvres complètes* [Paris: Gallimard, La Pléiade, 1959-1995], IV, 249). 'Good socialisation' thus effects the 'most remarkable change in man by substituting justice for instinct in his conduct, and endowing his actions with the morality they previously lacked', leaving him with 'his ideas enlarged, his sentiments ennobled, his entire soul elevated …' (Rousseau, *Du Contrat social* 1: 8, *Oeuvres complètes* III, 364). For Lardreau's early and emphatic affirmation of Rousseau, see in particular *Le Singe d'or: essai sur le concept d'étape du marxisme* (Paris: Mercure de France, 1973), 195–215.
4. Guy Lardreau, 'The Problem of Great Politics', trans. Peter Hallward, *Angelaki* 8:2 (2003), 90; FD, 14.
5. Immanuel Kant, *Groundwork of the Metaphysics of Morals*, in *Practical Philosophy*, ed. and trans. Mary Gregor (Cambridge: Cambridge University Press, 1996), 4:393 (references to Kant are to the standard pagination of the German Akademie edition).
6. Lardreau, 'The Problem of Great Politics', 90.
7. Cf. Alain Badiou, 'Roads to Renegacy', *New Left Review* II:52 (September 2008).

8. Lardreau, *Le Singe d'or*, 89; cf. 122–24.
9. In what follows, I use the following abbreviations within the text for references to these books: LA: *L'Ange. Ontologie de la révolution, tome 1: pour une cynégétique du semblant* (Paris: Grasset, 1976); LM: *Le Monde, Réponse à la question: qu'est-ce que les droits de l'homme?* (Paris: Grasset, 1978); LV: *La Véracité: essai d'une philosophie négative* (Lagrasse: Éditions Verdier, 1993). All translations are the author's own.
10. The same distribution of roles will allow Lardreau, later on, sharply to distinguish Foucault (who began as a communist and who remained a reader of Marx, a critic of '*progréssisme*' and of the parliamentary 'left', and who 'always embraced the point of view of the oppressed, of the rebels'), from Deleuze ('who, since he was late to wake up from the political indifference that academic study nurtures, since he was never a practising Marxist, conclude that one had to be "gauchiste" or "on the left" as a matter of course, in keeping with the 'soft rebellion' of the Mittérandistes), Guy Lardreau, *L'Exercice différé de la philosophie: à l'occasion de Deleuze* (Lagrasse: Verdier, 1999), 11, 84.
11. Guy Lardreau and Christian Jambet, 'Entretien avec Hertzog', *Magazine littéraire* 112–113 (May 1976), 56.
12. Even so severe a critic of Lardreau and Jambet as Alain Badiou acknowledged, in his review of *L'Ange*, that unlike 'so many of their former comrades', they refuse to 'falsify the force and novelty' of the Cultural Revolution and May '68. See Alain Badiou, 'Un Ange est passé', *La Situation actuelle sur le front philosophique* (Paris: Maspero, 1977), 66.
13. LA, 10, 91. Lardreau was always careful to distance himself from *la nouvelle philosophie* as an apparently 'collective' project, and still more as a media phenomenon (cf. Guy Lardreau and Christian Jambet, 'Une dernière fois, contre la "nouvelle philosophie"', *La Nef* 66 [January 1978], 35–40). It is hard to see how Lardreau's work in particular might be vulnerable to the main objection posed by Deleuze and other critics of the new philosophers, that they represent 'the submission of all thought to the media'. See Gilles Deleuze, "À propos des nouveaux philosophes et d'un problème plus général', *Deux Régimes de fous et autres textes [1975-1995]*, ed. David Lapoujade (Paris: Minuit, 2003), 134; cf. Dominique Lecourt, *Dissidence ou révolution?* (Paris: Maspero, 1978); François Aubral and Xavier Delcourt, *Contre la nouvelle philosophie* (Paris: Gallimard, 1977). Lardreau always protested against any interpretation of *L'Ange* as some sort of renegation or *retournement* (see Jean Birnbaum, 'Quand un absolu chasse l'autre', *Le Monde*, 28 avril 2008). Nevertheless, Bernard Henri-Lévy may still be entitled to see *L'Ange* as 'the real inspiration' for what he dubbed *la nouvelle philosophie*, insofar as he defines its first principle precisely as 'historical pessimism', i.e. 'the refusal of Providentialism and of the idea that History has a meaning or direction [*sens*]'. See Lévy, interview with Yorgos Archimandritis, 'BHMagazino' (November 2010), accessed 30 October 2018, http://www.bernard-henri-levy.com/bernard-henri-levy-et-michel-houellebecq-a-athenes-suite-11858.html
14. Lardreau and Jambet, 'Entretien avec Hertzog', 55.
15. Lardreau, *Le Singe d'or*, 229.
16. Lardreau and Jambet, 'Entretien avec Hertzog', 57.
17. 'We do not shy away from admitting it: we used to be Stalinists because we used to be political', and Lardreau's break with Stalinism, as he describes it in 1976, coincides with his renunciation of politics and of all *militantisme* (Lardreau and Jambet, 'Entretien avec Hertzog', 57).
18. Lardreau and Jambet, 'Entretien avec Hertzog', 55.
19. Jacques Lacan, *Le Séminaire, Livre XVII: L'Envers de la Psychanalyse* [1969-70]. : Seuil: 1991, 239; cf. Guy Lardreau, 'Un Paradoxe pratique: conférence prononcée à Lagrasse en août 1997' (unpublished; references are to the French typescript), 21.
20. Lardreau and Jambet, 'Entretien avec Hertzog', 55; cf. LM, 107.
21. Guy Lardreau and Christian Jambet, 'À propos du Cambodge' [originally published in Italian under the title 'A proposito della Cambogia', in *Spirali* (Janvier 1979), 25-27; references are to the French typescript], 1; cf. LM, 191–92.
22. Lardreau and Jambet, 'Une dernière fois, contre la "nouvelle philosophie"', 36–37.
23. Lardreau and Jambet, 'À propos du Cambodge', 2.
24. Lardreau and Jambet, 'Une dernière fois, contre la "nouvelle philosophie"', 40.
25. Guy Lardreau, 'Ne pas céder sur la pensée', *Le Débat* (September 1980), 45. Deleuze rephrased Lardreau's point more scornfully: 'This is also why the thinking Subject returns to the philosophical stage, since the only possibility of revolution, for the new philosophers, is the pure act of the thinker who thinks it to be impossible' (Deleuze, 'À propos des nouveaux philosophes', 131–2).
26. Alberto Toscano, 'Mao and Manichaeism: An Episode in the Politics of Purity', *Parallax* 17:2 (2011), 51.
27. Cf. Lardreau and Jambet, 'À propos du Cambodge' [1979], 3.
28. Kant, *Critique of Practical Reason*, AK 5:29. 'A free will and a will under moral laws are one and the same' (Kant, *Groundwork of the Metaphysics of Morals*, AK 4:447).
29. Kant, *Groundwork*, AK 4:433.
30. Lardreau, 'Un Paradoxe pratique' (1997), 13.
31. Guy Lardreau, 'Habent sua fata', *Filozofski Vestnik* 16:2 (1995) [references are to the French typescript], 4–5.
32. 'Unless pure willing', Heidegger continues, 'as the genuinely actual of all ethical action, actually wills itself, a material table of values however finely structured and comprehensive remains a pure phantom with no binding force. This willing of itself is ... what is most concrete in the lawfulness of ethical action. The ethicality of action does not consist in realising so-called values, but in the actual willing to take responsibility, in the decision to exist within this responsibility' (Martin Heidegger, *The Essence of Human Freedom* [1930], trans. Ted Sadler [London: Continuum, 2002], 193).
33. See, for instance, LM, 40; LV, 211; *L'Exercice différé de la philosophie*, 80–81; *Vive le matérialisme!* (Lagrasse: Verdier, 2001), 27.
34. Lardreau, 'Ne pas céder sur la pensée' (1980), 42.
35. Guy Lardreau, *Discours philosophique et discours spirituel: autour de la philosophie spirituelle de Philoxène de Mabboug*

36. Guy Lardreau, *Dialogues avec Georges Duby* (Paris: Les Dialogues des petits Platons, 2013), 79.
37. Ibid., 76-7.
38. Lardreau, *Discours philosophique et discours spiritual*, 138. As Mao put it in a formulation retained in the little red book, 'the masses are the real heroes, while we ourselves are often childish and ignorant, and without this understanding, it is impossible to acquire even the most rudimentary knowledge' (Mao Zedong, 'Preface and Postscript to Rural Surveys' [1941], *Selected Works* [Beijing: Foreign Languages Press, 1944-], III, 12).
39. Lardreau, *Discours philosophique et discours spiritual*, 119.
40. Ibid., 140.
41. Ibid., 132.
42. Ibid., 139.
43. Lardreau, *L'Exercice différé de la philosophie*, 11.
44. Guy Lardreau, 'Sur le bonheur' [unpublished], summer 1993, 1, accessed 30 October 2018, http://lesingedor.fr/wp-content/uploads/2014/03/Sur_le_bonheur_Guy_Lardreau_1993.pdf
45. Lardreau also continues, incidentally, to affirm Gauche Prolétarienne as 'the only Maoist organisation that ever counted,' but it counts, now, precisely because when it came to making a choice between pursuing the realisation of its actual political aims on the one hand and self-dissolution on the other, it concluded that only the latter course was consistent with a sustainable practice of revolt. Lardreau summarises its trajectory in a formulation that compresses much of the elusive logic of his own later work: Gauche Prolétarienne was a vanishing political moment, it was 'that instantaneous cut in which Veracity briefly exposed itself in a place in which it does not belong; it was, in the strongest sense of the word, discretion itself: an instant, of the kind in which animals fall silent, and an Angel passes' (LV, 273n.45; cf. 239-40).
46. Lardreau, *Discours philosophique et discours spiritual*, 133.
47. Guy Lardreau, *Fictions philosophiques et science-fiction* (Arles: Actes Sud, 1988), 271-2; cf. LA, 36.
48. Lardreau, *Fictions philosophiques et science-fiction* 145; 45-6.
49. Lardreau, 'Travail et paresse de la vérité' (1998), accessed 14 February 2014, http://www.editions-verdier.fr/banquet/n44/travail1.htm
50. 'I say without hesitation that whether Dreyfus was guilty or innocent was of no importance.... I do not know if Dreyfus was right; I know that his adversaries were wrong' (Lardreau, 'Travail et paresse de la vérité' [1998]).
51. LV, 260n.7; cf. LA, 217; *L'Exercice différé de la philosophie*, 47, 85.
52. Lardreau, 'Habent sua fata' (1995), 5.
53. Lardreau, *Vive le matérialisme!*, 27-28.
54. The French is typical of Lardreau's style, and reads: 'tout ne se ramène à ce que l'on pense, matière signifiant la butée que, quel que soit son progrès, l'esprit ne lève, parce qu'elle ne se résume pas à une insuffisance ordinaire, mais donne la loi de son activité, qui devant soi incessamment la construit. ... Matérialiste sera une philosophie qui représente à la pensée, au titre de dernière instance, l'irreprésentable, soit, qui prend le parti du Réel' (*L'Exercice différé de la philosophie*, 80–81; cf. *Vive le matérialisme!*, 27). Again, 'matter is that which refuses representation; that which cannot be imagined, or symbolised. ... It is not matter than engenders materialism, but materialism that allows matter to exist', i.e. to be posited as existent (*Vive le matérialisme!*, 22–23).
55. As far as theoretical reason is concerned, what can be known of the free or 'real subject' is simply that it must be 'non-constituent and non-constituted' (LV, 51), i.e. independent of the operations whereby, along conventional Kantian lines, the constituent subject orders its world: it endures in an excess in which any actual (constituted) subject counts for nothing, in which collapse all distinctions between matter and form, between the one and the multiple, between God and his creation (46).
56. Guy Lardreau, 'L'Universel et la différence', *La Nef*, Nouvelle série 4 (1981), 86; cf. LM, 24.
57. Lardreau, 'L'Universel et la différence', 84.
58. LM, 11, 83; cf. Lardreau, 'L'Universel et la différence', 78.
59. Cf. LV, 211; Lardreau, 'L'Universel et la différence', 79.
60. Lardreau, 'L'Universel et la différence', 85.
61. Ibid., 80.
62. There are some striking parallels between Laruelle's position here and that of his under-appreciated contemporary Françoise Proust's equally Kantian emphasis on freedom as pure beginning (without actual follow-through or consequence). See in particular Françoise Proust, *Kant: Le Ton de l'histoire* (Paris: Payot, 1991), 14–17 and *passim*.
63. Lardreau, 'Un Paradoxe pratique', 20.
64. Lardreau, 'The Problem of Great Politics', 92–93; cf. FD, 66–67.
65. LM, 19–20, 278–80; see in particular Christian Jambet, 'La Volonté de pureté et l'ange barbare', in LM, 175–223.
66. Lardreau, 'Un Paradoxe pratique', 20–21.
67. Lardreau, 'The Problem of Great Politics', 93; cf. LV, 195–202.
68. As Badiou summarises, Lardreau's argument here commits him to an 'abstract opposition: either politics wants to change the world, and so engages in a "final solution" – in which case it realises itself in barbarian immorality. Or else politics *wills* nothing, it is pure negation, and it is thus suited only to evanescent objects' (Badiou, 'The Imperative of Negation', in *The Adventure of French Philosophy*, trans. and ed. Bruno Bosteels [London: Verso, 2012], 304, trans. modified).
69. Late in his life, Lardreau was happy to admit to Jean Birnbaum that he considered himself 'to be a "an old follower of Maurice Barrès, or as more spiteful people might say, of [Charles] Maurras"'. See Jean Birnbaum, *Les Maoccidents: Un néoconservatisme à la française* (Paris: Editions Stock, 2009), epilogue.

# The politics of miscarriage
Victoria Browne

In 2015, Purvi Patel became the first person in the US to be charged, convicted and sentenced for 'feticide' in relation to her own pregnancy. In 2013, she had been admitted to an emergency room in Indiana after turning up with heavy bleeding and a severed umbilical cord. She claimed to have suffered a miscarriage and disposed of the foetal body on the way to the hospital. The prosecution, however, argued she had deliberately sought to terminate the pregnancy through taking abortion-inducing drugs ordered online (though the toxicology report found no evidence of the drugs in her body). Patel was also charged with neglect of a dependent, as the prosecution proposed that the foetus had in fact been born alive, and could have survived if medical attention had been sought.[1] Though the charges appear contradictory (and the evidence for both was fiercely contested), the prosecution contended that a person can be guilty of 'feticide' for deliberately trying to end a pregnancy by illegal means, even if the foetus survives; and that in such cases, a person can also be guilty of letting them die after birth. Patel was indeed found guilty of both crimes – class A felony 'neglect of a dependent' and class B felony 'feticide' – and sentenced to 20 years in prison.

Indiana's 'feticide' statute, introduced in 1979, refers to 'a person who knowingly or intentionally terminates a human pregnancy with an intention other than to produce a live birth or to remove a dead foetus', or to perform a legal abortion.[2] It was designed with violent third parties in mind whose actions cause a pregnancy to end in miscarriage or stillbirth (through intimate partner violence or assault for example), rather than those who attempt an illegal 'self-abortion'. Indeed, the Indiana Court of Appeals vacated the 'feticide' charge against Patel in 2016, stating that 'the legislature did not intend for the feticide statute to apply to illegal abortions or to be used to prosecute women for their own abortions'.[3] The Patel case, however, is by no means an isolated incident and stands testament to the increasing criminalisation of miscarriage in the US, as women – disproportionately poor and/or of colour – are considered suspect and punished for disguising illegal 'self-abortion' as involuntary miscarriage or stillbirth. Thirty-eight states have 'feticide' or 'fetal homicide' laws[4] that may be applied in cases of 'suspicious' miscarriage/stillbirth, and women have also been held criminally liable for 'reckless' behaviour, like drug use, that is deemed to play a causal role in adverse pregnancy outcomes.[5] Since 1973, at least 45 states in the US have sought to prosecute women for exposing their 'unborn child' to drugs under a variety of laws such as 'child endangerment' or 'child neglect'. In Oklahoma, a drug-addicted woman, Theresa Lee Hernandez, was sentenced to 15 years in prison for second-degree murder after her baby was stillborn in 2004 and tested positive for methamphetamine.[6] In February 2018, despite the clarification of the Indiana law, Kelli Leever-Driskel was arrested after a stillbirth and charged with 'feticide' and involuntary manslaughter based on her alleged drug use while pregnant, and remains in prison.[7]

Faced with these kinds of cases, the onus on the legal defence is to 'prove it's a miscarriage'[8] or stillbirth, and moreover an 'innocent' one, thereby summoning a series of binary distinctions – chosen versus unchosen, intentional versus spontaneous, voluntary versus involuntary, reckless versus responsible, and so on – that could hold the key to an individual's freedom from incarceration and other forms of punishment. But from a broader theoretical viewpoint, what kind of response might these criminal cases generate? What have feminists had to say about miscarriage and its place within the politics of pregnancy, and how might this inform the challenge to its criminalisation in the US and beyond?

Before proceeding further, it is important to address some terminological issues, given that there is no clear agreement on what a 'miscarriage' or a 'stillbirth' actually is. For example, the UK National Health Service defines 'miscarriage' as 'the loss of a pregnancy during the first 23 weeks', and a stillbirth as 'when a baby is born dead after 24 completed weeks of pregnancy';[9] but in the US, the point of distinction is usually 20 weeks.[10] The terms themselves are also contested, especially 'miscarriage' with its connotations of failure (e.g. a 'miscarriage of justice'), or implication that the pregnant person is somehow responsible (e.g. the 'mis' as in 'misplaced'). In light of these issues, 'pregnancy loss' is often used as an alternative by academics and support groups – a wide-ranging term that can cover the cessation of a pregnancy whatever its duration, as well as instances where a pregnancy has been terminated but loss is felt, as in a 'therapeutic abortion' for medical reasons. However, this more experientially laden term is not always appropriate, given that loss may not be felt when a pregnancy ends; and as will be discussed, there are political reasons to be wary of the language of loss within a 'pro-life' saturated political climate in which a sense of loss is more or less demanded as the only intelligible and proper response.[11] Accordingly, this article opts for the more colloquial term 'miscarriage' to speak in general terms of non-induced pregnancy cessation, as the priority in this instance is to avoid emotional implications regarding the highly variable subjective experience of this phenomenon.[12]

The designation of those who are/have been pregnant also runs into terminological difficulties, as speaking of 'pregnant women' can be taken as exclusionary of pregnant men or those who are gender non-binary.[13] More inclusive gender-neutral terms like 'pregnant people' are increasingly preferred,[14] and impatience has been expressed in relation to feminist critics who persist in referring to 'pregnant women' as a generic collective, or 'the pregnant woman' as an abstract singular.[15] Yet moving to gender-neutral language is by no means a simple fix. In the first instance, as Laura Briggs points out, the language of 'pregnant people' and 'non-pregnant people' has a history of reactionary usage: for instance, by those who seek to deny protections against pregnancy discrimination in the workplace by insisting it is not a form of illegal sex discrimination.[16] Moreover, the use of gender-neutral language can feel somewhat obfuscatory when pregnancy is hardly a gender-neutral affair. Just as the capacity for pregnancy has consistently been linked to femaleness and womanhood within the binary sex/gender model, normative and misogynist ideas about femaleness and womanhood – such as feminine self-sacrifice, the unruliness of female flesh, or the untrustworthiness of women's testimony and conduct – have in turn determined social expectations and regulations of pregnancy. Indeed, it is precisely this close association that makes male pregnancy such an 'unthinkable' phenomenon,[17] whilst at the same time, we see gendered notions of feminised pregnancy carrying over into the paternalistic, patronising and dismissive ways that non-female pregnant people are also treated.[18]

So whilst de-naturalising the circular link between 'pregnancy' and 'women' is essential to the project of transforming dominant imaginaries of pregnancy and overturning the patriarchal, heteronormative, cisnormative government of reproduction, it does not necessarily make sense to speak of pregnancy in gender-neutral terms, or to abandon 'pregnant women' as an analytical category. This is especially true when the intention is to examine how struggles for control of pregnancy and reproduction impact particularly upon people understood to be women and girls, although, as Michael Toze argues, 'feminist critiques of the regulation of female bodies can be expanded to offer a mechanism for analysing the ways in which trans masculine bodies are also regulated'.[19] With such considerations in mind, this article does use gendered terminology like 'pregnant women' when referring to gendered discourses and regimes of pregnancy that explicitly or implicitly evoke and impact upon pregnant women *qua* women. But when the use of gender-specific terminology is not vital to the point, more capacious terms like 'pregnant people' are used in a bid to expand the conceptual frame.

## Miscarriage and feminist philosophy

For something that affects so many women so directly, and is such a deeply gendered phenomenon, it is perhaps surprising that miscarriage has received little feminist attention. The reproductive justice movement has forcefully challenged the singular focus on abortion, highlighting systematic sterilisation abuse amongst other coercive reproductive practices by the state, and the continuing power of 'the story that says poor women and women of colour should not give birth'.[20] Accordingly, it has become more widely understood amongst feminists that the right *to* reproduce is as much at stake as the right *not* to.[21] But the place of non-intentional non-reproduction – or 'failed' reproduction – within a feminist politics of non/reproduction requires further theoretical elaboration. So often miscarriage is treated as a private or 'medical' problem, 'or worse "her fault"',[22] such that its social and political aspects are obscured. Yet, for many feminists, attending to miscarriage can feel like risky business, when acknowledging that the range of feelings it can entail – including sadness, loss and grief – might seem to give credibility to anti-abortion crusades that fetishise foetal life and tragedise its ending. The claim that pro-choice feminism straightforwardly dismisses the foetus as a 'bunch of cells' is, as Ann Cahill argues, something of a caricature; yet the continued patriarchal appropriation of pregnancy and assault on women's reproductive lives renders 'any attempt at subtlety politically dangerous'.[23] Just as 'speaking as an aborting body ... from within abortion can feel impossible',[24] speaking from 'within miscarriage' can feel equally so.

That said, work is being done to address this theoretical lacuna. Alongside work on miscarriage and stillbirth within feminist sociology and anthropology,[25] there has been a burgeoning interest within feminist philosophy in the last few years. A special issue of the *Journal of Social Philosophy* in 2015, for example, was devoted to 'Miscarriage, Reproductive Loss, and Fetal Death'.[26] The articles in this issue concentrate predominantly upon the ontological, ethical and social questions provoked by miscarriage and foetal death, rather than political or legal questions as such. The opening essay by Alison Reiheld, however, does venture into this territory with her argument that miscarriage has been 'enrolled' in political debates and laws around abortion and control over pregnancy due to its 'sequestered' nature and 'liminal' status.[27] As a state of being 'betwixt and between', she contends, miscarriage falls between a series of binaries including 'parent' and 'not-parent', 'not-having-procreated' and 'having procreated', 'life and death', 'abortion and pregnancy'. Its ambiguous ontological and social status, according to Reiheld, means that miscarriage is not often acknowledged or spoken of, which in turn makes it susceptible to being co-opted by discussions and legal battles over the control of pregnancy and abortion: 'A thing poorly understood but too-like states or events which we believe we understand is quite likely to be drawn into debates over those other states or events'.[28] Accordingly, she contends, miscarriage becomes subjected to sets of laws and policies (proposed or enacted) seeking to control abortion and pregnancy: those which require pregnant people to prove their pregnancy has ended involuntarily rather than voluntarily; those which allow health care providers to opt out of treating miscarriage because it can require similar techniques as abortion (most notably D&C);[29] and those which hold individuals criminally responsible for their own miscarriages or stillbirths where their actions or behaviours are deemed to have played a causal role.[30]

Reiheld's conclusion is that if miscarriage were better theorised and understood as a 'liminal event', it might not be so 'easily enrolled in these other debates' pertaining to control over pregnancy and abortion. She acknowledges that in light of the persistent obsession with 'fetal personhood' in the US, it is unlikely that we can 'avoid entirely' this kind of enrolment. Nonetheless, the task for philosophers, as well as law- and policy-makers, as Reiheld sees it, is to develop an understanding of miscarriage 'in its own right' as a liminal event that is 'clearly distinct from the binaries it falls in between. 'Without a clear notion of what miscarriage is', she asserts, 'I fear we will repeat again and again the negative ethical fallout of failure to understand miscarriage's liminality. The result? Women who miscarry will again and again be isolated, their troubles sequestered, their experiences and fates enrolled in debates which hardly bear on miscarriage at all.'[31]

The call to treat miscarriage as a case apart does make practical sense in certain situations. For example, people experiencing miscarriages or stillbirths often find it distressing to be treated in the same spaces within medical institutions as those having check-ups for ongoing pregnancies or those in labour. But at the level of principle, the argument to separate out miscarriage from pregnancy and abortion needs to be further questioned. What makes miscarriage 'clearly distinct' from pregnancy and abortion, as Reiheld contends? In what sense can debates around the control of pregnancy and abortion be considered as 'hardly bearing' on miscarriage? Or, if indeed it is 'too like' abortion, does this imply we should be devoting our theoretical energy to trying to separate them out?

## Miscarriage/pregnancy

The first point to take issue with is the idea that 'miscarriage' needs to be differentiated from 'pregnancy'. Is a pregnancy that ends in miscarriage not still a pregnancy? On what grounds can they be rendered distinct? One distinction drawn by Reiheld is that whilst miscarriage is 'liminal' in the sense of being socially marginalised or 'taboo', pregnancy is surrounded by a whole host of well-established, 'clear cultural scripts', and is therefore 'not liminal'.[32] But debates around the meaning of 'liminality' aside,[33] this claim obscures the fact that social support for pregnancy is highly conditional and variable, depending upon who is pregnant. It is certainly true that the lived experience of pregnancy tends to be a 'noisy one',[34] whilst the ending of a pregnancy through miscarriage is characterised more often by silence. Yet as feminist theory has long demonstrated, well-established cultural scripts do not necessarily have positive effects, nor do they impact upon different individuals and social groups in the same way.

The dominant scripts of pregnancy in the US overwhelmingly privilege a certain kind of white, well-off, straight, non-disabled, compliant, feminine pregnant subject. For those who measure up, pregnancy generates significant levels of social approval and support:

'Pregnancy is bathed in sunlight, moonlight, God light. What could be more beautiful than the pregnant woman, deliverer of pure promise?'[35] But pregnancy can also be the source of 'acute social shaming', as those who do not match this vision of pregnant femininity are consistently designated irresponsible and suspicious.[36] The figure of the pregnant teen, for example, is a ubiquitous symbol of problematic pregnancy, along with pregnant bodies of all ages marked by nonwhiteness, or a whiteness 'contaminated by poverty'.[37] The 'clear cultural scripts' of pregnancy thereby perpetuate a toxic pregnancy hierarchy that is absolutely central to the politics of miscarriage when, in a study of 413 arrests and forced interventions on pregnant women in the US between 1973 and 2005, 71% were living in poverty and 59% were women of colour.[38] In the past decade, arrests and forced interventions have 'skyrocketed' according to the National Advocates for Pregnant Women: at least 700 more cases have been reported, and those targeted continue to be 'overwhelmingly low income and a disproportionate number are women of colour'.[39]

It may seem contradictory that the same people whose pregnancies are marked as deviant and threatening to social/national futures are punished when their pregnancies are deemed to be in jeopardy or end without a live birth; but this apparent contradiction only lays bare how the professed concern for 'the child' functions as a smokescreen or 'cover story'[40] for wider political agendas and exercises of power. Scenes of criminalised pregnancy depicted in the news – like the disturbing images of Purvi Patel in handcuffs – may also seem a far cry from the frothy magazine articles and casual social interactions Reiheld has in mind when she speaks of 'pregnancy scripts'. But such banal discourses are a primary vehicle of what Jennifer Scuro refers to as 'childbearing ideology': the 'scripts and rituals that underwrite socio-political, gendered, and embodied expectations about pregnancy', differentiating the 'right' kind of pregnancy from the 'wrong' kind, and validating only its productive aspects.[41] Childbearing teleology promotes a normative model of pregnancy as 'all directed for the sake of a child produced', and is instilled through a 'medical and cultural complex of guidance and instruction'. Pregnancy guidebooks, for instance, align

the time of pregnancy to the expected linear development of the foetus, with routine temporal milestones – the successive weeks, months, or trimesters – serving as a 'countdown' to birth.[42] Indeed, the more proleptic versions of these narratives present the imagined baby or child as *already here,* and the pregnant person as 'already a mother embarked on a life trajectory of mothering'.[43] As feminist writer Angela Garbes recounts:

> When I first opened *The Healthy Pregnancy Book* ... I was startled by an image ... There on the second page was a gray, delicately shaded pencil illustration of a baby nestled cosily in a womb, its arms and legs crossed. A thought bubble emanated from the baby, carrying a firm message: 'Mama take good care of yourself so I can grow better'. I was only eight weeks pregnant (my foetus was kidney-bean size ...), and yet here was this fully formed baby admonishing me for mistakes I was already making. 'Do you really want to eat that'? the baby asked incredulously on page 54.[44]

To be sure, many pregnant people do think of themselves as mothers or parents to their foetuses, and of their foetuses as their babies or children, and engage in material and social practices that 'interpellate' them as such.[45] But as feminists have been arguing for decades now, the externally imposed logic that treats the foetus as a separate, autonomous being with interests, even 'rights' of its own, comes with serious consequences for pregnant people, especially when combined with ideologies of 'total motherhood'. The pregnant person, as Lauren Berlant contends, is expected to 'act like a mother' to the foetus, but at the same time, is effectively made a 'child to the foetus' through the de-legitimation of their agency and identity, as they become 'more minor and less politically represented than the foetus, which is in turn more privileged in law, paternity, and other less institutional family strategies of contemporary American culture'.[46] Another, less considered, consequence of childbearing teleology is that 'miscarried' pregnancies which do not result in a live birth are cast outside the world of normative pregnancy altogether, and shrouded in shame, stigma, silence or suspicion. If pregnancy is taken as equivalent to 'having a baby', then as Scuro writes, 'anything short of these expectations of equivalence becomes a site of harm and humiliation',[47] even evidence of 'child abuse' or criminal 'neglect'.

Defining miscarriage as a liminal event *in distinction* to pregnancy therefore seems to somewhat miss the point, as if the ubiquitous scripts and symbols of normative pregnancy were not themselves the source of the problem. 'There are no greeting cards' for pregnancy loss, writes feminist anthropologist Linda Layne,[48] but surely this is not a reason for lament? I am being somewhat facetious here, as the point of the statement is to draw attention to the general lack of social support for people who go through miscarriage – all the more jarring if it has been abundant during the pregnancy and is then suddenly withdrawn when the pregnancy ends unexpectedly with 'nothing to show for itself'.[49] But the problem, arguably, can be more squarely located in the dominant imagery and logic manifest in pregnancy greeting cards themselves, rather than the lack of an equivalent miscarriage range. It is precisely the depictions of pregnancy featured in greeting cards – where 'being pregnant' means 'having a baby' and 'holding the future' – that make miscarriage appear as a deviation from pregnancy's proper path. And however banal or seemingly benign, the imagery and 'noise' around pregnancy too often perpetuates the patriarchal convention of expropriating the 'unborn child' from the lived pregnant body, such that it apparently makes sense to proceed as if the gestating foetus might require 'protection' from the body that sustains it and with which it is intertwined. Indeed, the more banal and seemingly benign this symbolism is, the more ordinary and commonplace it becomes.

## Miscarriage/abortion

The second point to address is the idea that miscarriage should be properly distinguished from abortion, to ensure that those who go through miscarriage are shielded as much as possible from the negative 'fallout' from the 'abortion debate'. Both miscarriage and abortion have an abject status in a social context in which pregnancy is equated with childbearing and proleptic parenthood. Neither delivers up the 'the all-miraculous, all-coveted BABY'.[50] Yet they are often treated as oppositional phenomena, which stems from the centrality of 'choice' to the construction of abortion as a political issue. If abortion is framed as, above all, the chosen volitional act of an autonomous individual, then miscarriage becomes defined by its lack of chosenness and intentionality. Ann Cahill thus identifies a widespread assumption that 'whether a pregnancy is terminated voluntarily or not constitutes an enormous distinction between experiences',[51] which is presumably behind Reiheld's claim that 'the line between completing or accelerating a miscarriage and performing an induced abortion seems clear to me'.[52] But for as long as the rhetoric of individual choice and voluntarism has been attached to abortion, it has also been subject to feminist interrogation,[53] which gives us reason to hold this assumption up to closer inspection. This is not to say that chosenness and unchosenness are not significant or relevant to the discussion. In plenty of cases, abortion is experienced as an empowering exercise of choice, whilst many personal accounts of miscarriage describe it as an event that brings a depleted sense of control and agency. Jennifer Doyle, for example, writes of her sense that 'the abortion I had as a student at Rutgers in the 1980s was one of the most singularly empowering experiences I've had as a sexual subject',[54] whilst Angela Garbes describes feeling 'powerless' as her miscarriage occurred.[55] But the line between miscarriage and abortion can also feel much finer, as Scuro documents in her account of a 'therapeutic abortion' on medical grounds, which for years she had classified as a miscarriage, feeling it did not 'count' as an abortion because the pregnancy had been wanted.[56] Or as Barbara Katz Rothman argued in *The Tentative Pregnancy* over thirty years ago: 'The decision to abort a foetus with spina bifida when you live in a fourth-floor walkup in a city designed without access for wheelchairs is not really an exercise in free choice.'[57]

There is clearly a danger in highlighting these kinds of fine lines. In the first instance, the examples taken above from Scuro and Katz Rothman can easily be made to fit the normative narrative of the 'right' kind of abortion: the regretful one involving a moral dilemma, or a difficult and painful choice in response to extraneous circumstances.[58] This narrative belongs to what Erica Millar calls the 'mushy middle' that is 'at once pro-choice and anti-abortion', professing support for women to choose and have abortions, 'so long as they feel "really, really bad" about them'.⁵⁹ Narratives of abortion as a 'choiceless choice'⁶⁰ can also be summoned in support of the 'pro-life' claim that women are 'victims' of abortion as much as the 'unborn', as no woman in their right mind or in the right circumstances would ever choose abortion. As Millar demonstrates, since the early 1980s, the transnational anti-abortion movement has 'increasingly shifted rhetorical focus away from protecting foetal life to feigning equal concern with the impact of abortion on women'.⁶¹ This turns on reframing abortion as 'loss' rather than 'murder', and transposing the foetus into 'a constant, absent presence in the woman's life, constantly judging her for making the wrong decision and retrospectively organising her pregnancy as involving an eternal relationship between a mother and her child.'⁶² The 'wrongness' of the abortion choice is recast as a wrong against women themselves and their 'maternal nature', such that women need to be protected from the bad choices they might make under the spell of feminist doctrine. Choice is thereby voided through claims that abortion could never be a valid choice, and, further, that it is a 'loss even when it is chosen'.⁶³

So if the distinction between miscarriage and abortion hinges upon individual choice, voluntarism and intention, then in practice it is being eroded quite effectively by anti-abortion campaigners, through the language of loss and mobilisation of what Millar calls 'foetocentric grief'. At the same time, the presumption of miscarriage as a passive event that is *undergone* rather than chosen is being eroded through the regulatory discourses of 'foetal motherhood'⁶⁴ that not only maternalise abortion but responsibilise all pregnant people for the outcomes of their pregnancies. As Pam Lowe argues, 'every choice that a woman makes, from eating to prenatal testing, is taken as evidence of her willingness to perform idealised motherhood ... whilst nominally "choices" can be made, there is often only one "right" choice for responsible women to make'.⁶⁵ Hence, whilst it may be recognised that miscarriage itself is not actively chosen or intended, the pregnant person can nevertheless be held responsible for their 'choices' up to that point. This logic reaches its dreadful realisation through the criminal justice system when women are arrested, prosecuted and charged for 'culpable miscarriage', the message being that it does not matter whether the ending of a pregnancy was chosen, intended or undertaken deliberately, because a pregnant individual can still be held responsible for failing to 'act like a mother'. This is clearly recognised by Dennis Muñoz, a lawyer representing two imprisoned women in El Salvador (where there is a total ban on abortion), who contends that the miscarriage/abortion distinction has become essentially irrelevant in the eyes of police and prosecutors: 'They say women are responsible for care of the foetus ... There is a lot of ignorance and no intention to investigate. There's also religious dogma. I prove it's a miscarriage but the courts don't care.'⁶⁶

All this might well suggest that the feminist response to the 'merging' of miscarriage and abortion⁶⁷ should be to do just the opposite and reinforce the distinction between the two. But if such a distinction depends upon a reinforcement of chosenness/unchosenness as the decisive criterion, or presumptions about which pregnancies are 'willed' and 'wanted' and which are not, this only brings us back to all the problems that ensue when individual choice, action and emotion are placed front and centre of reproductive politics. The marshalling of individual autonomy – 'My body, My choice' – certainly carries a powerful charge as an act of reclaiming what patriarchal ideologies and laws seek to obliterate; and meaningful choice is an important condition of reproductive freedom. But as reproductive justice activists have tirelessly argued, in isolation from campaigns for 'enabling conditions',⁶⁸ the mantra of individual choice only serves to eclipse the gross structural inequalities that materialise through differential access to reproductive services including abortion, as well as through modes of reproductive coercion, censure and sanction. In practice, the apparatus of 'choice' works for some but against others, when the moralised and gendered responsibility to make the 'right' choices and want the 'right' things functions as a form of disciplinary power exercised particularly over the 'wrong' sort of women.⁶⁹ Further, as Millar points out, the tables are easily turned when 'choice' is appropriated and marshalled by anti-abortion activists. Whilst on the one hand they claim that women's choices to abort are against their 'maternal nature' and hence can never be genuine, they themselves deploy the discourse of choice when they assert that knowledge of 'post-abortion syndrome', as well as incremental restrictions on abortion, including mandatory counselling and 'cooling-off' periods, 'provide women with informed and "real" choices'.[70]

What we are dealing with, then, is a terrain in which 'chosen' and 'unchosen' may continue to hold subjective meaning (in terms of how an individual might understand and frame their own abortion or miscarriage), but their political meaning has become subsumed by powerful discourses of proper and responsible behaviour, and a consequentialist logic whereby outcome, above all, is deemed sufficient grounds for culpability. In response, what is required is not so much a renewed feminist defence of individual choice, but joined-up resistance to the mechanisms of responsibilisation that put people who experience both abortion *and* miscarriage at risk of censure and criminal punishment. This means suspending questions about choice and intent, and reckoning instead with the gendered, raced and classed norms that position certain individuals on the right side of social approval and the law whilst rendering others reckless or suspicious.[71] *Whose* miscarriage looks 'too like' abortion? If there is a 'right' and a 'wrong' kind of abortion, how does this relate to the 'right' and 'wrong' kind of miscarriage, and the 'right' and 'wrong' kind of pregnancy? How well is someone able to narrate their miscarriage or abortion to meet the requirements for 'responsible decision-making', 'conscientious pregnancy' or 'innocent loss'?

It also means treating miscarriage and abortion as issues of social justice, and reckoning with the impacts, implications and costs of abortion and miscarriage – quite literally for those without adequate medical insurance or who are gestating for money[72] – in light of how they map on to wider social inequalities. For instance, not only have impoverished and non-white women in the US been disproportionately affected by state-imposed restrictions on accessing abortion, by the denial of federal funds for abortion, by punitive welfare policies, and by the criminalisation of pregnancy, abortion and miscarriage; statistics also show that those same groups are more likely to experience miscarriage in the first place due to factors including inadequate or non-existent healthcare, housing conditions, and the 'weathering effect' of systemic racism.[73] When we widen the focus out like this, what appears most significant with regard to cases like Purvi Patel's is not so much what the individual in question may have chosen or intended – was it deliberate? – but the conditions that make adverse pregnancy outcomes, interventions and arrests far more likely for some than for others; in which pregnant people may refrain from seeking help for drug or alcohol addiction for fear of being reported to the police; and in which the options for some pregnant people are so severely constrained that risking a 'DIY abortion' may appear as the only option.[74]

## Conclusion: spectrum not separation

It is problematic to distinguish miscarriage from pregnancy on the presumption that miscarriage is socially marginalised whilst 'pregnancy' is socially supported; or on the grounds that 'pregnancy' is child-producing whilst miscarriage is not. It is also problematic to treat miscarriage and abortion as categorically separate on the grounds of choice, volition or intention. Not only do such distinctions frequently falter on further examination; they are also integral to oppressive social discourses of childbearing teleology and foetal motherhood which, to quote Berlant, 'retraumatise a set of already vulnerable bodies: the body of the woman unsettled by pregnancy and already exposed to misogyny and the state; the impoverished, the young, the often African American or Native American women who have had little access to reproductive health support apart from a scandalous history of state chicanery…'[75] From this perspective, it is not that miscarriage is wrongly 'enrolled' in laws and debates over the control of pregnancy and abortion due to conceptual error. It is rather that struggles over the criminalisation of miscarriage are *inextricable* from struggles over the control of pregnancy and abortion. When pregnant people are treated as dangerous subjects, it is inevitable that those who have experienced miscarriage or stillbirth will be 'swept up' into the criminal justice system, at least those whose reproductivity and existence have already been marked as a threat.

Accordingly, instead of trying to refine categorical

distinctions and treating miscarriage as a case apart, there is much more to gain from pursuing a politics of solidarity and considering different pregnant realities and outcomes together, and in relation to one another. A powerful example of this kind of approach is provided by the 'full spectrum' doula movement: a rising form of reproductive justice activism that seeks to provide non-judgmental support and care for pregnant people however their pregnancy proceeds or ends, whether in birth, abortion, miscarriage or stillbirth.[76] As Loretta Ross explains it, the intention is to 'weave diverse pregnancy experiences into a holistic service and advocacy model that challenges stigmatised, artificial divisions among pregnancy outcomes'.[77] For instance, abortion advocacy and birth advocacy are forms of activism that usually operate separately, or indeed are presumed to be in conflict; but full-spectrum doulas have promoted the idea that 'abortion should not stand alone', and instead be approached as 'one part of a person's entire reproductive life. The same individual may have an abortion, give birth, and then have a miscarriage', and support and care should be equally available in every case.[78]

The full-spectrum doulas provide a direct caregiving service that works with individuals, but in breaking down boundaries between birth, abortion, miscarriage and stillbirth, the movement also paves the way for pregnant/postpartum solidarity and co-ordinated struggle at a broader level. Though the 'abortion issue' operates as a pernicious mechanism of division, the full-spectrum approach enables us to see the damaging effects of 'pro-life' policies and logics upon all pregnant people and not only those who seek to terminate, as the logic of 'foetal rights' renders pregnant bodies increasingly vulnerable to unwanted interventions and procedures. Lynn Paltrow, for example, of the National Advocates for Pregnant Women, tells of an anti-abortion campaigner who found herself subjected to a forced C-section.[79] The full-spectrum approach can also mobilise collective resistance to the normative 'success model' of pregnancy as a 'trap' or 'set-up' that generates feelings of guilt and shame even amongst those who do deliver up the expected child.[80] To be sure, it is not uncommon for those who have been through a miscarriage or stillbirth to report feelings of resentment towards those whose pregnancies continue to term, as well as those who opt to abort. These are understandable emotional responses – especially within a culture that pits women against one another – and should not be weaponised as yet another source of gendered guilt. But at the same time, recognition of 'common threats and threads', in Paltrow's words, can serve as a uniting force to challenge the master narrative of productive pregnancy and sacrificial maternity. Scuro also proposes this kind of vision, writing that 'Perhaps instead solidarity will be found with the woman who has miscarried, as she might recognise herself in the woman who has aborted her pregnancy, and again each with the woman who has "successfully" given birth.'[81]

For feminist philosophy, then, the aim should be to explore what philosophical analysis can bring to the 'full-spectrum' framework, whilst also taking on the foetocentric logics and value systems that divide us and do such damage. The impulse to 'rescue' miscarriage from the 'fallout' of abortion politics through insisting upon its difference may be strong, but in 'turn[ing] away less from those who have experienced miscarriage',[82] it is vital not to turn away more from those who have experienced abortion. In particular, there is a need for vigilance concerning the assumptions and implications that lie behind the idea that it is *especially* bad for someone to be punished for inducing an abortion when in fact the cessation of pregnancy was involuntary. Of course there is a particular cruelty to being punished for something one did not do. This adds the injustice of wrongful accusation into the mix, and if the pregnant person did not want the pregnancy to end, a wretched kind of irony. But who is to say it is necessarily less painful to be punished for something that one has actually done, especially within a cultural climate that is so anti-abortion that even pro-choice activists refer to it as a 'necessary evil'?[83] And if we entertain, even for a second, the idea that abortion is something to distance ourselves from, or that punishing miscarriage is necessarily 'worse' than punishing abortion, we risk fuelling anti-abortion sentiment even further. Whether or not the 'crime' was committed, the focus should be squarely on challenging the brutality and injustice of the punishment full stop.

*Victoria Browne is Senior Lecturer in Politics at Oxford Brookes University and a member of the* Radical Philosophy *editorial collective. She is author of* Feminism, Time and Nonlinear History *(2014).*

**Notes**

1. The pathologist who testified for the defence told the court the foetus was at 23 or 24 weeks gestation and that its lungs were not developed enough to breathe. But the pathologist for the prosecution claimed that the foetus was further along than that – at 25 to 30 weeks gestation, which is treated as past the point of 'viability' – and was born alive. He also used the discredited 'lung float test' in making his determination. The idea behind the test (which dates from the seventeenth century) is that if the lungs float in water, the baby took at least one breath, but if they sink, then the foetus died before leaving the uterus. For more details, see Emily Bazelon, 'Purvi Patel Could Be Just the Beginning', *New York Times*, 1 April 2015, https://www.nytimes.com/2015/04/01/magazine/purvi-patel-could-be-just-the-beginning.html.

2. See http://www.in.gov/legislative/bills/2009/SE/SE0236.1.html

3. As for the neglect conviction, it was decided that 'the State presented sufficient evidence for a jury to find that Patel was subjectively aware that the baby was born alive and that she knowingly endangered the baby by failing to provide medical care, but that the State failed to prove beyond a reasonable doubt that the baby would not have died but for Patel's failure to provide medical care. Therefore, we vacate Patel's class A felony conviction and remand to the trial court with instructions to enter judgment of conviction for class D felony neglect of a dependent and resentence her accordingly'. See the Court of Appeals of Indiana case summary, Purvi Patel v. State of Indiana, 22 July 2016, https://www.in.gov/judiciary/opinions/pdf/07221601tac.pdf.

4. The National Conference of State Legislatures website claims that 'at least 38 states have fetal homicide laws'. See 'State Laws on Fetal Homicide and Penalty-Enhancement For Crimes Against Pregnant Women', National Conference of State Legislatures, 1 May 2018, http://www.ncsl.org/research/health/fetal-homicide-state-laws.aspx

5. The National Advocates for Pregnant Women contend that media reporting on the impact of drug ingestion upon foetal development is consistently misrepresentative. See 'Pregnancy and Drug Use: The Facts', accessed 30 October 2018, http://advocatesforpregnantwomen.org/issues/pregnancy_and_drug_use_the_facts/.

6. Leticia Miranda, Vince Dixon and Cecilia Reyes, 'How States Handle Drug Use During Pregnancy', ProPublica, 30 September 2015, https://projects.propublica.org/graphics/maternity-drug-policies-by-state.

7. 'NAPW Demands Indiana Prosecutor Drop Murder Charge Against Woman Who Had a Stillbirth at Home', National Advocates for Pregnant Women blog, 2 August 2018, http://advocatesforpregnantwomen.org/blog/2018/08/.

8. These are the words of lawyer Dennis Muñoz, who represents two imprisoned women in El Salvador where there is a total ban on abortion. Between 2000 and 2011, more than 200 women were reported to the police for suspected abortions, 49 of whom were convicted with seven more convicted since 2012. See Jonathan Watts, 'El Salvador: Where Women Are Thrown Into Jail For Losing a Baby', *The Guardian*, 17 December 2015, https://www.theguardian.com/global-development/2015/dec/17/el-salvador-anti-abortion-law-premature-birth-miscarriage-attempted-murder.

9. 'Miscarriage', last modified 1 June 2018, https://www.nhs.uk/conditions/miscarriage/.

10. This is arguably attributable to the greater traction of the 'foetal personhood' trope within the wider socio-political context of the US.

11. See Erica Millar, 'Mourned Choices and Grievable Lives: The Anti-Abortion Movement's Influence in Defining the Abortion Experience in Australia Since the 1960s', *Gender & History* 28: 2 (2016), 503.

12. For further clarification: the article tends to refer to 'miscarriage' rather than 'miscarriage/stillbirth' for ease of reading, but the argument pertains to the cessation of pregnancy at whatever stage.

13. The treatment of trans pregnancy in the media has been sensationalised and hysterical, but there are a growing number of academic articles available. See, for example, Paisley Currah, 'Expecting Bodies: The Pregnant Man and Transgender Exclusion from the Employment Non-Discrimination Act', *Women's Studies Quarterly* 36:3 (2008), 330–336; Damien W. Riggs, 'Transgender Men's Self-Representations Of Bearing Children Post-Transition', in *Chasing Rainbows: Exploring Gender Fluid Parenting Practices*, ed. Fiona Joy Green and May Friedman (Ontario: Demeter Press, 2013), 62–71; Michael Toze, 'The Risky Womb and the Unthinkability of the Pregnant Man: Addressing Trans Masculine Hysterectomy', *Feminism & Psychology* 28:2 (2018), 194–211. The University of Leeds has received funding from the UK Economic and Social Research Council for a three-year project on 'An International Exploration of Transmasculine Practices of Reproduction'. See https://transpregnancy.leeds.ac.uk/

14. In 2016, the British Medical Association produced a document, 'A Guide to Effective Communication: Inclusive Language in the Workplace', which states that 'A large majority of people that have been pregnant or have given birth identify as women. We can include intersex men and transmen who may get pregnant by saying 'pregnant people' instead of 'expectant mothers', accessed 30 October 2018, https://archive.org/details/2016BritishMedicalAssociationBMAGuideToEffectiveCommunication2016/page/n0. This predictably caused a media outcry, with Stephen Adams and Sanchez Manning from the *Daily Mail* reporting the story with the headline 'Doctors banned from using word "mothers"', 28 January 2017, https://www.dailymail.co.uk/news/article-4167632/Don-t-call-pregnant-patients-mothers.html. The *Telegraph* quoted the Conservative MP Philip Dav-

ies: 'If you can't call a pregnant woman an expectant mother, then what is the world coming to?' See Laura Donnelly, 'Don't call pregnant women "expectant mothers" as it might offend transgender people, BMA says', 29 January 2017, https://www.telegraph.co.uk/news/2017/01/29/dont-call-pregnant-women-expectant-mothers-might-offend-transgender/

15. See, for example, Sophie Lewis, 'Gestators of all Genders Unite!', Verso blog, 6 March 2018, https://www.versobooks.com/blogs/3654-gestators-of-all-genders-unite.

16. Laura Briggs, *How All Politics Became Reproductive Politics: From Welfare Reform to Foreclosure to Trump* (Oakland: University of California Press, 2017), 5.

17. Toze 'The Risky Womb and the Unthinkability of the Pregnant Man', 204–05.

18. For instance, the high-profile pregnancy of Thomas Beatie in the US in 2008 was the subject of much public 'concern' that his foetus might be negatively affected by previous testosterone use – he was instructed by an obstetrician via a television network (ABC TV) that it was 'really important' that he did not take any testosterone during the pregnancy – and that the future child would be 'confused' later in life about their parental situation. See Patrick Barkham, 'Being a pregnant man? It's incredible', *The Guardian*, 28 March 2008, https://www.theguardian.com/lifeandstyle/2008/mar/28/familyandrelationships.healthandwellbeing.

19. Toze, 'The Risky Womb', 204–05.

20. Alexis Pauline Gumbs, 'M/other ourselves: a Black queer feminist genealogy for radical mothering', in *Revolutionary Mothering: Love on the Front Lines*, eds. China Materns Gumbs and Mai'a Williams (Toronto: PM Press, 2016), 19.

21. Loretta Ross and Rickie Solinger, *Reproductive Justice: An Introduction* (Oakland: University of California Press, 2017).

22. Jennifer Scuro, *The Pregnancy [does-not-equal] Childbearing Project: A Phenomenology of Miscarriage* (London: Rowman & Littlefield, 2016), xiii.

23. Ann Cahill 'Miscarriage and Intercorporeality', *Journal of Social Philosophy* 46:1 (2015), 48.

24. Jennifer Doyle, 'Blind Spots and Failed Performance: Abortion, Feminism, and Queer Theory', *Critical Humanities and Social Sciences* 18:1 (2009), 25.

25. Best known amongst sociologists and anthropologists who have written on the subject of miscarriage and 'reproductive loss' are Gayle Letherby and Linda Layne. See, for example, Letherby's article 'The Meanings of Miscarriage', *Women's Studies International Forum* 16: 2 (1993), 165–180; and Layne's *Motherhood Lost: A Feminist Account of Pregnancy Loss in America* (Abingdon and New York: Routledge, 2002). See also Carol Komaromy and Sarah Earle (eds.), *Understanding Reproductive Loss: Perspectives on Life, Death and Fertility* (Abingdon and New York: Routledge, 2012). Miscarriage and stillbirth are also discussed in reproductive justice and advocacy publications such as Julia Chinyere Oparah et al, *Battling Over Birth: Black Women and the Maternal Healthcare Crisis* (Amarillo, TX: Praeclarus Press 2018).

26. See also Scuro, *Pregnancy [does-not-equal] Childbearing*; or Kate Parsons, 'Feminist Reflections on Miscarriage, in Light of Abortion', *International Journal of Feminist Approaches to Bioethics* 3:1 (2010), 1–22.

27. Alison Reiheld, '"The Event That Was Nothing": Miscarriage as a Liminal Event', *Journal of Social Philosophy* 46:1 (2015), 16.

28. Ibid., 23.

29. D&C, or Dilation and Cutterage, is the procedure of widening the cervix and surgically removing part of the lining and/or contents of the uterus.

30. Reiheld, '"The Event That Was Nothing"', 23.

31. Ibid., 23, 22.

32. Ibid., 13.

33. 'Liminality' was coined by anthropologist Arnold van Gennep in his 1909 text *Rites of Passage* and popularised by Victor Turner, both of whom use the term to refer to the transitional stage of a ritual initiation in which the 'liminar' is 'betwixt and between' fixed points in the social structure. But there are also ways of understanding liminality that are not wedded to the sequential linear structure of pre-liminal—liminal—post-liminal, where the 'liminal' names that which is excluded but remains on the margins as a perpetual threat to the stability and unity of the established symbolic or social order. The work of Julia Kristeva and Homi Bhabha can serve as illustrations here. I discuss the concept of liminality in more detail in relation to pregnancy and miscarriage in my forthcoming book *Pregnancy without Birth*.

34. Cahill, 'Miscarriage and Intercorporeality', 45.

35. Claudia Dey, 'Mothers as Makers of Death' *The Paris Review*, 14 August 2018, https://www.theparisreview.org/blog/2018/08/14/mothers-as-makers-of-death/.

36. Erica Millar, *Happy Abortions: Our Bodies in the Era of Choice* (London: Zed Books, 2017), 212.

37. Imogen Tyler, 'Chav Mum, Chav Scum: Class Disgust in Contemporary Britain', *Feminist Media Studies* 8:2 (2008), 30.

38. Lynn M. Paltrow and Jeanne Flavin, 'Arrests of and Forced Interventions on Pregnant Women in the United States, 1973-2005: Implications for Women's Legal Status and Public Health', *Journal of Health Politics, Policy and Law* 38:2 (2013), 299–343.

39. Lynn Paltrow, 'The dangerous state laws that are punishing pregnant people', Think Progress, 28 September 2016, accessed 30 October 2018, https://thinkprogress.org/criminalization-pregnancy-us-43e4741bb514/.

40. Briggs, *Reproductive Politics*, 71.

41. Scuro, *Pregnancy [does-not-equal] Childbearing*, 189.

42. Ibid., 234.

43. Lauren Berlant, 'America, "Fat", the Fetus', *boundary 2* 21:3 (1994), 148.

44. Angela Garbes, *Like a Mother: A Feminist Journey Through the Science and Culture of Pregnancy* (New York: HarperCollins, 2017), 19.

45. Catherine Mills, 'Technology, Embodiment and Abortion', *Internal Medicine Journal* 35:7 (2005), 428

46. Berlant, 'America, "Fat", the Fetus', 147.

47. Scuro, *Pregnancy [does-not-equal] Childbearing*, ix.

48. Layne, *Motherhood Lost*, 69.

49. Scuro, *Pregnancy [does-not-equal] Childbearing*, 209.

50. Maggie Nelson, *The Argonauts*, (Minneapolis: Graywolf Press, 2015), 109.
51. Cahill, Miscarriage and Intercorporeality', 57.
52. Reiheld, "'The Event That Was Nothing'", 23.
53. Millar, *Happy Abortions*, 29.
54. Jennifer Doyle, 'Blind Spots and Failed Performance', 26.
55. Garbes, *Like a Mother*, 76.
56. Scuro, *Pregnancy [does-not-equal] Childbearing*, x.
57. Barbara Katz Rothman, *The Tentative Pregnancy: How Amniocentesis Changes the Experience of Motherhood* (New York: W. W. Norton & Company, 1986), 9.
58. To illustrate, we might contrast two British MPs speaking out against Northern Ireland's abortion laws through reference to their own abortions. Conservative MP Heidi Allen's account fits the mould of the 'right' kind of narrative when she reports that her abortion was an 'incredibly hard decision' and explains she had been very ill with daily seizures and so reluctantly put her health first: https://www.independent.co.uk/news/uk/politics/nothern-ireland-abortion-irish-referndum-rules-pro-choice-life-pregnancy-mps-a8384976.html. Labour MP Jess Philips takes a bigger political risk in writing that 'my abortion was nothing special. I cannot remember the date it happened. I never wonder': https://www.theguardian.com/commentisfree/2018/may-/27/jess-phillips-i-had-an-abortion-and-will-fight-for-rights-for-everyone
59. Millar, *Happy Abortions*, 2 (quoting Katha Pollitt).
60. Ross and Solinger, *Reproductive Justice*, 102.
61. Millar, *Happy Abortions*, 501.
62. Ibid., 508.
63. Ibid., 507, quoting Selena Ewing, *Women and Abortion: An Evidence-Based Review* (Parramatta: Women's Forum Australia, 2005).
64. Berlant, 'America, "Fat", the Fetus', 147.
65. Pam Lowe, *Reproductive Health and Maternal Sacrifice: Women, Choice and Responsibility* (Palgrave Macmillan, 2016), 109.
66. Jonathan Watts, 'El Salvador', .https://www.theguardian.com/global-development/2015/dec/17/el-salvador-anti-abortion-law-premature-birth-miscarriage-attempted-murder
67. Millar, 'Mourned Choices', 506.
68. Ross and Solinger, *Reproductive Justice*, 122.
69. See Victoria Browne, "'The money follows the mum": Maternal Power as Consumer Power', *Radical Philosophy* 199 (2016), 2–7.
70. Millar, *Happy Abortions*, 508.
71. Penelope Deutscher, *Foucault's Futures: A Critique of Reproductive Reason* (New York: Columbia University Press, 2016).
72. One estimate is that uninsured women in the US are paying between $4,000 and $9,000 for medical treatment of miscarriage, whilst insured women are paying out-of-pocket expenses of between $250 and $1,200, depending upon their co-payments and deductibles. See Jessica Grose, 'The Cost of a Miscarriage', *The Slate*, 26 March 2015, http://www.slate.com/articles/double_x/doublex/2015/03/the_cost_of_a_miscarriage_we_talk_about_the_emotional_pain_but_not_the_financial.html.
73. See Oparah et al, *Battling Over Birth*. Briggs also cites a large study finding that after controlling for confounders, the rate of miscarriage for Black or African American women was 57% higher overall and 93% higher after week 10 of pregnancy, and another which shows that the mortality rate for Black infants is more than twice that for white infants. Briggs also notes that infant mortality rates are elevated for Native Americans, Asian Americans and Latinx people, particularly Puerto Ricans, but she explains that that this data set has greater variation because of the different health experiences of the different groups, which have not been made into coherent groups the way African Americans have. See *Reproductive Politics*, 129-34. Another devastating reality is that, according to the Centre for Disease Control and Prevention, Black women in the US die from pregnancy- or childbirth-related causes at three to four times the rate of white women.
74. To be clear: the 'DIY abortion' is not necessarily risky in itself, as argued by feminist campaigns to de-medicalise abortion or to legalise taking abortion pills in a home setting. See, for example, Lizzie Presser, 'Inside the secret network providing home abortions across the US', *The Guardian*, 27 August 2018, https://www.theguardian.com/world/2018/aug/27/inside--the-secret-network-providing-home-abortions-across-the-us. Or Claudia Craig, 'It's perfectly safe – so why can't women take abortion pills at home?', *The Guardian*, 1 August 2018, https://www.theguardian.com/commentisfree/2018/aug/01/abortion-pill-law-scotland-women-english.
75. Berlant, 'America, "Fat", the Fetus', 149.
76. 'Doula' is a term for birth attendant, though 'full-spectrum' doulas offer support for the full range of pregnancy outcomes including abortion, miscarriage and stillbirth.
77. Loretta Ross, 'Preface' to Mary Mahoney and Lauren Mitchell, *The Doulas: Radical Care for Pregnant People* (New York: Feminist Press at the City University of New York, 2016), x.
78. Mahoney and Mitchell, *The Doulas*, 5.
79. Lynn Paltrow, 'Abortion Issue Divides, Distracts Us From Common Threats and Threads', *Perspectives* 13:3 (2005), available at https://www.americanbar.org/content/dam/aba/publishing/perspectives_magazine/women_perspectives_voicesabortion.pdf.
80. Scuro, *Pregnancy [does-not-equal] Childbearing*, xiii.
81. Lynn Paltrow, 'Abortion Issue Divides'; Scuro, *Pregnancy [does-not-equal] Childbearing*, xiii-iv; see also Mahoney and Mitchell, 10.
82. Reiheld, "'The Event That Was Nothing'", 22.
83. Millar, *Happy Abortions*, 2.

# Agustin García Calvo in our time
Vicente Ordóñez

The Spanish philosopher and writer Agustín García Calvo, who died in 2012, was a thinker who tried to provoke people into thinking about the problems posed by neoliberal globalisation. He thought that this global ideology was made to appear self-imposed, a kind of *hyper ouranos topos* (or ideal realm) pervading everything and from which everything emanates, and his works represent and raise awareness of the experience and effects of its absolute ideological hegemony. His political thought was inspired, in this respect, by the Presocratic thinkers, whom he had studied deeply.

Yet this raises an obvious question: how could a group of thinkers apparently concerned exclusively with theoretical aspects of reality offer the basis for a political agenda for the Left? I think they might, as Engels argued a long time ago[1] – for the Presocratics attempt also to untie the slipknot of cultural and religious prejudices and to challenge power relationships, exposing, among other things, unconsciously assumed ideological positions that contribute to submission and dispossession. Certainly Heidegger's hermeneutical work – reading the Presocratics in terms of 'power', 'struggle' or 'strength' – problematises any simple appropriation of their ideas for the Left.[2] But Heidegger's is not the only possible analysis: García Calvo offers an interpretation of the Presocratic thinkers that has in fact permeated left-wing politics in Spain over recent decades. Specifically, he has had a notable influence in the anti-Francoist struggle, the anarcho-syndicalist union CNT, social movements such as the 15m and political parties such as Podemos, among others.

Born in Zamora in 1926, García Calvo studied classical philology at the University of Salamanca. In 1964 he was appointed to a university chair of Classical Languages at Madrid's Universidad Complutense. After supporting the student revolt in 1965, he was removed from his professorship and lived in self-imposed exile in Paris. In 1970 he was appointed professor at Lille University and at the Collège de France. He also worked as a translator for the exiled Spanish publishing house Ruedo Ibérico. In 1976, following the death of General Franco, he recovered his chair in Madrid, where he remained teaching ancient philology until his retirement in 1992. He was emeritus professor at the Universidad Complutense until 1997 and remained active as a lecturer, writer and columnist until his death in 2012.

In his work, García Calvo proposes a hypercritical model of political action that focuses on discovering the falsehoods on which our reality is built, condemning them and insisting on saying 'no' to any form of imposition. He argues that this is the only realistic political tactic that can be cultivated in our circumstances: to bring to the surface the commands that the ruling social order imposes; to show that these commands are not to be confused with our own impulses, desires or wills; and thus to begin to realistically resist.[3] He is well aware of how restricted his programme is, but insists that that is precisely its strength, being rigorously realistic about how what are described as *our* desires, and so on, are always integrated and assimilated by the existing social order. He thus maintains that it is not possible in this conjuncture to draw any kind of positive theoretical conclusions at all. Rather, all we can do is to insist on being resolutely negative. We must simply give up the production of theory, together with any plans, strategies or proposals to which such theory might give rise, in order to focus entirely on negative action, struggle and praxis. His political project may be said to resemble the attitude of the gentleman in Kafka's tale, of whom the servant, when he sees him saddle up and about to leave, asks, 'Where is the master going?', to which his answer is: 'Just out of here.'[4] 'Just out of here' is at once all we can say and a sufficient basis for action. That is to say that to condemn the ideas and forms imposed from above, to break these forms and ideas and to uncover what lies behind them is – however apparently purely negative – already a worthwhile step. In fact, it is not only worthwhile, but necessary.

So how might García Calvo's strategy be integrated into a coherent and consistent left-wing programme? The first thing to understand is that it is not a question of what one speaks *for*, but only of what one speaks *against*. García Calvo starts with an indefinite pronoun and impersonal speech, from which the *subject* has been eliminated. When 'one' intends to 'be against', there are neither guides nor rules: the important point is to fight against what is being imposed and what is being presented as what 'one' desires.[5] Paraphrasing one of his favourite poets, Antonio Machado, one might say that for García Calvo it is the struggle itself that lights up the road. In this struggle it is supremely important to know what one is against; it is all that finally matters. García Calvo is in no doubt whatsoever about this. He is against any and all plans and projects, against any and every authority and dogma; in short, against all the falsehoods on which life today is based – the State, the capitalist production regime, representative democracy and patriarchy. So, if in political terms the intention is a left-wing transformation of reality – or, as he insisted, transformation from 'below' – the first and most urgent task is to bring to light the contradictions on which the present social order is based. In fact, we need to impose a self-limiting ordinance on ourselves and refuse to do anything *more* than that. Otherwise we risk both neoliberal assimilation and outright rejection by those whose 'utopias' or 'positive' proposals fail to match our own, thus fragmenting opposition from the very outset. García Calvo makes no concessions: for him discontent is both the beginning and end. The struggle is a war against every aspect of reality as currently constructed.[6] Negation is the only viable path towards liberation.

## Presocratic logic

But García Calvo's position is not merely a tactical political response to present conditions. It is rooted in the Presocratic philosophers' logical speculations and it is on this basis that he approaches the contemporary political world. What, then, does he take from Presocratic logic? Certainly not an *apodeiktikes epistemes* or a demonstrative science in the style of Aristotle, nor a formal science intended to formalise principles of valid reasoning. Rather, García Calvo understood Presocratic logic as an activity through which one might explore some of the mechanisms of language and follow those mechanisms through to their ultimate consequences. For him, Presocratic logic is pre-philosophical: it reveals the discontinuities that make up that which constitutes us and the essentially contradictory character of the real.[7] It does not therefore – and of course this is what is crucial for García Calvo – present any positive doctrine. It is a constant questioning that does not seek to come to any agreement that would connect or annul the differences that reason encounters when it strikes out to investigate reality.

So how exactly is Presocratic thought political? Certainly not as a political aetiology which allows one to infer how to rule, of the sort one finds in what remains of Presocratic fragments. But Presocratic thought may nonetheless be political inasmuch as it insists that reality is made up of contradictions, that reality is genuinely contradictory. For García Calvo, this logic of contradiction is the foundational example of a non-submissive thinking that can help develop a politically – because negative – position. Anaximander's *apeiron* (unlimited or boundless), Heraclitus' *logos* (reason) or even Parmenides' *to eon* (what it is) bring to light latent contradictions between language and reality. I draw attention here to the apparently less negative thinker of those mentioned: Parmenides. After hearing the first of the ways that one can conceive – 'the one that it is and that it is not possible not to be' – Parmenides is witness to the second way – 'that it is not and that it is right it should not be'. The testimonial word of Parmenides, the word that he hears and that asserts non-being in order to negate it, evokes non-being, and on evoking it makes possible the passage that goes from being to non-being. The 'is' that the goddess proffers seeks to define itself as apart from all negation.

Nevertheless, upon showing him the road of 'is-not' the goddess converts it into a case of 'is'. 'This IS that has no IS NOT that counterbalances it', writes García Calvo, 'is in fact also a negation of negation'.[8] The attempt to assure the identity of 'being' meta-logically (a = a) ends up strengthening the contradiction that one wanted to escape (a = ¬(¬a)): the opposition between 'a' and '¬a' reveals the identity of the substance 'a', but the substance is also revealed to be contradiction. What does this 'no' do? What's so radical about that? Presocratic denial can only negate what is established as real. By denying reality, Presocratic logic takes a stand against the ideas that constitute reality and destroys the very reality it denies. The destruction of what appears to be leaves breaks and pathways for 'what is not' to arise – '"what is not" which we clumsily call life, love, happiness or pleasure'.[9]

The unveiling of the fundamental contradiction that our thought rests upon is an example of what García Calvo seeks to recuperate for reflection: *wounding logic* – which is 'what Presocratic thought represents for philosophy (and its history)'[10] – needs again to be heard in public. This is the task that García Calvo makes his own. He develops a conception of contradiction that does not deny the truth of things and their relations, does not seek to hide or harmonise the living contradiction that beats at the foundation of the real, but rather shows that these are the very contradictions in which human life is grounded.

## No

García Calvo carried out a large portion of his public activities in anarchist cultural centres linked to the CNT (Confederación Nacional del Trabajo, or National Confederation of Labour), despite the fact that he was not affiliated to any anarchist group or trade union. In anarchism, García Calvo found people he could speak with and listen to, and it would be in part in libertarian milieux that he tested the constant practice of logos, or common reason.[11] For instance, his political ideas had a powerful impact on the anti-Franco resistance group los Ácratas (the Anarchists). This group had the Francoist authorities on tenterhooks between 1965 and 1969, and succeeded in putting an end to the Falangist SEU (Sindicato Español Universitario, or Spanish Students' Trade Union), the only legal student organisation in Spain since 1939. According to Miquel Amorós, one of the most rigorous historians of anarchism, García Calvo was their leading influence.[12] Although in some respects they had diametrically opposed points of view – mainly concerning García Calvo's total rejection of the use of violence to achieve political aims – los Ácratas were nonetheless inspired by García Calvo's *via negativa*: they refused to obey orders, did not recognise courts, rejected paying taxes, avoided military service and promoted a rhetoric of confrontation with the state. Tellingly, this was based directly on García Calvo's interpretation of the Presocratics.[13]

This proximity to anarchism, however, did not mean that he ceased to point out the imbalances that were at the foundation of its project, beginning with the negative particle 'an-' that the term itself incorporates. 'No' is, for García Calvo, the voice of common reason, the voice of protest, one of the few tools with which the people can destroy the ideas that have been developed to create and defend reality. Incorporated as the negation of authority or power (*arché*), 'an-archy' becomes loaded with meaning, becomes something positive and ceases thereby to serve as a critique of reality. Negation is in this way domesticated: 'avoiding this subjection of the No to some kind of future plan like Theirs, that of those that rule, is elemental, it is the most elemental thing that one can say in politics'.[14] Presocratic logic is the guide here, for its essential mechanism is negation.[15] And since a simple negation, saying 'no' to what occurs, has no substantive content of its own it cannot be integrated into any system.

The influence of that 'no' with which García Calvo confronts what has been established as real can be felt in various political, social and cultural phenomena. Within anarchism, sympathisers with anarcho-syndicalism, activists and those connected with libertarian anti-political groups have all shown themselves to be in tune with the political attitude of García Calvo, holding that ideologies play various functions within the complex machinery that assures social control – including the manufacture of lies. The only legitimate political tactic is, for them, saying 'no': no to the future, to computed time; no to progress; no to representative democracy; no to any 'ism', including anarchism. In addition, activists in citizens' movements like the 15M *indignados* have followed García Calvo in his politics of 'no', although these activists represent only the most radical minority sector within the movement. Finally, this 'no' should be noted in artists such as Chicho Sánchez Ferlosio, Isabel Escudero or Santiago Sierra, all of whom have developed a hypercritical attitude towards systems and social institutions – state, church, economic system and political powers.[16]

## Above/below

Despite his instrumental characterisation of ideologies, left-wing parties have been inspired by, and have used, some of the concepts that García Calvo developed. I have room here to explore only the most important of these: 'those below'. For García Calvo, 'those below' are one and the same as those who are 'the people': the term points to the *to xynon* of Heraclitus. In one of the plazas occupied during the events of 15 May 2011 in Spain, García Calvo declared:

> Therefore, when amongst ourselves we say and repeat that war is not about left or right, but rather is about below against above, we should not misunderstand … We must try to avoid confusion about above and below. Clearly and most immediately, above means cabinet ministers, top banking executives, all of that that you know is above – 'above': people say it like that, as we have no need to say it differently. Those who are high up are puppets that can be swapped in a couple of years or less, but that doesn't matter; they are those who are above. They are those who control. And below are those of us who are not them, to the degree to which we are not, because each of us is a little bit that – we are all of us a little bit of a banker and a little bit of a leader, and what are we going to do? There is a part of us that tends to that, but is not that, it is what is below: the people that does not exist but is, is simply what is below, below the government, below the oppression of capital, below money.[17]

It is worth paying attention to the contradiction between the polarities of 'above' and 'below', which are nothing but another manifestation of the movement to which things and processes are subjected. For García Calvo, the point, however, is that this dichotomy leads to a conflict that cannot be remedied. First, 'above' points to the space of power; second, it shows the teleological process of power since any power needs a direction and thus prescribes an imperative sequence of events. 'Below', on the contrary, points to what is common and public, to what is everybody's because it is not anybody's.

According to scholars such as Ruiz Fernández, Podemos, the most successful political party emerging from the demonstrations in Spain of 15 May 2011, has directly appropriated García Calvo's 'above'/'below' idea.[18] While Juan Carlos Monedero, one of the leaders of Podemos until his resignation in 2015, denies Ruiz Fernández's claim,[19] it seems no coincidence that the leaders of the three principal currents that now converge in Podemos – Pablo Iglesias, General Secretary of the group, Íñigo Errejón, ex-Podemos spokesman in Congress, and Miguel Urbán, chief representative of the 'Anticapitalists' current – continue to make use of this idea of 'above/below'.

Despite this adoption by Podemos, and also despite the admiration that Pablo Iglesias has for García Calvo,[20] there is nothing further from the political logic of the latter than a standard political party. García Calvo holds that people tend to fetishise stable and hierarchical organisations: they think that a group has to organise itself after the manner of a political party because it is the only way to be effective in social struggle. Nevertheless, history is obstinate in demonstrating the contrary, manifesting over and over again the toxicity of such options.[21] And that is something the Left would do well to ponder.

*Vicente Ordóñez is Lecturer in Political Philosophy at Universitat Jaume I, Spain. His book* El ridículo como instrumento politico *[Political uses of ridicule] was awarded the Universidad Computense de Madrid National Essay Prize 2014.*

**Notes**

1. Friedrich Engels, *Socialism: Utopian and Scientific*, trans. Edward Aveling (New York: Mondial, 2006), 45.
2. Martin Heidegger, *Heraklit*, in *Gesamtausgabe II. Abteilung: Vorlesungen 1923-1944*, vol. 55, ed. Manfred S. Frings (Frankfurt: Vittorio Klostermann, 1994), 158; Martin Heidegger, *Parmenides*, trans. André Schuwer and Richard Rojcewicz (Bloomington: Indiana University Press, 1998), 17.
3. Agustín García Calvo, *De Dios* (Zamora: Lucina, 1996), 85. All translations of García Calvo are the author's.
4. Franz Kafka, 'The Departure', in *The Complete Stories*, trans. Tania and James Stern (New York: Schocken Books, 1971), 497.
5. Agustín García Calvo, *Qué es el Estado* (Barcelona: La Gaya Ciencia, 1977), 8.
6. See García Calvo's talks at the Athenæum of Madrid: *Tertulia Política number 11 and 80* (2006, 2007), accessed 10 April 2018, http://bauldetrompetillas.es/agustin-garcia-calvo/tertulias/en-el-ateneo/
7. García Calvo studied logical contradiction in depth in his essay *Contra el Tiempo* (Zamora: Lucina, 1993).
8. Agustín García Calvo, *Lecturas presocráticas I* (Zamora: Lucina, 2001), 176.
9. Agustín García Calvo, 'Placer y negación' [Pleasure and Denial], *Conference*, 25 March 1992, accessed 29 March 2018, http://bauldetrompetillas.es/wp-content/uploads/pdf/Placerynegacion.pdf
10. Agustín García Calvo, *Lecturas presocráticas II. Razón Común: edición crítica, ordenación, traducción y comentario de los restos del libro de Heraclito* (Zamora: Lucina, 1985), 12.
11. García Calvo sometimes refers to his anarchic heart, 'a heart that has no ends, but only means, because its ends are nothing but its means. Its aim is above al the enemy order which is all constituted of ends and causes, of evolution towards ideal goals.' Agustín García Calvo, 'Carta a Carlos Semprún y Javier Domingo: contra la idea de hacer la Historia del Anarquismo' [Letter to Carlos Semprún and Javier Domingo: Against the Purpose of Publishing a History of Anarchism], *Historia Libertaria* 1:6 (1978).
12. Miquel Amorós, *1968. El año sublime de la acracia* [1968: The superb year of anarchy] (Bilbao, Muturreko Burutazioak, 2014), 71.
13. Agustín García Calvo, *De los modos de integración del pronunciamiento estudiantil* [Different ways to integrate the students' movement] (Madrid: La Banda de Moebius, 1979), 8.
14. M.C. García and P. Nacarino, 'Contra la Realidad: entrevista a Agustín García, *Periódico CNT* 324 (2006), http://www.cnt.es/noticias/contra-la-realidad
15. García Calvo, *De Dios*, 293. See also Agustín García Calvo, 'Heráclito y la lógica' [Heraclitus and Logic] (1991), accessed 10 April 2018, http://bauldetrompetillas.es/agustin-garcia-calvo/conferencias/
16. For the influence of García Calvo's ideas on Spanish anarchism, see for instance Octavio Alberola, *La revolución: entre el azar y la necesidad* [Revolution: Between Randomness and Necessity] (Buenos Aires: Libros de Anarres, 2017),
17. To understand the connections between García Calvo and the Free Assembly of Puerta del Sol in Madrid on 15 May, see María del Consuelo Ahijado, *Enseñar a No Saber: la Contra-Educación como Acción Política en Agustín García Calvo* [Teaching Not Knowing: Counter-Education as Political Action in Agustín García Calvo] (Doctoral Dissertation, 2015), 391, accessed 12 March 2018, http://www.tesiserred.net/handle/10803/365568. On the links between García Calvo and artists, see Chicho Sánchez Ferlosio, *A contratiempo* (Madrid: Diapasón, 1978); Isabel Escudero, *Coser y cantar* (Zamora: Lucina, 1990); Santiago Sierra, noglobaltour.com (2009), accessed 12 March 2018.
17. Agustín García Calvo, 'Asamblea de la Puerta del Sol' (16 June 2011), accessed 17 March 2018, http://bauldetrompetillas.es/agustin-garcia-calvo/tertulias/en-sol/
18. Jesús Ruiz, 'Agustín García Calvo en el 15-M' [Agustín García Calvo at the 15-M], *Las Torres de Lucca* 8 (January–June 2016), 261. On the basis of discussions with those involved in the 15m Free Assembly of Puerta del Sol in Madrid, Ruiz Fernández feels that the 'above/below' polarity has been appropriated by Podemos leaders.
19. Personal communication, 18 November 2017.
20. See 'La banda sonora de la campaña de Podemos', *Sabemos*, 22 May 2015, accessed 30 March 2018, http://sabemos.es/2015/05/22/la-banda-sonora-de-la-campana-de-podemos_2063/
21. Agustín García Calvo, 'Ateneo de Madrid. Tertulia Política no. 283' (2011), accessed 2 April 2018, http://bauldetrompetillas.es/agustin-garcia-calvo/tertulias/en-el-ateneo/

# Forgetting Vietnam

Trinh T. Minh-ha with Lucie Kim-Chi Mercier

Trinh T. Minh-ha teaches in the University of California, Berkeley's departments of Rhetoric, and Gender and Women's Studies. Born in Hanoi in 1952, Trinh emigrated to the United States in 1970 where she studied musical composition, ethnomusicology and French literature, completing her PhD dissertation in 1977 under the title: *Un Art sans Oeuvre: l'Anonymat dans les Arts Contemporains* [*An Art Without Oeuvre: Anonymity in Contemporary Arts*]. Since the early 1980s she has developed a complex theoretical, visual and poetic response to the implicit politics regulating the production of discourses and images of cultural difference. Working through the multidimensional effects of imperialism and neo-colonial modernity, her works played a pivotal role in the emergence of postcolonial theory and critique. Her now canonical 1989 book, *Woman, Native, Other*, investigates the contradictory imperatives faced by an 'I' positioned 'in difference' as a 'Third World woman' in the act of writing, as well as in critiquing the roles of the creator, intellectual and anthropologist. But aside from the critique of mechanisms of cultural representations, Trinh's works experiment with deconstructive and transgressive ways of questioning their own classifications. They play on, with and across cultural and national boundaries. Alongside films and installations, Trinh has published numerous essays and books on cinema, cultural politics, feminism and the arts.

The interview took place in London in December 2017, when the London premiere of *Forgetting Vietnam* at Tate Modern was programmed in parallel with a full retrospective of Trinh's films at the Institute of Contemporary Arts.

**Lucie Kim-Chi Mercier [LM]** You made three films around Vietnam; can you speak a little about the process that led you from one to the next? Is there a thread running through the different films, namely *Surname Viet Given Name Nam* (1989), *A Tale of Love* (1995) and *Forgetting Vietnam* (2015)?

**Trinh T. Minh-ha [TMH]** In terms of realisation they are three very different films, but certainly, there are threads linking them together because they are all about 'culture' in the largest sense of the term. Whenever I go to places and shoot in cultures different than my own, I'm not interested at all in 'covering a story' – an individual's story or an individualist subject. I never work that way. I'd rather come into places and events with questions like: What characterises a culture? What is its everyday reality? What leads a country to be seen as such? And importantly, *how* do we show and tell (from what position, with what tools)?

*Surname Viet Given Name Nam*, as you can tell from the title, concerns the naming of a country. It has to do with gender and national identity, as well as with the politics of naming, translating and interviewing. *Forgetting Vietnam*, which engages with the process of remembering and forgetting, also relates to the naming of a country, by featuring the multi-dimensional roles of land and water. In Vietnamese, *đất nước*, the term for country, designates 'land' and 'water', but just saying '*nước*' or 'water' already refers to a country (for example '*nước ta*' means both 'our water' or 'our country').

I start from there, from Vietnam as a body of water – in its geological formation and via its people's economic and cultural activities – to commemorate its fiftieth anniversary of the end of the War. *A Tale of Love* is a film based on the national poem of Vietnam, *Kim Vân Kieu*. If there's one thing the Vietnamese diaspora across all nations remembers of the culture, it's this poem. It's unique because it speaks to people from all classes in all walks of life. Villagers know verses of it. They've become popular sayings and are widely cited in a host of circumstances, especially situations related to questions of gender and nation, virtue and loyalty. Even if people don't remember all 3,254 verses of the epic love poem (none could do so in any case), they do remember fragments pertaining to the distinct roles and deeds of the characters in the poem.

This was what I adopted in approaching the poem with my film: not illustrating it; not manufacturing a realist representation of it; not narrating it linearly from beginning to end, but offering a multi-time, multi-layered, music-for-the-eye work. Therefore, coming in from the middle, opening with the ear via the poem's closing verse which deliberately states its function as a fabulation for beguiling the long night. What is emphasised is the nature of the poetic, hence the singing and recitation against a visual work that also invokes the olfactory dimension of experiencing love. And what is retained from the poem are only those instances that highlight the 'scents of a narrative' – here, as I have it, the conflicted loyalties and the nonconforming choices of the woman protagonist who, despite her sacrifice and impeccable ethics in love, does not fit squarely into patriarchal norms and ideology.

In other words, when I approach culture, what appeals to me is not the search for 'a good story', the individual story, or the clear message that marks our consumerist society's media productions. The ubiquitous demand for a centralised story sets the mould for funding and exhibition networks whose criteria for what is 'good,' and 'clear' serve to promote a monolithic, domination-subordination mode of storytelling. What appeals to me, however, is a making that maintains at core a relation to infinity: a focus that is vast in scope yet specific to the culture observed; situations that pertain to local people and at the same time speak to those from elsewhere; women whose peculiar conditions do not merely represent those of their peers—in this case, Vietnamese women. So when people say 'it's a film on Vietnamese women', I would say yes, *but* ... For example, I remember well when I presented and showed *Surname Viet* in Bologna in Italy, some women from the audience told me how moved they were by what they had heard in the film. They felt that it was their own condition that was being addressed. And this, I was told, also occurred with a group of Palestinian women who discussed my book *Woman, Native, Other*. So when you choose something specific it could be at the same time locally precise and very wide in scope.

**LM:** Let me linger a little bit on this question of the 'name', and the paradox that in order to deconstruct or undo the idea of a specific place or nation state you have to reassert its name. For instance in a lot of these films you name 'Vietnam' in the title. In *Reassemblage*, you narrate that someone asked you: You want to make a film on Senegal, but *what* in Senegal? A signifier of a nation state seems to be very important both as the locus of a de-figuration and, at the same time, a locus of play.

**TMH:** Absolutely. It tells us something about our compartmentalised world – how knowledge is forcibly compartmentalised for control purposes, and how, even with the constant talk about virtual boundlessness in globalisation, the world we live is a world of proliferating fences and walls. Boundaries are all over in our language, in the way we relate to people and events in life.

In remote villages of West Africa, where lived 'Africa' is not divided into nations, people identify mainly in terms of genealogy, ethnicity and linguistic belonging, and it's not at all uncommon for these villagers to speak four to six African languages. In other words, they are fluent across geographical and ethnic borders. They speak the languages of their neighbours in addition to their native language and the trade language of their region. So the system of the nation state and its derivative notion of nationalism remain quite disconnected, at odds with this cultural context – something like an exogenous imposition, a hard line drawn over the map of precolonial African kingdoms.

Such a structure of governance taken for granted as the norm is not unrelated to the way we consume film in general. In a story-driven approach to documentary for example, it is often thought that if you cover a subject, you have to focus on a specific topic, a 'case study' – something finite like an individual's story, a conflict, a ceremony, an incidence within a village or a community, or else a family drama– but if you are focusing on everyday life, building on the gestures of a culture via ordinary activities, and composing a distinct tapestry of sense, sight and sound as you go, it doesn't seem like a subject for a number of film consumers, especially film programmers and funders, who always ask for 'a story' (obviously, not the kind of cosmic, spiritual indigenous storytelling whose scope reaches across generations, which I discussed in *Woman, Native, Other*). So even when you make a documentary they beg you to develop an individualist, character-bound story with a beginning, middle and end, abiding by the normative theatrical three acts and its conflict-driven climax. For me, filmmaking is not at all about stories or messages. Those come along, but they can't define cinema.

Why not approach filmically a country, a people, a culture by starting with what comes with an image (mental, material, digital) or with a name like 'Vietnam', 'China', 'Japan', or 'Senegal', for example – as explicitly asked in my earlier film, *Reassemblage* (1982). What exactly stands for, characterises and speaks to a cultural and political event? Through the specific apparatus of film and video, how does one show, tell and receive while refusing merely to represent? In other words, the given name or the recorded sound image is a site of departure, where one takes off rather than arrives.

The focus here is on the play between seeing and not seeing; on the work of the invisible within the visible, and vice versa; or else, on how the seen both displays and veils, and how what is necessarily left unseen in each instance of the seen could contribute to bringing about *another seeing*. Questioning the prevailing claim to visibility, such a seeing acknowledges its limits while inducing one to *see anew*, not only with eyes wide open, but also with eyes wide shut. Of course, this is only one way of questioning the established tendency to reduce reality to the realm of the visible. Another way would be to address the other senses involved since cinema is not a mere art for the eye but an experience of the whole body.

**LM:** I was struck by the multiple facets and ambivalence of the title, *Forgetting Vietnam*. So, with 'forgetting' you highlight the act by which one might attempt to forget, the paradox of acting the forgetting, and you give us this beautiful quotation: '"To really forget, we must fully know what we want to forget"' (Pham Thi Hoài). But how to remember the face of a war?' This runs against the idea of a *devoir de mémoire*, in the sense of memorialisation. Indeed, it inverts it: what's at stake is not a determinate form of remembrance, as in Walter Benjamin's idea of the Proustian image, but a determinate forgetting... So, I'm interested in how you treat memory and forgetting via image and sound.

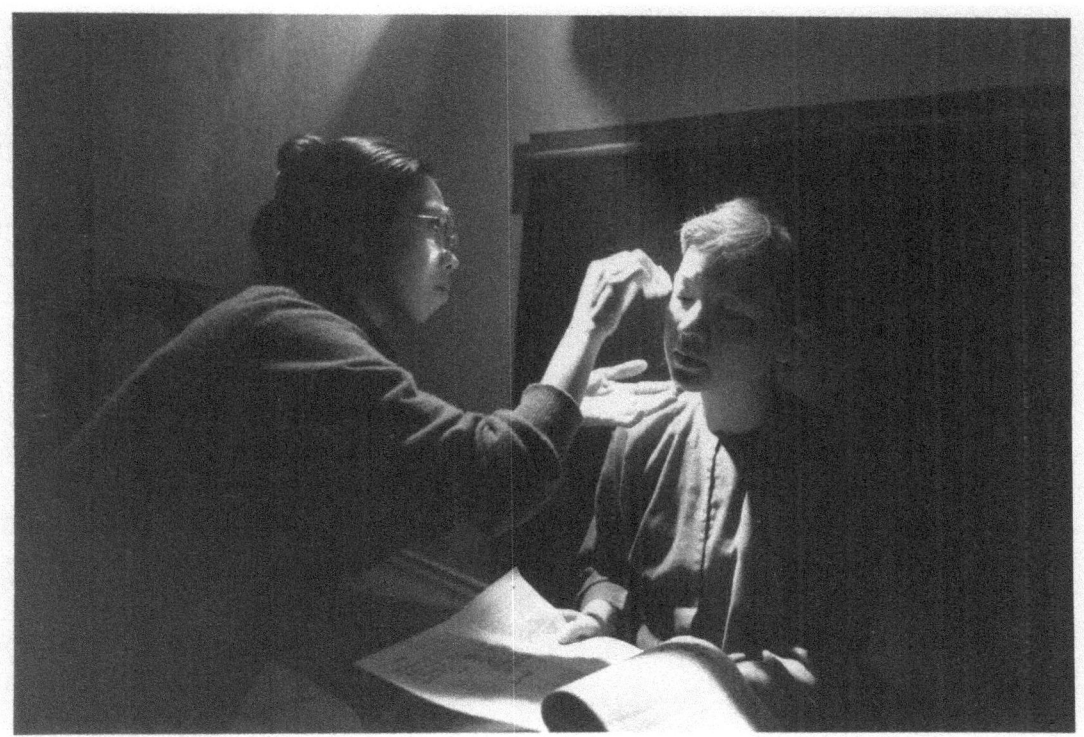

Image: Trinh T. Minh-ha, Surname Viet Given Name Nam (1989)

**TMH:** This follows nicely from the earlier discussion concerning the land-water pair *đất nước*) that defines Vietnam as a country. A common place to start would be to say: land records, water dissolves. The forces of preservation and oblivion go hand-in-hand. As stated at the beginning of *Forgetting Vietnam*, 'It all begins with Two.' Non-binary pairs multiply in unexpected courses and there are always at least two ways to enter my films.

To return differently to what I said about my three films on Vietnam being very distinct from one another, *Surname Viet Given Name Nam* is a 16mm film in which the stories of women interviewed in Vietnam by a French-based Vietnamese writer, Mai Thu Van, were first translated and published in French, then retranslated by myself into English and made into a 'script' for the film. Through the condition of women both in Vietnam and in the diaspora, the work features the historical multi-naming of a country and the politics of translation and interview – or documentary's antiquated devices.

Shot in 35mm, *A Tale of Love* deals with the genre commonly called 'fiction' or 'narrative feature' in which the love story is requisite. With the love story comes a whole process of voyeurism, for every story of love on screen is a story of voyeurism. The more of a voyeur you are in a feature narrative, the more intimate the view you offer to the spectator, right? So the camera would follow people everywhere. In their bathroom, in their shower, in their bed, in their nudity, but also in their terminal illness, in their hunger, in their suffering. It is an extreme form of voyeurism which I literally and provocatively exposed and incorporated into the role of one of the main characters of the film: the photographer. *A Tale of Love* is structured in such a way as to give you at first the feeling that you have a story, but as the film moves on, the story seems to disappear. As it loses its linearity and is made to dissolve, the viewer is invited to follow the narrative threads the way a deer would track a scent. 'Narrative, in her world, is a track of scents passed on from lover to lover', says a character in the film.

In *Forgetting Vietnam*, I was dealing with footage shot in 1995, with the advent of Hi8 video, and footage shot in 2012, with the advent of High Definition (HD) video. So you have low and high technology, tradition and modernity, rural and urban, and it's arduous to make them work together. Like other Third World countries, this is a problem that Vietnam is struggling with, not only because the leap required to bridge the gap between old and new is much more abrupt than in European countries, but also because the concept regulating the relation between low tech and high tech in today's consumer society is *incompatibility*. Everything is linearly made incompatible between past and present, North and South, East and West, so that we are constantly compelled to keep on consuming in our throwaway society.

The three films are therefore different from one another in their treatment, approach and concerns, even though this may escape many viewers. It's interesting to see how curators tend to program them. They usually put my African films on the same bill, and my two last Vietnam films would often be screened in consecutive order, one after the other with barely a break in between; and that's because they go by subject. But if, instead of content, they were to go by cinematic concerns, they wouldn't program them together. For me, lumping them together would make it impossible for the viewer to open up and take in their autonomy and integrity as film.

I mention all this to give you the wider context required to respond to your question about the complex relation between forgetting and remembering. In the making of *Forgetting Vietnam* one of the commitments I kept in relation to war images was the following: most of the films made on the war in Vietnam show you the horrors of war mainly through what constitutes the sensational in cinema. So: explosions, bombings, killings, bodies, buildings and environment being burned, mutilated and blasted; violent, bloody scenes with wounds oozing open (blood as depicted in mainstream films is cheap), and then suffering that is strident – noisy, and loud. Such a depiction of war amply exploited on screen for spectacular effect is something that I do not want at all to have in my films. Showing brutality has its journalistic function, but violence for violence's sake is how the media continue to desensitise human suffering and distress, as well as how the entertainment industry claims to serve a consumer society steeped in violent media.

And then you have the other kinds of films evolving from this war, of which you really have to ask: Whose interest does it serve? For most of the time what's covertly at stake are American interests. Whether their politics is liberal or conservative, mainstream films made in the name of the war in Vietnam speak to one side of the war and contribute to sustaining American hegemony. So, sometimes during one of these films' screenings, I would be sitting in the audience with other Vietnamese people, and they would look at me and say: Do you think it has anything to do with us? [Laughter]

With *Forgetting Vietnam*, viewers often wonder why there are no images of the war, but the war is all over, whether visible or otherwise. Its traces are everywhere, present in the environment, in people's memory, in their speech and daily rituals. For example, the poets quoted in the film are mostly young -- those whose generation has not known the war. Yet their thoughts and feelings are full of it, like this young woman poet, Phan Huyền Thư, who, writing about Huế – the ancient imperial city in central Vietnam whose traumatised inhabitants silently endured the mass killings perpetrated during the historical Offensive of Tết Mậu Thân 1968 – would disclose her sentiments as follows: '*I want to murmur to Huế and to caress it / But I'm afraid to touch the sensitive spot on Vietnam's body.*'

The War's affect still runs deep within the young generations born after it or at its end.. On the surface, everything seems to have returned to normalcy today, and ironically, in the current era of terror, Vietnam is reportedly one of the safest places to travel to. But the War is all-permeating, very present in its absence, and not just present the way the media represents it. The commitment to not use any footage of the War that has been taken and circulated on the media in *Forgetting Vietnam* was a question both of ethics and of *intense remembering in forgetting*. In *Surname Viet Given name Nam* I deliberately used some archival footage of the refugees in the 1950s with the stories of refugees in the late 1970s and 1980s so as to remember rape as a national and yet gender-specific problem across times of war. But in *Forgetting Vietnam*, I didn't want any war footage because as soon as you have 'Vietnam' in a film, people would expect to see these kind of images, and when these are not there, they feel somehow lost, as if Vietnam as a war is the only way they could relate to the country. So this is one way of forgetting.

Another more obvious way to forget could be seen in what has happened with tourism since the end of the War. There are many American soldiers who travelled there, not so much to remember Vietnam as to forget the Vietnam they knew, which is partly understandable. They are likely interested in returning to learn about the country of which they knew so little when they first came, deluded by their might, to eradicate an enemy force via military power. However, there is also a nostalgic side to it. They return to their battlefields, but this time as a tourist, as a consumer, so of course the Vietnamese folks would immediately oblige. Today in the flourishing industry of war tourism, the complex interwoven tunnel system in southern Vietnam, which bears witness to the guerillas' unmatched ingenuity and endurance, has become a source of investment. The multileveled subterranean structure that allowed the Vietnamese to gain victory over the Americans is precisely now part of the exoticism of war in the tropics, and the very places for touristic …

**LM:** You can even shoot a gun right, you can shoot a gun as part of the experience?

**TMH:** It's incredible. That's a second aspect of the forgetting. This being said, what is equally important to me is that when you go to a place with a camera, you rely on the camera to remember for you. And with new technologies – the iPhone being a popular example – you can select, delete, trash, edit, collect, keep whatever you want. This is how memory is treated today through digital technology. The difference between old and new technology is all about systems of memory. However, when I don't have a camera I remember very intensely the experience of an event, a place, a culture, a people. Relying on the camera to capture and record has led people to think that they can preserve memories with a camera. But actually, what they preserve is of a different nature than what they experience and remember. In that sense, one can talk about a 'memory for forgetfulness', since forgetting here means engaging critically with the world of camera and iPhone ever-faster memory. Show, tell, record. On the one hand, such an unquestioned economy of display-so-as-to-remember should be problematised in relation to everyday practices of forgetfulness and to indigenous economies of preservation-through-burial, for example. On the other hand, the more you attempt to forget and evade what you try to forget, the more it comes back to haunt you. Vietnam's spectre still haunts the White House, as it has the world at large. The question of remembering and forgetfulness could never be separated. For me, it remains a non-binary pair, two faces of the same coin.

**LM:** I would like to discuss the problem of heroism because it appears to stretch all the way back in your work to *Lovecidal: Walking with the Disappeared* (2016), which articulates a critique of the heroic version of war, war seen in terms of victory vs. defeat. The discourse on heroism seems to lock memory on every side. Memory is locked by the discourses of victory, that is, in the official Vietnamese discourses of history and state, as well as in a left-wing discourse which maintains a melancholic relationship to that moment – with its strong internationalist commitment against the war that hasn't since achieved comparable momentum. In the US, you also have the two sides of, if you will, 'defeat': the Vietnamese diaspora for whom it is still difficult to speak about the war now, as well as the American veteran's side.

**TMH:** Your take on heroism in this context is pertinent, and I can see the link with *Surname Viet Given Name Nam,* in which the women interviewed criticise the way they were presented by the foreign media, that is, always as 'heroic fighters'. In *Forgetting Vietnam* and especially in my last book *Lovecidal*, it is the victory mindset that I see regulating war, paradoxically bringing together the two warring sides. It is a mindset that divides the world into winners and losers. When you think about it, it is absurd to always want to be the winner and to always consider the other to be the loser. Heroism righteously trotted out to disavow suffering and distress partakes in such inanity. In today's 'new wars' it might be more appropriate to say that the line between winning and losing has been so muddled that there is no longer a loser. Every war champion claims victory at all cost, and hence, battles are only fought between victor and victor.

For example, one of the most striking and puzzling moments for me during the 1991 Gulf War was when the Americans were declaring victory over Iraq. As television screens were filled with talk about the war coming to an end, thanks to the glorious results of Operation Desert Storm and the swift victory by American-led coalition forces, we, earnest spectators, were briefly shown images of Iraqi's celebrating their own 'victory'. This is what in *Lovecidal* I call the 'Twin Victories'. Of course, for Western media reporters, it was mind-boggling to see such a celebration when Iraq had lost the war. Everyone said at the time that Saddam Hussein was deceiving his people. For me, it's not the same concept of victory. Same word, similar striving, but not the same thing. The West is always probing and measuring the other in their terms, but it would be more relevant to ask seriously why Iraq claimed victory where the Western world only saw defeat. As with the Algerian or the Vietnam wars, the West may obtain military victory temporarily via a power from the sky, but nations of lesser means ultimately gain political victory via a power from the underground. These persist through elaborate subterranean structures built to fight those who claim to see everything from the sky.

Victory can also be a victory like 9/11. Who is winning? Who is losing? Such senseless questions evade the full significance of war. There is political victory, there is symbolic victory, and then there is this victory achieved by force of arms, which ultimately serves the military empire, allowing those considered all-powerful to prevail over those fighting through guerrilla means. It is this imbalance of asymmetrical warfare and the rise of singular forms of everyday resistance that I raised in *Lovecidal*. Not only do they speak to the absurdity of war, they carry the potential to change the landscape of struggles for justice.

In the war against the French, the moment I focused on was also the moment of victory and defeat at Dien Bien Phu – that memorable closing instance when a Viet Minh combatant asked the French colonel, *in French*, '*c'est fini?*' and the officer replied, '*Oui, c'est fini.*' It's like hearing two children play fighting and then turning to one another as they end the game: 'Is it over?' 'Yes, time's up.' War comes down to something so infantile, so insignificant. You lose so many lives just for that moment of victory. Together with the affective dimension of war, this is the absurdity that I wanted to highlight. The same thing goes with the so-called 'end of the war' in Iraq. The Americans' exit strategy was to pull out during the night so that you couldn't see their withdrawal. Then they continued the war through means which were not explicitly martial, but were fed by their military-industrial complex: arms industries promoting not only the circulation of American weapons, but also private security contractors and more.

It is interesting that you link heroism to memory in the context of state discourse (the official voice of Vietnam) as well as left-wing discourse. The orthodox Left could not hear women speaking critically within their midst; it could not tolerate the complex positioning of Mai Thu Van, whose interviews I adapted for *Surname Viet Given Name Nam*. She's a well-informed Marxist herself, but her book was shunned by Leftists because she exposed the shortcomings of the system through the voices of women – from both North and South -- who dared express their discontent and call into doubt the Party's patriarchal structures and State feminism. Of course, the absurd question that arises in these cases is: Who is more Marxist than whom? Is *her* stance more Marxist, because she is critical and she remains true to these heroic fighters' voices? Or is it the oblivious dogmatic Left that can just unfold its own narrative, without having to involve themselves in the struggle of women throughout history and His-story (history by and for men)?

**LM:** If you don't mind, as we are currently celebrating the 50$^{th}$ anniversary of 1968, I would be interested in shifting this reflection back in time. I'm thinking of two works that were made around '68 on the Vietnam War that explicitly tackled the issue of heroism. Firstly, the film *Loin du Vietnam* [*Far from Vietnam*] (1967) – collectively realised by Joris Ivens, William Klein, Claude Lelouch, Chris Marker, Alain Resnais, Agnès Varda and Jean-Luc Godard – a film in which, in a striking scene, Bernard Fresson monologues to a completely silent Karen Blanguert about the heroism of the Vietnamese people, the rightness of their cause, and the impossibility of living with the idea that he cannot prove his own heroism. The problem of being 'far' from Vietnam, which Godard develops. Secondly, Susan Sontag's text *Trip to Hanoi* (1969), in which she spends a good half of her narrative complaining that her trip is a sort of anti-climax because she was expecting to see a heroic people in action and is disappointed. They are living a great destiny but they don't seem quite to grasp what is happening to them.... And the tension is very much about communication; she finds it really hard to communicate with them. In the end she reconciles herself with her ideal and she ends on a praise of their 'laconic', 'flat' form of communication as a model of 'economy of words'. In your own trajectory, how did you react to these kinds of engagements with the Vietnam War?

**TMH:** We're not dealing here with Left versus Right, but rather with a left within the Left, with the issue of gender looming large. This fight is much more challenging. Sometimes we speak the same language, and yet we feel as if we were dispossessed of the very tools that enable us to have a voice. The rhetoric of equality and justice is readily appropriated by the Left's 'old boys club', which is why the 'linguistic self' (Gloria Anzaldúa), the 'verbal struggle' (Mao) and the politics of representation continue to be fought on the feminist front.

When I made *Surname Viet*, I did initially get hostile reactions from both the Left and the Right. But the more vicious ones were from the Left, not from so-called 'rednecks' as one might expect, but from righteous people who didn't want to hear any of the views put forth in the film: partly, it seems, because women didn't really count and their voices didn't score with theirs; partly because the history of the war in Vietnam is a territory they authoritatively owned and controlled. The only thing they would hear was that the Communist Party was criticised, which they immediately interpreted as a stance against the revolution and socialist Vietnam, which was not at all the point. There was no room in their mind for difference, only for opposition. A film on the plight and suffering of women in the war is commonly viewed as being partial, but it doesn't seem to cross many viewers' minds to regard as biased and chauvinist all the films made on the War which almost exclusively feature male anguish and male heroism.

Image: Trinh T. Minh-ha, A Tale of Love (1995)

In the aftermath of Vietnam's victory, many people who fought dearly for socialist Vietnam couldn't voice their thoughts. They spoke almost as if they were muzzled. You couldn't speak unless you did so about the fatherland in positive terms. Even sadness and mourning were state-mediated; it took decades of struggle for writers in Vietnam to concede with quiet laughter that they have at long last 'gained permission to be sad' and 'can now weep without being gagged.' I'm thinking here of the wonderful writer, archivist and translator Pham Thi Hoài, whose novel *The Crystal Messenger* (1988) was banned in Vietnam, and who is now living in Berlin. During wartime she was an enthusiastic revolutionary of North Vietnam and yet she has come around since then to asking aloud the question: What happened to that revolutionary spirit? What is left from that revolution?

This is where we can situate my response to a work like *Loin du Vietnam*. I don't want to comment too much on Susan Sontag because the kind of expectation she had for 'a heroic people' in action could, at best, be qualified as naive, and, at worst, as arrogant in its paternalism. This is the tension around communication, which is somewhat similar to the early situation of feminism, or should I specify 'white feminism', in which the fight for 'women' excluded or barely acknowledged the plight and contributions of women of colour. So in its exclusive claim for equality, 'woman' could remain oppositional and discriminatory from within. Going to Vietnam with a superiority complex and a preconceived idea of what the revolution should look like, and expecting communication with the locals to be readily friendly and forward to an American foreigner, is much less interesting to pay attention to because, as an attitude, it is highly patronising.

But Godard is an interesting case. Although *Loin du Vietnam* is a collective work that seemed to be put together quite expeditiously, it was an activist gesture of support. The short section titled 'Camera Eye' that Godard contributed, appearing on screen with his camera – lens and apparatus – was quite to the point. Unlike some of the other sections that endorse unquestioningly the norms of reportage (omniscient voice-over running throughout the footage, in which the relation between the verbal and the visual was not thought through), Godard's section critically deals with the core of reportage. For this kind of eye-witness genre, being present and shooting on site is essential. But Godard told us from the outset that he was denied permission to go to Vietnam to shoot and he accepted the North-Vietnamese government's refusal because, as he interpreted it, his politics were rather vague and that perhaps what he would come up with might do more harm than good for their cause. Rather than abandon the project, however, he offered a work that spoke to his being 'far from Vietnam'. Such a position has disadvantages, but it could open up a wealth of possibilities such as acknowledging that 'Vietnam is in us' and that one should create three or four Vietnams...

More generally speaking, and just like with the film Godard made on the Palestinian struggle, *Ici et ailleurs*, [*Here and Elsewhere*], whatever he is critical of, he is right in the midst of it. He is reckless in the way he attacks and exposes himself as a film director. The criticism is not pointed outward, it is pointed right at himself. Sometimes what he offers can be offensive but it is actually offensive – with him right in the middle of the picture, so to speak. For me this is far more dangerously challenging than the position in which criticism is voiced from a safe place, as if what one points to is outside, external to oneself and to where one stands. As I just mentioned, Godard actually put to use the government's rejection to assume his position as outsider and his being genuinely 'far from Vietnam.' He is not claiming to speak and show from 'inside' Vietnam.

When I came up with the title 'Forgetting Vietnam', I was staying away from the righteous, moralistic connotation of one like 'Remember Vietnam'. With all the wars going on today, the White House is not remembering well. Every time war looms, the spectre of Vietnam haunts the President's speeches, even though he may assert that no, this is not its repetition. But the mere fact that its name repeatedly crops up means that the spectre of the Vietnam War still walks the halls of the White House.

Contextually, Godard is explicit in his positioning. He is far from Vietnam. In *Ici et ailleurs* he makes us smile and cringe at the kind of grandiose speech that struggles of liberation and socialist regimes are so fond of, and with that the grandiose notion of heroism. It's discomforting to listen to grandiosity in its in-progress construct: militant speech coming out of a child's mouth innocently performed with pompous gestures, its being awkwardly rehearsed by a woman on screen.

**LM:** It seems to me that with this question we are really in the midst of your own research into another way of relating to politics. Do you feel that the critique of anthropology and ethnography that you were leading in the early 1980s is still current? Is it still urgent for you? Or has it lost some of its urgency?

**TMH:** Well, the first thing to recall is the link between anthropology and colonialism. Anthropology has done a lot to disengage itself from the fact that it was born with Europe's colonial expansions, but in its pseudo-scientific claims anthropology remains steeped in a colonial ethos. The questioning of the anthropological apparatus and its essentialising constructs was urgent when I was living in Senegal and doing research in West Africa. It was not as if I didn't encounter such a colonialism-inflected discourse in Vietnam, but I was very young at the time and was not as puzzled as I had been in Senegal by a discourse that turned you into an 'other'. What was so baffling for me in Senegal was not just the white administration or the white anthropologists and researchers who carried on this colonial structure of the mind, but actually the insiders themselves, African intellectuals and city-dwellers who often enacted the anthropologist's mindset in speaking authoritatively about their own culture. So at the time it was urgent for me, and especially when making the film *Reassemblage* (1981).

I've moved on since, and today when some viewers tell me they find my films to be 'ethnographic', I take it positively, especially when coming from an ethnographer. You can be ethnographic without making an ethnographic film, not because you adopt a process recognised or approved by anthropology, but because of the rigour you bring into your work when you look at another culture. Having learnt to see anthropology through my studies and research in ethnomusicology, I think anthropology is at its best when it acknowledges the crisis at the core of its being, and when it assumes the precariousness of its status, rather than evade or deny this by trying to institute its authority. It is a vulnerable field because you are trying to do research in a context that is unfamiliar to you, and then trying to share it, to translate it to another context. You are constantly in the position of mediator and translator. If one recognises the impossibility of the task of translation (the way Walter Benjamin discusses it) and the impossibility of translation in one's work, it becomes an interesting work — one that is situated at the edge of being no longer valid. Offering something valuable while questioning its validation is a way of de-positioning while positioning. So that's where anthropology could be at its best. And I do find a small number of scholars and young people working in that direction today.

**LM:** In order to bring the different threads of our conversation together, I'd like to ask you to say a bit more on the way in which you reflect on 1968 today, and in relation to the Vietnam War?

**TMH:** There are many ways to answer such a vast question. I'll give it a try, first by drawing on the context of our discussion, taking Vietnam as an example to relate to the revolutionary spirit of that transnational moment. On the one hand, as stated in *Forgetting Vietnam*, 'can one simply place the War in a museum?' Through what is made visible and put on display for memory, what precisely is kept invisible and erased from memory? In other words, how to remember the historical 'defeat' of '68's emancipatory ideas so as to keep their legacy alive in today's so-called 'free-market' ideology (a mere alias for corporate greed)?

For example in Vietnam, 1968 was the memorable year when the Offensive of Tết Mậu Thân was launched. The message which informed North Vietnamese forces that they were about to inaugurate the largest campaign of surprise attacks against South Vietnam's military and civilian control centres was relevant enough: 'Crack the sky, shake the earth.' In its zealous mission of liberation, Hanoi firmly believed that the Offensive would trigger a spontaneous, supportive uprising of the population which would lead to a quick, sweeping victory. But the outcome of the Offensive was far from what was expected: the loss of lives – mainly civilians, but also troops from both sides of the battle – was staggering. Nonetheless, the failure to achieve their main objective of spurring uprisings throughout the South was still translated into a victory for the North, as the media's coverage of the atrocities and the extent of these human losses during the Offensive exposed the truth of war in all its messiness and changed the American public's perception of their role in Vietnam.

Today, the 1968 Huế carnage allegedly perpetrated by the National Liberation Front during their occupation, as well as by America's firepower in their resolution to recapture the city, remains a 'most sensitive case'. On the one hand, placed into oblivion in the official version of War history and conveniently absented from the government-operated War Remnants Museum in Ho Chi Minh City. On the other, persisting in people's collective memory, thereby revealing the utter delusion of war when to win and regain control means to destroy what one set out to protect. In this bitter lesson of war, victory in defeat for the Northern forces was followed by defeat in victory for the Southern forces and the US. As stated in the film, no matter how carefully selective memory is in rewriting history, the 'scars of war have surfaced publicly'. The survivors' harrowing testimonies as well as the mass graves discovered in and around the city, which revealed victims buried alive in addition to those clubbed or shot dead, have had a massive impact on the 1975 refugees exodus. They have also triggered the exodus of human remains since the 1990s. The War's many faces cannot be reduced nor simply buried.

Must victory thrive on selective forgetfulness and the erasure of its defeats? The socialist Vietnamese government has never acknowledged the slow but unprecedented exodus of 'boat people' and refugees – some two million persons by 2001 – who continued to leave Vietnam following the War's end. As Pham Thi Hoài remarked, 'It took the winners ten years to realise that victory was not something that could be eaten ... It took the US twenty years to sign a peace treaty with its own past.' Her analysis also informed how the War provided the Communist Party with justifications to fight and rule with 'the mandate of Heaven' – a principle borrowed from China whose legitimacy must constantly be reified and deified. This is how the war-heroes' monopolising authority and the war-military leadership, turned now into totalitarian control, continue to thrive.

Decades after the Vietnam War, the foundational cultural values of the revolutionary cause have lost their validity and the consecrated ideas of communist ideology have become a farce – blatantly betrayed, at best relegated to die-hard nostalgia. Social inequality has increased at full speed. To give you an example of the Vietnamese flavour of state capitalism today: while foreigners talk avidly about a booming real estate market and the new Housing Law which allows them to invest in Vietnamese property, to the consternation of Los Angeles' South Vietnamese diaspora, the upper echelons of *socialist* Vietnam's ruling class are buying up luxury properties in Orange County and elsewhere in the US. When this crony class comes to America for a visit, they reportedly bring regiments of house servants, moving in *with style*.

Whose victory is it? This is a question one could also ask in relation to the '68 of the West and the rest of the world, whose notions of 'revolution' have since been so hollowed out by racial, sexual and fiscal backlash that rather than radically changing, for one, America, the old values have been comprehensively reiterated. With the 'Alt-white' effect and the dire political situation in the US today, the country continues at core to be a 'nation at war' – not only abroad, but also, more destructively, at home. We are undergoing a virulent revival of the old orthodoxy. There's no voice of reason, no discursive logic, no psychiatric name-calling that could be effectively used in response to the kind of belligerently segregative rhetoric coming from the Oval Office, and its Alt-right mouthpieces, which is tearing the country apart and letting loose all forms of bigotry and human debasement in social relations.

What happened to 'the revolution of values,' which Martin Luther King Jr. used to dream of, during which the established political and cultural institutions lost their legitimacy and patriarchal colonial systems came under attack, triggering the decline of Western hegemony? In the present climate of disappearing ethics, of an unbridled revival of sexism, racism, homophobia, xenophobia and Islamophobia, to mention a few examples, America's heartsick society is suffering a huge throwback to its past. However, to acknowledge this state of things is not to assume a defeatist stance. As I discussed in *Lovecidal*, the transgressive phenomenon of women marching across nations in their struggles for justice has now amplified in scope to become the Women's March, built on diverse alliances around the world. Highlighting a different focus each year, it contributes to changing the way people take up political action as they become aware of their agency as political and social actors.

# Reviews

## Anthropology beginning again

Pierre Charbonnier, Gildas Salmon and Peter Skafish, eds, *Comparative Metaphysics: Ontology after Anthropology* (London: Rowman and Littlefield, 2016). 364pp., £95.00 hb., £31.95 pb., 978 1 78348 857 5 hb., 978 1 78348 858 2 pb.

'Sometimes one feels like one has nothing "new" to say,' writes Eduardo Vivieros de Castro in his contribution to *Comparative Metaphysics: Ontology after Anthropology*. Yet new things must, nevertheless, be said – or so insists this collection of essays, which bears the dual purpose of taking stock of a project already well underway, known in anthropology for the past decade or so as the 'ontological turn', and re-announcing its coming in the form of a profound disciplinary recomposition arising from the encounter between anthropology and philosophy. To these ends, the collection assembles an impressive cast of anthropologists and philosophers from across the Anglo-French academic divide – aside from Vivieros de Castro, there are chapters by Philippe Descola, Marilyn Strathern and Eduardo Kohn, among others, and an interview with Bruno Latour – encompassing a range of interpretations of the proposition contained in the title. Anthropology is metamorphosing, the volume suggests, into our new, planetary-crisis-era metaphysics.

Our metaphysics – as in, *all* of ours. Or rather, none of ours. For the point is to wrench 'metaphysics', which bears something of an unstable meaning across this collection of essays, from its European locus and to remake it on the shifting grounds of comparison itself. In this way, the project of *Comparative Metaphysics* positions itself as the latest charge in the ongoing battle with a philosophical canon resistant to decentering. Anthropology has played this revitalising, or relativising, role in relation to philosophy before: from the 1960s onwards, following in the footsteps of Claude Lévi-Strauss in particular, a generation of young French philosophy students turned their backs on their discipline, which they considered to have grown repetitive and stale, to try their hand at ethnography. Many worked with indigenous peoples in remote parts of the Amazon; if a concern common to structuralist projects was to associate the conditions of science with an epistemological *décalage*, or displacement, then for structural anthropology this was conceived in quite literal, geographical terms. Cultural difference – provided the emphasis was placed on the play of difference itself rather than a substantialist notion of culture – was viewed as the terrain upon which speculative thought could flourish.

By the 1980s, however, cultural difference had become a problem. Lévi-Strauss's project had revealed itself, in the eyes of its many critics, to be a troubled enterprise: structuralism, they argued, had rendered cultures as closed systems operating behind the backs of their bearers yet visible to the omnipotent anthropologist. Accordingly, as Étienne Balibar noted, culture had assumed the determining function previously played by nature. In the end, culture wasn't much better than race, and it served many of the same ideological functions. Anthropology in turn plunged into a crisis of self-criticism from which it could only emerge (so goes the 'ontological' line) by destroying the concept of culture altogether. This is where the work of ontological anthropology is at its most astute, on a political level – in realising that even a concept of culture reformed by reflexivity and intertextuality was complicit in the ethnocentrism it claimed to overcome. For as long as difference was concentrated in culture, the former remained confined to the level of representation, as a matter of belief or a set of 'worldviews' variously adequate to a nature whose order was adjudicated by the natural sciences. If cultures were so many ways of 'making sense of the world' – or so many mediations between humanity and a universal Nature, the truth of which only the 'moderns' knew – the subtext would always be that some of these ways made more sense than others. The multiculturalist gesture did little to conceal the fact that the management of the planet and access to its resources, including simply inhabitable space, would be differentiated accordingly.

Ontological anthropology hopes to disrupt this order of things by taking aim at some of its key epistemological assumptions. It entreats us to think that there is nothing 'beneath' what we inadequately call culture: neither nature, nor mode of production – nor even, it would seem, history. Or rather, the essence of the ontologising gesture is to 'provoke a crisis', as the editors put it, in such categories, by letting the thought of the subjects of that anthropology invade the workings of its conceptual construction. This is what many in the collection call 'reverse anthropology'; it is the essence of Vivieros de Castro's claim that the coming anthropology will facilitate the 'ontological self-determination' of those studied. But if the positions assembled in the book can agree up to this point, the project thereafter splits into two. On the one hand we have the comparison *of* metaphysics – of metaphysical systems, that is, assigned to the many different 'worlds' in existence. Placing indigenous metaphysical systems alongside those of the moderns seeks to force revisions of the central categories of the latter, such as nature and culture, human and nonhuman, and life and nonlife. This first project is exemplified by Philippe Descola's major work, *Beyond Nature and Culture*, in which he constructs a four-fold schema composed of 'modes of identification' that he terms animism, totemism, analogism and naturalism. In the useful set of methodological reflections he contributes to this collection, Descola defends this approach as closest to the original structuralist aim of constructing a 'combinatory matrix' facilitating the comparison of formal properties of phenomena, which he insists is 'in no way a grid for describing empirical situations', but rather a model for an always-incomplete comparative endeavour.

But if this still feels too foundational, as a number of those in the book suggest, we can move to an epistemologically more ambitious operation. This is comparison *as* metaphysics, in which the foundation – that which is known to be true – ascends to the realm of the virtual, such that the truth of the actual is only the possibility of alteration, as Patrice Maniglier puts it, or 'being otherwise'.

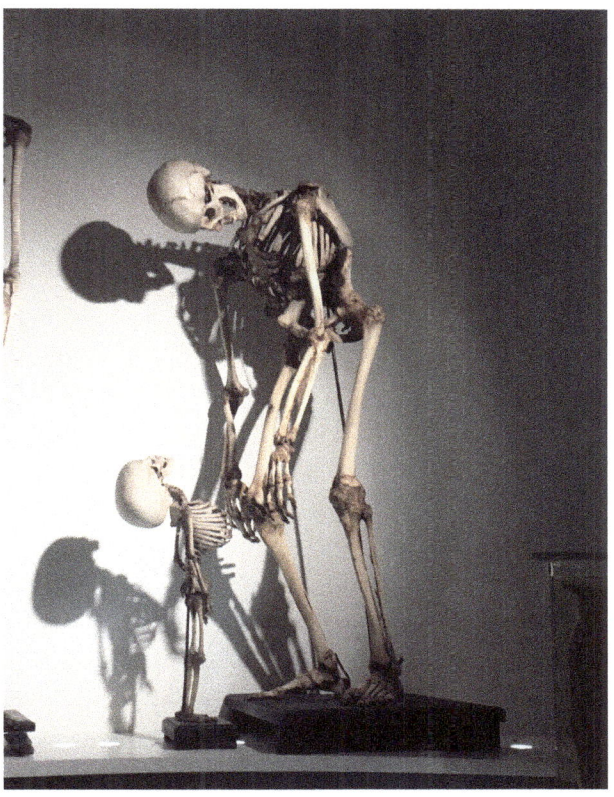

As well as providing the most systematic set of reflections on this second operation, Maniglier offers a rare determination of the term 'metaphysics', whose baggage in the history of philosophy otherwise goes unacknowledged in the volume; he takes it in the sense of Descartes' metaphysical reasons for doubt. Titling his chapter 'Anthropological Meditations', Maniglier argues that anthropology, as the science of comparison par excellence, *is* metaphysics not because it has found a new object in questions of being, but because the two 'share the same *epistemological situation*', existing likewise in the shadow of radical doubt. The difference is that while Descartes took this kind of doubt as the point of departure from which to ascertain the indubitable, the anthropologist stays with it, allowing it to transform any putative identity into a 'variant': a peculiar ontological entity that exists only by way of its differentiation from other entities.

But if anthropology is on its way to becoming comparative metaphysics, the nature of this transformation is yet to cohere, at least across this collection, at a philosophical level. For Martin Holbraad, the 'radical reflexivity of conceptualization' associated with the work of Marilyn Strathern, Roy Wagner and Vivieros de Castro might be understood as a variant of the Kantian transcendental deduction, 'multipl[ied] kaleidoscopically' along ethnographic lines. Morten Axel Pedersen, on the other hand, suggests the likeness between the ontological turn and the *departure* from the Kantian project in the work of those such as Quentin Meillassoux. And while many of the contributors insist on the 'critical' import of ontological anthropology, the jury is certainly still out on the question of critique. For despite the array of philosophical points of reference in the volume, the underlying conviction of the project is that critique alone can only take one back to where they began. As Charbonnier, Salmon and Skafish write in their introduction: 'You want to think modernity? You had better start from the outside – the concrete outside of an era and a people, not that of thought in the abstract.' It is this will to take leave of the work of negation, and instead seek out positive representatives of what Ghassan Hage calls elsewhere an 'alter-modernity', that draws this anthropological tendency toward those forms of cultural alterity apparently most unscathed by capitalist modernity; that is, to regain – however self-consciously or ironically – a *primitivist* imagination.

The charge of primitivism is by no means new to the ontological turn. It is first on the list of the critiques coming out of what Holbraad terms a 'veritable industry' of commentary, from within anthropology, on this body of work. For many anthropologists, ontological anthropology signals a violent reduction of heterogeneous modes of thought and life in the interests of creating a new grand narrative of the (especially Amazonian) primitive, whose world persists somehow unchanged on the sidelines of world history. It is all the more strange, then, that within philosophy, where the work of Vivieros de Castro in particular has begun to be taken up enthusiastically as part of both a philosophy of nature and a broader 'metaphysical turn', these criticisms should so rarely make an appearance. Is this perhaps because they miss the (philosophical) point? After all, any science of comparison must work at some level through reduction and schematisation, or it must be willing to take a leap of faith, grabbing at a conceptual problem and working it in new directions. On the other hand, perhaps it is because the project of turning anthropology into philosophy, or the reverse, circulates on *one* conception of philosophy at the expense of others.

If so, this would appear to be a philosophy on the hunt for new beginnings. This is one response to the problem of philosophy's corruption by its own history, a glance at which makes evident the inextricability of ideas such as universalism with their apparent contraries – such as racism, a term whose complete absence from this collection is striking. It is a response which also risks isolating itself from the work of indigenous intellectuals who have recognised themselves to be somewhere within this history, for better or worse, and sought to work its contradictions to crisis point – work which underpins fields such as indigenous studies, black studies and anticolonial thought. Ontological anthropology effectively seals itself off from these fields, perhaps because they would prompt difficult, but vital, questions: can the 'outside' to modernity on which comparison is to be grounded really be present under global capitalism? Is seeking it out really such a novel project, or is it rather part of an older philosophical imaginary in which thought persists autonomously from (its) history? And in engaging this imaginary are we not participating, whether we mean to or not, in a remaking of indigenous and modern thought as uncomplicated and non-dynamic categories?

The ontological project, however novel it appears, certainly has *its* own history. It tends to present itself as the endpoint of such, following Vivieros de Castro's notion in his *Cannibal Metaphysics* of a closure of anthropology's 'karmic circle'. To do this, it must construct certain histories of anthropology: notably, the one in which a high structuralism of the 1960s was gradually torn down by postmodern anthropology from the 1980s onward. Yet anthropology, even in its French variant, was not *only* going through this dialectic of theoreticism and penitent reflexivity. For example, while Lévi-Strauss institutionalised the discipline around the study of indigenous peoples in the Americas, far from the disasters of French colonisation, a parallel current of 'Africanists' maintained a rather different relationship with their imperial history. This current worked, in opposition to Lévi-Strauss, under the tutelage of the 'political anthropology' of Georges Balandier, a student of Michel Leiris and anticolonial militant who had realised early on that the colonial situation made it impossible to do ethnography in the synchronic, depoliticised manner of Lévi-Strauss and his followers. In light of this minor history, it is notable that most of the proponents of today's comparative metaphysics appear little interested in probing the relationship between their effervescent new discipline and the memory apparatus of the French state. If anthropology is set to change the future of philosophy, including its most foundational questions such as universalism, then we had better make sure it's the right kind of anthropology.

Miri Davidson

# Who is the subject of violence?

François Cusset, *Le déchaînement du monde. Logique nouvelle de la violence* (Paris: La Découverte, 2018). 240pp., 20.00 euro pb., 978 2 70719 815 0

Elsa Dorlin, *Se défendre. Une philosophie de la violence* (Paris: Zones, 2017). 200pp., 18.00 euro pb., 978 2 35522 1103

Just over two years ago, on 19 July 2016, Adama Traoré died in custody after being suffocated by three members of the *gendarmerie*, a branch of the French military that also possesses a policing power. Adama died in the yard of the police station of Persan, in the region of Paris, on his 24th birthday. His brother – who was also under arrest – and the firemen who were called by the *gendarmes* to give first aid to the young black man testified that Adama, who had passed out, was still handcuffed, face against the ground, when the latter arrived and that they had to insist the policemen take the cuffs off in order to revive him. Yet, despite their efforts, it was too late. To the family, who arrived rapidly at Persan, the police initially maintained that Adama was still alive. They kept up this lie for four hours before allowing his mother and his brother Yacouba to enter the station, where they were asked: 'If we tell you something, will you take it badly?'

While neither addresses the Adama Traoré affair specifically, it is in the context of deaths like this, and the responses that they have engendered, that two books on violence, by François Cusset and Elsa Dorlin, have recently been published in France. Each helps us to better understand the case by analysing both state violence and violence as resistance outside of the common frames of an opposition between violence and non-violence or in relation to a notion of legitimacy. At the same time, they also raise awareness of the ways in which the government of the suburbs in contemporary France shares much with the government of former French colonies.

In *Le déchaînement du monde. Logique nouvelle de la violence* [A Ruthless World: New Forces of Violence], François Cusset identifies three minorities that are, today, subjected to what he calls a 'postcolonial violence': black people, the majority of Muslim people and indigenous people in the former colonies. Adama Traoré was French, black and Muslim. It should come as no surprise, then, that in a country where those who have power generally try to prevent a debate about postcolonialism from happening at all, he was used to facing systemic violence from the state. Cusset reminds us that the law of the 'imperial man', according to which 'might is right', is not an accidental and unfortunate flaw of power, but its rule. The failure of the state to provide protection to some of its citizens – most obviously, the residents of the suburbs – rather than acting only to control and assault them, means the state is not a third party which helps to resolve social conflict for such residents, but a stakeholder in such conflict and confrontation. In Adama Traoré's case, the state has too much to lose. Indeed, the judges deliberately neglected to interrogate the gendarmes involved. Cusset links this situation, in turn, to the neoliberal world-system which has turned the state into the operator of two logics: those of finance and police. The impoverishment of the suburbs at the expense of their inhabitants and the daily instances of police brutality there tend to confirm this. The state is 'depoliticised', as Cusset puts it, explaining the deafening silence of two successive Presidents of the Republic – François Hollande and Emmanuel Macron – in the face of the Traoré family's calls for a commitment to justice. For the population of the popular and multi-ethnic neighbourhoods, Cusset argues, the state's 'repressive stalemates are incomprehensible' unless one remembers that what is now applied there was first tested in the former colonies, where 'the worst of the twentieth century was developed … in order to quash any mere wish to revolt.'

Against this systemic violence, Cusset thinks that it is important to establish, explicitly, those who are responsible, to name the agents of violence, not as part of an individualising approach (which would be complicit with power), but in order to act collectively so as to open up the fight against the institutionalised powerlessness of minorities. In the wake of Adama's death, his sister, Assa Traoré, formed a collective demanding 'Truth and Justice for Adama' and has become one of the faces of the struggle against police brutality and anti-racism. Assa Traoré is, to be sure, asking for the conviction of the three individual *gendarmes* who caused her brother's death, but she also aims further, targeting the police force, its command, law, the judiciary, prisons and the state. With regards to any actualisation of the ideal of justice through rights, minorities have a singular relation to the law: they know that to emancipate themselves, they have to denounce, often physically, the limits or the lies inscribed in some rights. Truth and Justice for Adama did this brilliantly when they decided to walk at the head of a demonstration against Emmanuel Macron's economic and social policies on 26 May 2018, leaving the usual representatives of the 'social movements' (and any other demonstrator) with no choice but to walk behind the inhabitants of the suburbs and therefore symbolically support their fights.

As much as violence has been durably 'integrated' (*incorporée*) as a form of subjectification for the inhabitants of the suburbs, the latter can also 'stick together' (*faire corps*, literally 'become one body') in order to resist, in Cusset's words, state violence 'below politics, through a subversive and non-programmatic logic'. Two months after her brother's death, Assa Traoré was interviewed on TV about what happened to her brother. While she walks around Beaumont-sur-Oise, the city where she was raised with her siblings, she is joined by her friends and family members who walk behind her, silently and with determination. For many people, this footage showed the latent, almost intrinsic aggressiveness of 'uncivilised' bodies. All those racialised bodies going forwards in solidarity could not but constitute a threat. Yet, following Cusset, one can see instead here 'a new ritual which proceeds from a collective self-governance of violence', one that is very different from traditional political forms of organisation that have always excluded young suburban people – mainly because the old ideals of 'democracy' that they represent have never taken such people into account. Nonetheless, Cusset insists on the role that young people, in particular, might play in the corporeal struggle for emancipation, in so far as, he argues, they have always been at the core of insurrections and at the centre of major historical change. Cusset suggests a need to 'politicise biology' in order to counter, at once, ageism, political exploitation or betrayal by elders, and the supposed link between the temporary nature of youth and equally temporary left-wing convictions. As Cusset argues, 'joining forces through generations has always been one of the only means likely to challenge the order of things.' Notably, Truth and Justice for Adama produces this kind of generational conjunction by situating their struggle in line with the struggles for independence in the former colonies and with the American Black Power movement – Assa Traoré and Angela Davis were recently interviewed together by *Ballast* – as well as by gathering together the families of victims of police brutality (of whom there are several generations in France), and by paying tribute to the memory of those who have died over a number of decades. In doing so, they foster what Cusset calls a 'memory with archives' which is necessary to maintain the energy and intensity of struggle.

At the same time, they also fight against what Cusset describes as a 'triple violence': first, 'a violence *upon us*, caused by the structural constraints and arbitrariness of power'; second, 'a violence *among us*, caused by the unquestioned rivalry between economic subjects'; and, third, 'a violence *within us*, caused by the unknown and untreated psychic ravages of the nightmare that working can become' and by a symbolic violence that causes the dominated to endorse the way in which the dominant see them. The refusal to give up on Adama's case, the now famous 'Without justice, you will never get peace' that is inscribed on the supporters' t-shirts, the black pride asserted in their press releases, social network posts or pictures, and their physical occupation of an alternative political scene, show how they are able to fight against feelings of shame, helplessness and self-hate – thus experiencing, through this resistance, a powerful form of subjectification.

Cusset's argument echoes, in this respect, Elsa Dorlin's in *Se défendre. Une philosophie de la violence* [Self-Defence: A Philosophy of Violence]. Indeed, both authors assert that what Cusset calls a 'collective subject', and Dorlin 'the subject of self-defence', each come into being through their self-defence within a space of confrontation. At the same time, each analyses a (state) power that meticulously targets this political subject's ability to act or react in order to reduce this to the point of its complete annihilation.

On 19 July 2016, Adama was with his brother, Bagui, in the town centre of Beaumont-sur-Oise when they saw policemen walking in their direction. Since Adama did not have his ID card – which is mandatory in France; one of the extensions of colonial techniques over the entire population – and since it was his birthday, he decided to run away. This attitude is rarely understood by white French people: 'Why would he run, they ask, if he did nothing wrong?' The answer probably lies in what Elsa Dorlin calls 'dirty care'. Such 'negative care' is the result of 'a long process of sidestepping, of taking distance, of withdrawing, of preparing for confrontation' in which the members of an oppressed minority forget themselves and develop an acute knowledge of their persecutors, but not to their own benefit. Indeed, what Dorlin terms 'dirty care' implies the oppressed's ignorance of their potential power. As such, an ethics of care is necessarily linked with 'an ethics of impotence', with 'a dirty care for oneself'. Racialised men and boys in the French suburbs know precisely how any stop and search can end – especially if they do not have their ID, or are more than three in the hallway of their block of flats, and so on. They have known the characteristic ways in which the police act and react towards them from their earliest days. They know what to say, how to behave in order to avoid an escalation of the situation, to apparently defend themselves. So, if there is an exceptional reason not to go through an umpteenth public humiliation – like his birthday for Adama, or the breaking of the fast during the Ramadan month for Zyed Benna and Bouna Traoré who were killed running from the police in 2005 – then they run away.

Yet Dorlin notes that this 'dirty care' is not empowering for the members of minorities, but rather gives a tremendous power to their aggressors. Chased by police, Zyed and Bouna, 17 and 15 years old, ran away, hid in an electricity substation and were electrocuted. Their deaths led to the 2005 suburban revolts, which were, in turn, repressed by considerable police force and the imposition of a state of emergency – a process that dates back to the 1950s and the Algerian War of Independence. In the words of Garnette Cadogan, 'walking' or, even more so, running 'while Black' is enough to be considered a threat and to trigger an irrational, disproportionate, but perfectly legitimated cycle of violence for which the black person is ultimately considered responsible. As Dorlin writes, black people 'are the cause and the effect of violence, its beginning and its end. ... Violence is the one and only intentional action of a black body, which forbids them to legitimately defend themselves.' Hence the fact that, although they had absolutely no reason to chase Adama, the policemen still pursued him and, when they finally found him at a friend's place, unarmed and ready to surrender, three men enforced a prone position on him which caused positional asphyxia – the weight of three equipped *gendarmes* is close to 530 pounds – which caused his death. Every one of Adama's acts, from the moment he started running till the moment he was asphyxiated, was interpreted as violent – he pushed one of the men who were chasing him, hid himself and resisted the prone position because he felt he 'ha[d] trouble breathing', according to one of the policemen – rather than as a form of self-defence or resistance to arbitrary power. As Dorlin observes, the possibility of self-defence is denied to resisting bodies like Adama's, while police violence is almost never considered that of an aggressor. Typically, the prosecutor of Pontoise first claimed that Adama died of a blood infection, then of a weak heart and finally – when the Traorés asked for a second autopsy – of positional asphyxia. On 26 June 2018, the French equivalent to the UK's IPCC (Independent Police Complaints Commission) released its first – and incomplete – report on the number of deaths and injuries caused by the police in France. Introducing the 14 deaths and over 100 injuries, the head of the commission immediately warned 'this report is not an inventory of police blunders', and, arguing that the police killed terrorists, added that the commission 'did not presume the illegitimacy of those deaths and injuries.'

Adama's family, led publicly by his sister Assa Traoré, has not given up on his case and still asks for truth and justice. Yet, as Dorlin argues, the repression of power is proportional to the strength of the victims and the more they defend themselves, the more they are attacked and suffer. As of today, five Traoré brothers are in jail. Bagui, who was the main witness to his brother's death, has been sentenced to 30 months with no remission for extortion. Yacouba is in detention pending trial for allegedly setting a bus on fire (after another detention for intrusion into the Persan police station where he assaulted the *gendarme* who told him that his brother had died); so is Youssouf, but for drug trafficking. Serene has been sentenced to four months with no remission for insulting the mayor of Beaumont-sur-Oise the night she irregularly refused access to the town council to the collective Truth and Justice for Adama. Finally, Samba has been sentenced to 30 months with no remission for severe aggression. Whether those five men actually committed what they are accused of is not what matters here, because their very 'interpellation' is enough to justify the violence that killed Adama and the violence the Traorés are exposed to today. The police, legal and penal harassment directed against a family whose spokeswoman 'makes too much noise' tells us much about the French legal system's priorities and about the way this repressive and colonially-inspired *dispositif* 'considers', in Dorlin's words, 'that the one who is submitted to it *can do something*, so it precisely targets, stimulates, incites this last momentum of power and pushes into a corner in order to interpellate it as *un*-efficient, to make it powerless.' Dorlin argues that resisting this power therefore implies '*un*learning how to *not* fight' rather than 'learning how to fight'. Indeed, if racialised people are not expected to know how to fight, it is because, like women and LGBTQI people, they have been forbidden to do so. When they carry on regardless of this interdiction, their defensive and/or violent potential is acknowledged, and they are represented as intentionally aggressive and therefore legitimately stoppable.

On 29 April 2018, the collective Truth and Justice for Adama organised a day of activities in Beaumont-sur-Oise in order to raise funds and awareness of their case. Among the activities on offer, the female world champion Aya Cissoko conducted a boxing workshop for local kids. As soon as the workshop started, the organisers observed several trucks of soldiers – not the *gendarmerie*, but the actual army – arriving, and driving in circles around them, before armed soldiers came to meet the members of the collective. (See the Justice et Vérité pour Adama Instagram page.) The presence of the army in the suburbs is more proof, if it were needed, of the still essentially colonial approach taken by the French state when it comes to popular and multi-ethnic neighbourhoods. Of course, the only people who did not see the powerful potential of young racialised kids learning how to box were the kids themselves or, rather, the youngest among them. When the organisers and the elders probably looked at those beloved young bodies learning how to defend themselves against police brutality in the future – Dorlin talks in this context about the British suffragists who learned jujitsu but also of the Warsaw Ghetto insurgents, the Black Panther Party for Self-Defense, and of queer self-defence patrols – the representatives of the government (and a lot of people in France) saw only training for violence and criminality.

Dorlin argues that when 'a politics of self-defence' and 'a politics of self-representation and self-affirmation' are articulated, 'an explosive-defence' occurs. The subjects thus produced 'declare war ... that is, establish the modalities of an equal fight.' If Dorlin adds that this hope to restore equality often mobilises people in vain, she also notes that such a 'war' 'makes the now-belligerent persecuted minorities proud and honourable' and it allows them to use 'violence and its semiology as long as the revolutionary struggle demands it.' Thus, if self-defence is 'a lever for political awareness' and a (re)action through which a more emancipated subject can come into being, one can also appreciate how significant it is that such collective self-defence should be led by a black Muslim woman – Assa Traoré. A social worker who quit her job after Adama's death, she is also the mother of three children. Assa Traoré is the archetype of what a defensive government hates. Being black, it is true that, as Dorlin argues, she is less protectable and protected than a white woman. But while many would like to regard her as defenceless – and, indeed, actually 'in danger' among the suburban racialised men that centuries of racism have pictured as the only figures of patriarchy and the only agents of sexual violence in France – she is impressively consistent, proud and respected. While she should be submissive according to the mainstream representation of her cultural background and her religion, she leads an anti-racist movement, challenges the penal system and the political authorities, faces the media and allies with people she should supposedly not be able to reach or convince.

Among the improbable allies that the suburban collective Truth and Justice for Adama have been able to gather around them are the Bernanoses (a white upper-class family whose well-educated sons have been sent to prison for demonstrating against François Hollande's Job Act), Geoffroy de Lagasnerie (a white philosopher and sociologist who has stated on several occasions that 'the system who made [him] an intellectual is the same system that puts black and Arab men in prison'), and Edouard Louis (a white writer who comes from a lower-class family). The latter two are both well-known supporters of LGBTQI self-emancipation. Thus, led by Assa Traoré, the collective has managed to reach beyond their 'natural' (that is, constructed) political sphere in a way that is particularly unsettling for a power that has ended up believing its own lies according to which racialised men must inherently be sexist and homophobic, and, indeed, 'racist' against white people. This is not to deny the actuality of sexism or homophobia in the French suburbs (although it is important to contest the validity of the notion of 'racism' towards whites). But it reveals how racialised men, on the one hand, and women and LGBTQI people, on the other, have been made mutually threatening. It helps us to understand the conditions of possibility of femonationalism, or homonationalism, and of the feeling described by Huey Newton in a 1970 speech, 'The Women's Liberation and Gay Liberation Movements', which is cited by Dorlin: 'We want to hit a homosexual in the mouth because we are afraid that we might be homosexual; and we want to hit the women or shut her up because we are afraid that she might castrate us.' Following Dorlin, one could argue that Assa Traoré, her family, her collective and their friends manage to produce – through self-defence and against systemic violence – 'a "we" who, because it is nothing without the action that is realised in its name, possesses nothing, a "we" who can do anything.'

**Emmanuel Jouai**

# Inside families

Laura Briggs, *How All Politics Became Reproductive Politics: From Welfare Reform to Foreclosure to Trump* (Oakland: University of California Press, 2017). 304 pp., £24.95 hb., £20.00 pb., 978 0 52028 191 2 hb., 978 0 52029 994 8 pb.

The shift to neoliberalism is rarely narrated from the vantage point of the household, but it is here – in the realm of unpaid bills and mounting laundry – that the contradictions of our political moment are felt most forcefully, writes Laura Briggs. Her US-focused book, *How All Politics Became Reproductive Politics*, retells the story of neoliberal economics 'from inside families' and reframes its legacy through the lens of the care crisis. How did it get so hard, Briggs asks, to find the time and resources to do the necessary work of reproduction? The institutionalisation of the 'double day' – the site of one of feminism's great unfinished battles – has, she observes, eroded Americans' collective capacity to have and raise children, care for the elderly and support the sick and disabled. In Briggs' account, the neoliberal economic reforms of the 1980s and 1990s curtailed the dissenting energies of twentieth-century radical protest movements: this is the historical moment at which 'all politics became reproductive politics'. It is a controversial headline claim: after all, has there *ever* been a time under capitalism when 'all politics' were not shot through with the contradictions of social reproduction? The book never fully confronts this question, though it does paint a dynamic portrait of the structural contradictions that attend the contemporary organisation of care work in America.

Of course, to merely acknowledge the existence of a contemporary 'care crisis' is neither new nor necessarily radical. Briggs knows this: it is why she gives space in the first chapter to Gavin McInnes, the far-right founder of Vice Media, who told a *Fox News* host in 2015: 'Feminism has made women miserable. Women were much happier when housewives were glorified.' McInnes' comment epitomises a historically illiterate right-wing narrative that blames feminism for the withdrawal of social support for domestic work. In fact, Briggs contends, feminists were central to a broad field of twentieth-century left-wing struggles around social reproduction, from the labour movement fight for an eight-hour working day to the wages for housework campaigns and the Black Panthers' free breakfast programmes. The book's focus on the 'deep, and intimate links – including failure and betrayal, but also support [and] solidarity' across feminist, labour and racial justice movements is a powerful rejoinder to those who would reduce these movements to insipid calls for diverse boardrooms.

It is the truncation of such twentieth-century reproductive labour struggles that has brought us to the current precipice: a contemporary order in which it is 'impossible for any member of a household to stay home and do reproductive labour, much less do paid work and still have the time, space, and resources to care for dependents, households, and communities'. This situation is new only in its generalisation to the whole population. Black women in America have been denied the rights, time or resources to mother their children since the era of enslavement, when, as Hortense Spillers states in her essay 'Mama's Baby, Papa's Maybe: An American Grammar Book' (1987), 'the female could not, in fact, claim her child'. One of the most compelling threads of Briggs' book reveals how racism continues to function as a sticking plaster and alibi for the deficiencies of privatised care. Drawing on the work of Wahneema Lubiano, Briggs explores the construction of the 'welfare queen' stereotype as a 'cover story for reducing government programs in general': in short, teenage mothers were scapegoated so welfare could be gutted. The racist myth-making of the 1990s provided lessons for the financial crash of 2008, when banks courted Black, Latinx and female-headed households for subprime mortgages, then retrospectively smeared them as irresponsible borrowers who caused the recession.

If welfare reform rode the coat-tails of racist fearmongering about so-called 'cultures of poverty', it did so in order to construct new moral imperatives around work in an era of wage stagnation. In the wake of these shifts, US immigration policy has overseen a process of 'offshoring' reproductive labour. Briggs saliently points out that the management of migration to the US is 'significantly a question about how household and child care work are getting done in the aftermath of the neoliberal push to get all mothers and other caregivers into the workforce for 40 and more hours a week'. Almost a million women migrants in the US, many of them undocumented, are employed as domestic workers and vulnerable to low wages, abuse by employers and chronic health problems. Joining the dots between anti-union laws, wage cuts and immigration control, Briggs shows that it is through racism that the system – barely – sustains itself.

New forms of what the book terms 'structural infertility' have developed along racialised lines too. Black infant and maternal mortality is roughly double the white rate – a disparity thought to endure across social classes, whether because of racism within the healthcare system or the toll of the everyday experience of being black in America. Briggs juxtaposes this disparity in mortality rates with the case of Silicon Valley, where wealthy and often white employees are urged to freeze their eggs on the company dollar and devote their fertile years to work. The book treads a careful line here: acknowledging that funding for and access to assisted reproductive technologies (ARTs) is 'precisely eugenic' in its privileging of a majority white professional class, Briggs nevertheless maintains that black infant mortality and ARTs are two dimensions of the same trend: the rise of 'involuntary, structural infertility as a result of economic changes and unsafe jobs'.

The final chapter turns to gay marriage, which resembles egg freezing as an ostensibly progressive policy that, in Briggs' analysis, in fact bolsters the 'privatisation of dependency'. Twentieth-century queer politics had imagined and enacted new configurations of kinship and community beyond the nuclear family. But by the end of the century, 'the persistent, growing, and widespread absence of a social safety net together with active hostility from institutions like hospitals and schools to recognising gay kinship meant that, increasingly, family was the only obvious means for queer folks to care for dependents, and it needed to be a "legal" family.' In this telling, gay marriage expanded access to the nuclear family in order to further entrench it as the site of privatised and unremunerated reproductive labour.

Briggs is nostalgic for the radical visions of twentieth-century protest movements. As she writes, 'While in many ways the sixties and seventies had been no better in reality, there had been optimism and momentum to build public support for care.' But the book's focus on the present moment of reproductive crisis evades a recognition that the disavowal of social reproduction has endured as a problem across all stages of capitalist development – that it is, in fact, a problem *produced* by capitalism. As Nancy Fraser puts it in 'Crisis of Care?', her contribution to Tithi Bhattacharya's *Social Reproduction Theory* (2017), 'the present crisis of social reproduction indicates something rotten not only in capitalism's current, financialised form but in capitalist society per se.' This rot, as Fraser outlines, can be detected in the 'separate spheres' ideology of the nineteenth century and the social democracy of the mid-twentieth century, as well as the present stage of financialised capitalism. Each era has developed a different way of organising and naturalising the reproductive labour on which capital depends. Briggs defines reproductive labour as 'the work necessary to the reproduction of human life', but it is also, of course, the work necessary to the reproduction of capital: reproductive labour supplies new workers and replenishes their energies at the end of the day, all without commanding a wage. By conceptualising household labour as 'the reproduction of things we value', the book glosses over the tensions between the imperatives of capital and the desires, frustrations, projects, imaginaries and pleasures that stir outside or against those imperatives.

One result of this perspective is a tendency to flatten out the dissent internal to feminism, softening the edges of liberal-capitalist, socialist and Marxist feminisms to draw them all into a reformist consensus. The book mounts a surprising defence of two high-profile commentators on the 'care crisis': Facebook's Sheryl Sandberg, who notoriously advised women to combat structurally sexist workplaces by 'leaning in' to power, and Anne-Marie Slaughter, the Obama administration policy director who has publicly criticised the structural barriers she had faced as a successful woman with children. To Briggs, both Sandberg and Slaughter have been unfairly maligned because they are 'women talking about reproductive labour' – but neither commentator has framed her intervention in these terms, perhaps because doing so would mean negotiating the antagonism between work-life balance reforms *within* capitalism and reproductive labour struggles *against* capitalism. While Briggs recognises the limitations of both women's recommendations for reform, she does not pursue the deeper implications of this antagonism.

A similar flattening takes place in the book's discussion of the wages for housework movement, which finds its revolutionary horizon reduced to a demand for a '40-hour workweek that enables people to get paid and still have time to do essential care work'. This description fails to capture the autonomist critique of work that drove the campaign. Wages for housework was also wages *against* housework, as Silvia Federici affirmed when she wrote: 'To say that we want money for housework is the first step towards refusing to do it, because the demand for a wage makes our work visible, which is the most indispensable condition to begin to struggle against it, both in its immediate aspect as housework and its more insidious character as femininity' ('Wages Against Housework', 1975). At its most radical moments, the campaign called not for more time to do housework, but for its abolition. The demand for wages, as antagonistic to the state as to the private home, was the impossible claim that would fracture the whole order of things. In her book *The Problem With Work* (2011), Kathi Weeks draws a parallel between wages for housework and contemporary movements for universal basic income (UBI). Like the demand for wages for housework, UBI has its reformist and its revolutionary modes, but in its strongest form it would detach the means to live and thrive from the system of waged work. Set against current debates around UBI, Briggs' closing list of 'things that would help' – including a 40-hour workweek and school schedules to match – is striking for its timidity in the face of the crisis she has so cogently diagnosed.

The concept of wages against housework is valuable because it sutures a framework for resisting pronatalism to a critique of the devaluation of maternal labour. In 'Women and the Subversion of the Community', Selma James and Mariarosa Dalla Costa targeted the way 'women have been forced to have children and were forbidden the right to have abortions when, as was to be expected, the most primitive techniques of birth control failed.' Briggs, by comparison, tends to pit campaigns around abortion and contraception against struggles for the rights and resources to parent. She writes that 'we have been debating abortion, birth control, and the means of preventing unwanted pregnancies vigorously and at length for two generations, but while we were looking there, many people lost the ability to have the children they wanted'. It is certainly true that reproductive rights activism has often been narrowly focused on abortion and contraception rights, which are too readily conceived in abstract legal terms and divorced from material circumstances. At the same time, the rights and access to abortion and contraception are extremely limited in the US and around the world – this is hardly a battle that has been won. Commenting on the conservative rollback of the welfare state and the removal of workplace protections for pregnant women, Briggs writes, 'This was the real war on women'. The comment not only risks downplaying the Trump administration's renewed attack on the minimal freedoms secured by *Roe* v. *Wade*: it also misses an opportunity to show how pronatalism and anti-natalism reinforce each other. The task of a materialist feminism is, surely, to conceive of reproductive freedom as an expanded field in which child-rearing is chosen, not enforced; shared and resourced, not privatised; refused by some, taken up by others, and detached from gender roles, racist coercion and moralising imperatives.

*How All Politics Became Reproductive Politics* offers a valuable description of the social reproductive contradictions of the present state of things, and rightly emphasises the tightly bound relation of racism and reproductive politics. Briggs' conception of the scope of change is, however, disappointingly narrow, especially compared to some of the historical movements it invokes. The book's closing pages note that 'even major corporations have long since realised that easing work/life burdens improves productivity'. In light of the immiserating social conditions sketched in this book, it is surely time to question whether the drive to improve productivity will ever be compatible with the movement for reproductive freedom.

Sophie Jones

# Terror of the social

Galen Strawson, *Things That Bother Me: Death, Freedom, the Self, Etc.* (New York: New York Review of Books, 2018). 236pp., £11.99 pb., 978 1 68237 220 4

In his most recent book, apparently meant for a general audience and made up of essays previously appearing in non-scholarly publications, Galen Strawson has provided a nice recap of his general philosophical position. Most importantly, he has provided an opportunity to assess the relationship between philosophical discourse and what we might call common sense or everyday concepts. Strawson exactly captures the aporias and contradictions that are inherent, if often unnoticed, in the concepts with which we ordinarily operate in our everyday lives. However, I will also argue that we must treat these aporias and contradictions not as proven truths about reality, but as indications of where our common-sense understanding is in error. If we fail to notice these errors, as Strawson does, we are inevitably led to accept a certain amount of magical thinking and, more problematically, be convinced that we have no capacity to alter our lives, or the world, for the better.

Strawson is probably best known for his argument against free will, and so against the possibility of moral responsibility. In the introduction to *Things That Bother Me*, Strawson notes the angry response he has gotten to this argument over the years from those unable to refute it: 'The virulence of the messages suggests that those who send them think that the argument is sound, and this makes their anger a little odd … after all, they hold the same view themselves'. Strawson's rhetoric leads inexorably to conclusions most find troubling. However, few are able to interrogate the premises on which they are based, because they are premises on which almost everyone operates in everyday life. The point is that once we have accepted Strawson's use of our own everyday conceptions of free will, consciousness and determinism, then his conclusions *are* irrefutable. We must then accept the absence of all agency, the concept of the mind as a passive observer, and, most absurdly of all, panpsychism. However, if it is possible to examine these premises, so it is also possible to demonstrate the very different possibilities for human life that are revealed once we have corrected, or at least questioned, these assumptions.

In this collection, the concept of free will – the basis of Strawson's most troubling and best known arguments – is most explicitly addressed in two essays: 'Luck Swallows Everything' and 'You Cannot Make Yourself the Way You Are'. I take it that Strawson's idea of free will in these essays is precisely the one most people do indeed ordinarily operate under. Put most strongly, it is something like this:

> One's mental nature *inclines* one to do A rather than B (to use Leibniz's terms), but it doesn't thereby *necessitate* one to do A rather than B. As an agent-self, one incorporates a power of free decision that is independent of all the particularities of one's mental nature, in such a way that one can after all count as ultimately morally responsible in one's decisions and actions even though one isn't ultimately responsible for any aspects of one's mental nature.

Strawson easily points out that this position is untenable, because of course the 'agent-self' then needs to provide an explanation of how it makes its choices, and, as such, an infinite regress ensues. Yet most people probably do believe that they have some extra or surplus self, separate from their mental nature, above and beyond all their thoughts, beliefs, dispositions, emotions, etc., which can come in to freely choose between desirable options. This belief is the problem that we need to address if we are to avoid the morass of free-will debates.

This concept of a surplus self beyond the contents of our mind is certainly central to all Lockean empiricist theories of the subject, although it clearly predates Locke. Servais Pinckaers, for instance, in his 2001 book *Morality*, locates the origin of the problem with William of Ockham, arguing that the idea that 'free choice is the first faculty of the human person', the belief that we can even 'choose to think or not to think, to will or not to will', is an error that is not yet common before the fourteenth century. Pinckaers refers to this as 'freedom of indifference', and his discussion of the alternative to this idea of free will can serve as a useful guide to escaping the dead end into which we are led by this concept.

How might we hope to reject the common assumptions about free will without merely demonstrating its logical impossibility and so leaving us with the worst kind of fatalism? We can begin by considering other ways of conceiving of freedom that were common in the past: for instance, what Pinckaers calls 'freedom for excellence', a concept he suggests would have appeared true to Thomists a century before Ockham's position became dominant. For Thomists, it is essential that our freedom follows from, rather than precedes, both our reason and our intentions. We cannot choose to think or not think, we can only think and in that thinking arrive at an understanding of what is best to do. Freedom would then consist, as Pinckaers puts it, of 'the capacity to bring to good completion works of long duration that bear fruit for many.' This is not a matter of some kind of pure choice of an undetermined surplus self, a choice to tip to the side of good or evil when faced with alternatives. Instead, we must understand freedom as the increase of knowledge about the way the world about us works, which in turn increases our power to act in the world. Of course, this isn't what we normally think of as free will. Freedom to work long and hard at projects which are constrained by the way the world really is doesn't fit what we normally mean by freedom. We normally mean something like freedom *from* such effort and such constraints. And that is exactly the point. We need to abandon the mistaken idea of freedom, in order to grasp the kind of freedom we actually can have.

However, in order to understand just how we need to rethink these things, we need to first become more cognizant of the fundamental errors in at least two more of our most deeply held assumptions. This is essential if we hope to change the world rather than merely observe it. To that end, it is worth considering two deeply interconnected concepts: consciousness and determinism.

Strawson devotes perhaps his most impassioned arguments in this book to refuting the idea – which he calls the 'silliest claim that has ever been made' – that consciousness does not exist. As he writes: '[W]hen people say that consciousness is a mystery they're wrong, because we all know what it is. In fact we know exactly what it is. It's the most familiar thing there is, although that doesn't mean we can easily put it into words.' In what sense can we know *exactly* what something is, but be unable to explain it in language? There is a nice bit of equivocation here, concerning the different meanings of the word 'know'. For instance, consider something like an ordinary modern automobile. We would all say we 'know' how the car works, because we get in one and drive it successfully every day. But most of us don't 'know' how the engine actually operates, and could not hope to successfully design a working car given any amount of time and

access to Google. The point is, we 'know' how and when to use the *word* 'consciousness', but we don't actually have any clear idea of what it *means*.

I would suggest that it actually 'means' nothing, that it functions as a kind of floating signifier useful to cover over an aporia in the empiricist ideology of the subject. And we have all learned to use it in exactly that way, usually without being bothered at all by the lack of a concept behind the term (this is just how floating signifiers work). Although it ought to be obvious to scholars working in the field of philosophy of mind, surprisingly few people even in that field have noticed that the concept was simply invented by John Locke in *An Essay Concerning Human Understanding*. The term was a neologism in the seventeenth century, first appearing just over a decade before Locke published his work, and he gives it a new function which it continues to serve to this day. (On this, see Stella Sandford's 2013 introduction to Etienne Balibar's *Identity and Difference: John Locke & the Invention of Consciousness*.) The word serves to cover over a difficulty in the empiricist project, specifically the difficulty of accounting for the nature of the subject if it must be conceived of as *preceding* all sociality. If the subject must arise from sensory experience organised into concepts *prior to* entering any social dimension, then we are left with an enormous explanatory gap, the one we are still struggling with today: how exactly can this deterministic material body and brain give rise to anything like a mind? This perennial problem arises, then, only once we assume an atomistic subject, preexisting the social dimension, which can freely choose to enter into relationships with others. Locke's solution is to assert the existence of a consciousness (and a 'self', another neologism at the time), and give it domain over its empirical experiences.

Locke's concept of consciousness serves to avoid the aspect of the subject most troubling to reductivist materialisms from empiricism up to today's reductive neurocognitivism: the sociality of the human mind. We are left puzzling over how things like the experience of 'redness' can exist because we cannot conceive that in such experiences there are two components: the biological sensory experiences *and* the socially produced concept of redness that exists in our language and places that sensory experience in a context that is not solely dependent on the passive empirical reception of light waves. This social aspect cannot be eliminated from our experience, because it precedes and shapes our experience. The Lockean model of the subject helped remove the social from epistemology, from thought, and even from ethics. However, once we have removed the social aspect of consciousness, we are left with a mechanistically determined subject, whose consciousness plays no significant role in the world. In making his argument against free will, Strawson makes the claim that 'determinism is unfalsifiable', and that once we accept that assertion we are led inevitably to deny any kind of free will, to accept that absolutely everything about 'the way you are is, in every last detail, a matter of luck'. But it also means, I would point out, that we must accept his panpsychism, since it follows from his definition of determinism.

What does Strawson mean by 'determinism' then? Simply that 'One is the way one is, initially, as a result of heredity and early experience.' The determinism Strawson finds unfalsifiable is dependent on his very specific concept of 'experience'. In the essay 'Real Naturalism', in which Strawson argues that panpsychism is a necessary correlate of realism, he explains what he means by 'experience' this way:

> One way to convey what it is to be a realist about experience is to say that it's to continue to take colour experience or taste experience or pain experience, considered just as a mental occurrence, *to be exactly what one took it to be, quite unreflectively, simply in having it, before one did any philosophy:* when one was six, for example, and was given a food one didn't like.

This definition assumes that all experience is only empirical, that there is in fact experience 'before one did any philosophy'. But there isn't, if we think of 'did any philosophy' in the broadest sense, since that philosophising has already been done and is included in the socially constructed language in which we know our experiences of taste or colour or even pain – maybe not for a newborn infant, but certainly for the six-year-old that Strawson has in mind as his primitive subject. Once we've accepted this definition of experience, however, it seems logically to follow that determinism must be what Strawson understands it to be. It is then no leap at all to panpsychism, because if one kind of mechanistically determined matter (us) clearly has experience, we can't come up with any possible reason to suggest that conscious experience is not a property of all matter: 'nothing in physics requires or entails that the structure-transcendent nature of concrete reality is or must be fundamentally or irreducibly nonexperiential in character.' No, it doesn't, on this definition of experience. But we need not think of experience this way, if we lose our fear of recognising the socially-constructed nature of the mind. We could simply suggest that 'conscious' experience is a power that *emerges* because of the particular nature of human beings as social animals making use of and dependent on language.

Strawson seems to be as bothered by emergence as he is by sociality. He suggests that any alternative to his panpsychism would require that we 'posit some sort of "radical emergence"'. But it wouldn't. It only seems so if we think, like Strawson does, that 'some physical stuff is experiential in nature', that experience is a property of matter, something matter *has*, like mass. But if we understand that 'conscious' experience is something we *do*, not something we *have*, we aren't stuck in Strawson's dilemma. In this case, we would not need to suggest that subatomic particles or stones or galaxies have experience, any more than we would suggest that they have the capacity to build nests or make honey just because we know birds and bees have these capacities. Experience is not a property of matter, but an emergent capacity of a particular form of matter, and it need not seem any more 'radical' than a bee's ability to make honey unless we make the mistake of assuming that 'consciousness' is somehow essential to the existence of the universe. Once we eliminate this concept of experience, we are no longer stuck in Strawson's deterministic world in which everything about our lives is purely a matter of luck, with nothing at all we can do about it.

It is worth thinking here about the ideological

function of these fundamental concepts, as of much of the discourse of philosophy. When we think of free will in the manner Pinckaers refers to as 'freedom of indifference', we are left with a kind of fatalism about the world. We can at best respond, individually, to the world as it is, but we can never hope to transform it. That is, we are excluded from the realm of the structures of social formations, left only with the limited freedom to choose to stop thinking altogether. 'Freedom for excellence' – however little it sounds like what we usually mean by freedom – would leave us able, by contrast, to understand and transform the social world around us. Most of us use the term 'free' only in the former sense, because that is the sense it has taken on in most Western languages. When philosophers debate free will, they assume the same meaning of the term, and debate whether and how we might have it rather than whether it is the correct concept of freedom to have. Every new essay or book or college course on the free will problem, then, only reifies this concept, and works to reproduce an ideology in which our social world is of the same kind as the natural world, and not something we can do anything to change.

Similarly, the common concept of consciousness, essentially a floating signifier functioning to close a gap in a particular ideology of the subject, is almost never interrogated critically. As Strawson, and many others, have pointed out, this term is originally part of a forensic concept of personal identity, meant to define the legal status of individuals, and to proclaim their moral responsibility for participation in social formations that must remain beyond their power to change – in fact, beyond their capacity to think of as *social* at all. It is perhaps time to stop writing books trying futilely to explain the ineffability of consciousness, and just point out the ideological function of the term. Mechanistic determinism, of the kind so popular today in all forms of reductionism, and which implicitly informs the current popularity of theories about our inability to think rationally and the purportedly inborn predispositions that do all our thinking for us, is the most crippling of these fundamental concepts. However, terror of the social perhaps makes it the most difficult assumption to question, because how can we possibly accept that the only alternative to mechanistic determinism is that our agency requires the social negotiation of meaning, goals and intentions?

The task of philosophy ought to be to expose and critique the ideological concepts which inform our everyday practices. Unfortunately, much philosophical discourse has largely taken as given the concepts we use in our everyday thought about the world, our common sense understanding embedded in our language. This is why a book like Strawson's can cross the usually unbridgeable divide between professional philosophy and mainstream non-fiction. The assumptions of the discourse of philosophy just *are* the assumptions of common sense. What we need are more attempts to cross this divide, but to do so in an attempt to demystify these unquestioned assumptions. Every time we recycle the old debates about the mind-body problem or free will, we simply reify the ideological concepts fundamental to the functioning of the current social formation. Critiquing, but more importantly *replacing*, these concepts is thus the only way in which we can enable the functioning of our emergent capacity to know, and so effectively transform, the world we live in. That we can do this should be completely obvious to anyone who drives a car, talks on a cell phone, or lives in a city. Why we deny that we have that power is no mystery: it results from accepting the assumptions we have been examining here. Strawson says that the most absurd claim of all is the denial of consciousness; I would suggest that instead it is Strawson's own belief that everything we 'are' can only be left up to luck.

**W. Thomas Pepper**

# Strategies of debilitation

Jasbir K. Puar, *The Right to Maim: Debility, Capacity, Disability* (Durham, NC: Duke University Press, 2017). 296pp., £76.00 hb., £20.99 pb., 978 0 82236 892 2 hb., 978 0 82236 918 9 pb.

On March 30th 2018, Palestinian activists in Gaza began what they called The Great March of Return. Throughout a period beginning on Land Day and ending on Nakba Day, thousands of Palestinians marched towards the fence separating Gaza from the rest of Palestine and attempted to return to the family homes they lost in 1948. In response, Israel's military designated the marchers a threat to the State, branding them terrorists, and gave orders to fire upon demonstrators. Over the ensuing weeks, more than 120 Palestinians were killed by Israeli live fire. Just as striking was the sheer number of Palestinians injured – some 15,000 according to the Gaza Ministry of Health. Palestinian doctors observed that Israel appeared to have used sniper rounds with an expanding 'butterfly effect', which were designed to permanently disable targets. Indeed, a notable feature of the marchers was the prominence of those with existing disabilities among them, including many amputees who had lost limbs at the hands of previous rounds of Israeli military violence. An iconic image of double amputee Saber al-Ashqar launching a rock from a slingshot in his wheelchair circulated widely on social media. Another double amputee, Fadi Abu Saleh, was one of the many fatalities.

Watching these events unfold, I almost found it hard to believe that Jasbir Puar had written and published her book well in advance of the Great March of Return. It was as if *The Right to Maim* had anticipated these developments. Puar's work, bringing together disability studies, queer theory, Foucauldian biopolitics and settler colonial studies, focuses for the most part on Palestine and reveals the centrality of the phenomena of debility, disability and capacity for understanding contemporary politics there. Reading her text in conjunction with current events, it becomes tempting to interpret the Palestinian struggle not only as a globally significant national liberation movement, but also as one of the most radical disability justice campaigns in the world. Or at least it would be, were it not for the fact that Puar's work also successfully challenges the very framework of disability justice itself, pushing, dismantling and reassembling it to encompass a far broader terrain of struggle.

At the heart of the analysis is Puar's distinction between disability and debility. In disability studies, 'disability' usually denotes a differential bodily capacity hailed in dominant social frames as non-normative. Traditional disability rights activism, and more recent radical crip activism, challenges the basis of this non-normativity, arguing either for measures to include people with disabilities in society, or, more radically, challenging the very distinction between normative and non-normative capacities as the basis for social organisation. Puar does not reject this framework, but she does note the many exclusions and hierarchies which the framework of disability risks engendering. She proposes 'debility' as a necessary supplement to this analysis, by which she means the general societal production of differential capacities in ways not traditionally captured by the notion of disability, such as unequal access to healthcare, working in dangerous conditions or living under military occupation. Very often, she argues, the selective recapacitation of people identified as disabled is accompanied by the continued production of debility elsewhere.

Access to opportunities for inclusion, or even for more far-reaching transformative resignifications of disability, are stratified by race, class, nationality, gender, sexuality and colonial difference. And forms of debility which are not usually hailed as disability often continue undisturbed alongside these stratifications, and may even be perpetuated by them. Readers will recognise here the same critical impulse that animated Puar's first book *Terrorist Assemblages*, which examined the co-optation of Westernised gay rights struggles under the banner of imperialist homonationalism and the simultaneous stigmatisation of racialised groups as monstrous queers. In *The Right to Maim*, Puar builds on existing scholarship in critical disability studies, such as that of Robert McRuer and David Mitchell and Sharon Snyder, which adapted the insights of her earlier work to develop the concepts of 'disability nationalism', 'able-nationalism' and 'crip-nationalism'.

Thought-provoking examples of her argument are explored throughout the book. For instance, when capacitating technologies or social policies are made available in Western countries, this depends on patterns of production in an uneven global political economy which systematically incapacitates working class and racialised bodies, especially in the Global South. When the US military celebrates the bodily recapacitation and recruitment of trans* soldiers, this move relies on the continued functioning of American imperialism and militarism for success. When potentially suicidal young gay men are targeted with publicity campaigns for therapy, these initiatives often invoke a neoliberal affective and political economy (characterised by Lauren Berlant as 'cruel optimism') that ruins lives as it offers (often illusory) pathways to salvation.

However, it is in Palestine that Puar is most concerned to demonstrate the mutual imbrications of disability, debility and capacity. She shows that while Israeli families struggling to conceive can expect generous fertility treatment and Israeli military veterans receive generous compensation for their injuries, Palestinians are systematically denied the same opportunities. Meanwhile they must subsist under conditions of military occupation, restricted mobility, a devastated local economy, ruined infrastructure and aid dependency. Puar also argues, in a refinement of the insights of settler colonial studies, that Israel's logic of elimination unfolds as a logic of deliberate debilitation. Riffing on Foucault's theory of biopolitics and Mbembe's account of necropolitics, she terms this strategy a practice of 'will not let die', whereby military violence can be more easily internationally legitimated if it slowly incapacitates Palestinian society while holding back from total slaughter. In such conditions, she demonstrates, it is meaningless for Palestinians simply to demand biomedical interventions, reasonable adjustments or the exploration of radical crip subjectivities as correctives to disability injustice. In Palestine, meaningful disability justice also involves fighting Israeli practices of debilitation – and that means decolonisation. This inseparability is a vital lesson which the Palestinian struggle can teach disability campaigning elsewhere.

The real strengths of this book lie in the extremely broad range of conceptual sources and theoretical debates it engages, and Puar's ability to combine these multiple vectors into her argument. Central to this is the deployment of her own brand of assemblage theory, which constantly proliferates the possible points of contact between racialisation, disability, gender, sexuality, political economy, colonialism, and more, to present an often kaleidoscopic analysis. The attempt to combine these elements and still further to apply them to a context which has not been fully theorised in this way is what delivers the book's most significant achievements. This approach is, however, also the source of several limitations, which occasionally prevent the book from being equal to the sum of its constituent parts. In places the book simply attempts too much and becomes either bewildering (at least to this reader) or unsatisfying as a result. The forays into engagements with animal studies are a case in point. This is not to say that such an engagement could not be fruitful. However, there is insufficient space to do it justice within the confines of this project. A more charitable reading would account for these diversions as Deleuzian lines of flight which reflect Puar's analytic method, but there should be no necessity for this approach to trade off with thoroughness. Indeed, it is not a surprise to read in the acknowledgements that Puar originally thought she was writing two books before condensing them into one. This is reflected in the slightly awkward structure: the text seems to begin at least three times, with a preface, followed by acknowledgements, followed by an introduction and chapter one which feel more like distinct empirical case studies and which oddly precede the theoretical overview that appears in its fullest form in chapter two.

Another dimension to the book's overambitious tendencies is a preference for synthesis over new analysis. The temptation to combine ever more components into the assemblage often swamps the most novel contributions of the book. At one point, Puar professes neither 'to approximate nor replicate an ethnographic or area studies analysis', but some of the book's strongest elements do just that. For example, one of the most effective and elegant sections uses original fieldwork in the West Bank and observation of disability activists there to brilliantly crystallise the overall argument. However, rather than taking centre stage, this analysis is confined to a brief Postscript. By contrast, an entire chapter is devoted to reproductive politics in Palestine-Israel, even though this analysis is much more dependent on existing scholarship. This reflects a wider difficulty with the text. While the disability/debility distinction is a new and brilliant formulation, the bulk of the theoretical argument is indebted to existing work in disability studies, especially that of Nirmala Erevelles. This means that one of the main potential contributions of the project was to take this analysis beyond 'Euro-American framings' and to explore the new ramifications of this argument when considered in relation to Palestine. Puar appears more than capable of this, perhaps more than she allows herself; yet the book's startling transdisciplinary and synthetic ambitions mean that it cannot fully deliver the sustained treatment that her chosen empirical context invites and deserves. One should not force this point too far, however. In some ways, this is a great gift to future scholars who should find in the book rich inspiration for further work. A fascinating intellectual agenda has been demarcated, and a prescient window into the politics of the colonisation of Palestine has been opened here.

**James Eastwood**

# Without further ado

Theodor W. Adorno, *Aesthetics*, ed. Eberhard Ortland, trans. Wieland Hoban (Cambridge: Polity Press, 2017). 376pp., £55.00 hb., £18.99 pb., 978 0 74567 939 6 hb., 978 0 74567 940 2 pb.

Amongst the writings of canonised thinkers, there often exist ambiguous yet generative gaps between those works published during their lifetime and those made posthumously available. The task of bridging these two bodies of work, and according philosophical intent, is one fraught with complications. Questions as to the 'authentic' kernel of a thought, the marginal history of a concept or the speculative shape of unrealised work remain open and contestable. The stakes are heightened when, for instance, the border between published and unpublished is complicated by historical dramas and institutional positioning, as in the case of Walter Benjamin, or when archival or private material is said to unsettle otherwise rehearsed conceptual formations, as in the case of Martin Heidegger. When it comes to the work of Theodor W. Adorno, one of the most testing divides is the one that separates his *Gesammelte Schriften* [Collected Writings] from the *Nachgelassene Schriften* [Posthumous Writings]. If it is clear that such a divide cannot settle in either direction each and every dispute, it does, for a Germanophone audience at least, raise the distinction to the point of articulation. In an Anglophone context, despite the well-known shortcomings of existing translations of major works, it is becoming something of a tradition to pursue those works contained in the latter of these two, his *Nachgelassene Schriften*. The latest book-length work to be published in English falls squarely within this tradition.

Delivered during the winter semester of 1958–59, Adorno's *Aesthetics* is the eighth lecture course to have been translated and published by Polity, with one other announced (the 1960–61 course *Ontology and Dialectics*, edited by Rolf Tiedemann) and several more (possibly nine) likely to follow. The course documents the fourth of six occasions in which Adorno lectured students on the topic of art and philosophical aesthetics between 1950 and 1968, and, of all six, it is the earliest to have been recorded on tape and transcribed in full (the fifth occasion, delivered during the winter semester of 1961–62, exists as a transcript and will be published by Suhrkamp in the future).

As the book's editor, Eberhard Ortland, underscores in his German-afterword-cum-English-introduction, there are several points of theoretical interest in these lectures, three of which he selects as the most prominent. First, Adorno's demanding concept of aesthetic experience, fleshed out from the opening to the closing lectures, as an accompaniment to its use in other works; second, the discussion of Plato's *Phaedrus*, most fully examined in lectures nine and ten, is perhaps Adorno's most express analysis of pre-Modern philosophical notions of beauty; and, third, the references to John Cage in lecture eight, whose work, importantly, Adorno had engaged with during the 1957 and 1958 Darmstadt International Summer Courses for New Music. The *Aesthetics* discusses each of these to a degree either greater than or different to that found in his wider, published oeuvre, providing richer character to statements that might otherwise remain elliptical, technical or unjustified. In addition to Ortland's list, many readers will find the opening lectures dedicated to artistic and natural beauty, as well as his claims – repeated and qualified – as to art's capacity to help the 'suppressed and suffering to find its voice', illuminating and reassuring. Equally advisable, one should be alert, especially in lectures six to eight, to the categories of construction and expression; to consider the sustained argument against the sufficiency of subjectivist aesthetics, a corrective that remains poignant; to trace his early, although not first, diagnosis of art's historical 'crisis of meaning'; and finally but not exhaustively, to note his attacks on defensive reactions against modern art found in the work of Georg Lukács and Hans Sedlmayr alike. Accordingly, there are a number of conceptual contributions that the 1958–59 *Aesthetics* course introduce into the Anglophone philosophy of art and, if handled correctly, to our understanding of Adorno's positions and thought. Due credit must be granted here both to Ortland's editorial work and Wieland Hoban's translation. Not only does Ortland resist including any pantomime laughter and jeering (compare the *Introduction to Sociology*, edited by Christoph Gödde), but the endnote editorial commentary and the inclusion of Adorno's lecture notes are worthwhile. And in a situation where no translation can win, Hoban's attempt doesn't lose too badly.

For those unfamiliar with Adorno's lecture courses it may come as a surprise to find that he appears so engaged with his students, not only insofar as his intellectual demands are matched by patient elaboration and argumentation, but also insofar as the students' problems, questions and concerns often dictate the content of the lectures. As to the growing chorus that sings the lectures' praise as a gentler way into Adorno's written work, they are liable to find the 1958–59 *Aesthetics* an exemplary score. For, in contrast to many of the existing courses, what is historically and theoretically remarkable about the *Aesthetics* is that it is one of the few published transcripts that shows substantial evidence of having been consulted and annotated by Adorno himself. He returned to the transcript during the preparation of later editions of the course and through the period in which he wrote drafts of what was to be posthumously published as *Aesthetic Theory*. The years immediately succeeding this lecture course thus figure heavily in the afterlife of its transcript, for it is this period, as Gretel Adorno and Rolf Tiedemann note, that inaugurates early attempts towards *Aesthetic Theory*, formally christened by the first dictation of draft paragraphs in May 1961. Ortland's editing ensures that readers of the 1958–59 *Aesthetics* can participate in this origin story of *Aesthetic Theory* by tracing those passages and thoughts that Adorno felt worthy of marking and marginalia.

Taking this into account, as some prominent commentators have already suggested, it may be tempting to figure the *Aesthetics* as an introduction to, or identikit sketch of, *Aesthetic Theory* itself, a rudimentary but otherwise faithful likeness. As such, the relation between these two texts acts in part as a test case for the wider problem of how Adorno's *Nachgelassene Schriften* is to be thought alongside his *Gesammelte Schriften*. Many of the *Nachgelassene Schriften* editors are acutely aware of this issue, repeating the sediment problems that come with the publishing project. However, too often this is forgotten in secondary philosophical work that furiously grabs at exegesis or an unplumbed term. As regards relating the *Aesthetics* to *Aesthetic Theory*, legitimacy for such a manoeuvre may be sought in their shared intellectual content such that one could turn, for instance, to lectures one and five for some remarks on 'technique' or four and eleven for clarification of the notion of 'ugliness'. Straightforwardly to follow through on this, however, would be myopic on at least two counts: on one side, it limits the possibility for wider systematic connection and mediation; on the other side, it produces a false conceptual equivocation based on superficial similarity.

In the first instance, it risks distancing the 1958–59 *Aesthetics* from his longstanding writings on musicology and music criticism, as well as the important post-War dispute with Sedlmayr during the 1950 *Darmstädter Gespräch* on 'The Image of Man in our Time'. It risks severing ties to the extensive 1950s writings that form the 1958 publication of *Notes to Literature I*. It risks forgetting that 1958 marked the year that Adorno was commissioned by the *Schweizer Monatshefte* to write an essay on the sociology of music, signalling what was to become a public dispute with Alphons Silbermann. And, it risks occluding from view the three studies on Hegel delivered on each side of the lecture course. Where *Aesthetic Theory* is concerned, it risks failing adequately to mediate it through the 1960s, through the heavy edits, deletions and revisions that drafts went through, and through that extended set of activities that would interrupt, obstruct and distract from its completion. On this latter point, not only should we have in mind the increasing demands and interests from Adorno's radicalised students, and the infamous tensions that this brought with it, but also his increasingly public role in German sociological debates and, of course, the intellectual work that went into *Negative Dialectics*. This without mentioning any of the developments in 1960s art practice, music composition and film direction of which he was not unaware.

In the second instance, through a flagrant betrayal of those familiar comments made in the 1969 preface to the *Dialectic of Enlightenment* – comments that admit the authors' commitment to 'a theory which attributes a temporal core to truth instead of contrasting truth as something invariable to the movement of history' – there is a danger of stripping the two texts of their differing historical context, character and specificity. The *Aesthetics* lectures and *Aesthetic Theory* are not readily equivalent or interchangeable, and the force required to make them so is subtle but decisive. To make a quick conceptual comparison, or to view one as the other made simple, is to assume a base historical stasis between the respective positions. Equally problematically, one would have to lose a sense that the lectures are informally sequential and, despite being terminated early owing to poor health, generally followed a preconceived argumentative arc. *Aesthetic Theory*, as Adorno himself claimed, is decidedly fragmentary and paratactic. To hastily align the two would be to underestimate the strict argumentative organisation and presentation of the mature work that, however clichéd it might sound, causes such productive interpretative difficulties. Commenting on the editorial challenges that *Aesthetic Theory* presented, Gretel Adorno and Tiedemann remind us that '[t]he problems of a paratactical form of presentation, such as they appear in the last version of *Aesthetic Theory*, with which Adorno would not have said he was content, are objectively determined: They are the expression of the attitude of thought to objectivity.' To overlook this is to forego Adorno's thought itself.

In an aphorism positioned against the mediation of two thinkers, Friedrich Nietzsche writes in *The Gay Science* that 'seeing things as similar and making things the same is the sign of weak eyes.' His comments, aimed at those with 'no eye for the unique', critique a variation of a familiar conceptual-methodological flaw: the false attribution of identity in an unwitting denial of the dissimilar. Although the work of mediation (*vermitteln*) does not necessarily conform to the error of reduction in the way Nietzsche wants to claim, losing sight of a thinker's thought by only recognising resemblances does. Striking, *mutatis mutandis*, at the issues at hand, there may then be some merit to viewing Adorno as two separate thinkers, neither reducible to the other. More accurately, by reading the *Aesthetics* as elementary movements toward *Aesthetic Theory* and not a crude form of it, more may be gained in thinking their systematic connection through argumentative disjunction than there would be in suturing them together. To undertake this one would have to inquire into the problems Adorno encountered, for instance, in the notion of world-feeling (*Weltgefühl*), to account for the relative demotion of the role of co-enactment (*mitvollziehen*), or to register any other remarks that were abandoned or deemed insufficiently defensible to be included in *Aesthetic Theory*'s drafts. In reverse, one could treat the *Aesthetics* as a prompt to consider the absence in the lectures of his claims on the double character of art as autonomous and *fait social*, and the various post-1959 conditions that would ensure its introduction. Perhaps providing a better model for thinking the *Nachgelassene Schriften* and *Gesammelte Schriften* relation, any attempts of this sort would enrich its philosophical content by way of the necessary intellectual history and division. But the temptation to trade having to labour over Adorno's written prose for the comparative ease of turning to his lectures persists, and with it the danger that patient interpretive work will be sacrificed in the process. Whether such a sacrifice is executed for the sake of pedagogy or to soften the welcome to a general audience, obscuration or avoidance of intellectual difficulty harbours nothing more than the base theoretical conservatism contained in an injunction to digestible reception.

**Louis Hartnoll**

# Rebellious admiration

Clare Hemmings, *Considering Emma Goldman: Feminist Political Ambivalence and the Imaginative Archive* (Durham NC: Duke University Press, 2018). 304pp., £80.00 hb., £19.99 pb., 978 0 82236 998 1 hb., 978 0 82237 003 1 pb.

Clare Hemmings is one of the most innovative and original voices in contemporary feminist theory. Her work cuts across disciplinary boundaries and is largely concerned with an ongoing and wide-ranging critical reflection on the production of 'feminist theory' as a field. *Considering Emma Goldman* offers a continuation of this project in a new and provocative direction. In her previous book, *Why Stories Matter*, Hemmings focused on the pervasive historiographical assumptions underlying feminist theory's interpretive framing of feminism's past, present and future. In *Considering Emma Goldman*, Hemmings switches her focus to addressing the theoretical impasses and sites of political struggle that continue to shape feminist and queer theory in the present. At the same time, *Considering Emma Goldman* is also a personal project – a critical reflection on how Emma Goldman partly inspired Hemmings to become a feminist, and how she continues to animate Hemmings' conflicted if committed relationship to feminism. Hemmings' attachment to Goldman also allows her to take more seriously than she did in *Why Stories Matter* the powerful lure of the past or lost object. Here, nostalgia gets its due, albeit renamed as wonder. Finally, *Considering Emma Goldman* is an experiment in thinking through how a figure of the feminist past – in this case, one not easily or entirely claimed by feminism – can be both resource and method for accessing the complexity and messiness of feminism as a political project with a multivalent history and a varied set of ideas.

The kaleidoscopic approach of the book draws upon three distinct archives: the 'subjective' archive of Goldman's letters and political writings, the 'critical' archive through which Goldman's work has been interpreted, especially by feminist critics, and the feminist and queer 'theoretical' archive with which, and against which, Hemmings reads Goldman. Most provocatively, Hemmings also offers, in the fourth chapter, an example of what she calls the 'imaginative archive', in which she presents a series of letters written by Almeda Sperry, a correspondent, friend and sometime lover of Goldman's, with Goldman's missing responses penned by Hemmings. With these four archives Hemmings orients her readers to think about Goldman as a figure of attachment and defamiliarisation for feminist politics and theory in the present. As a political thinker and writer who was both highly skeptical of the political goals of organised feminism in her own time, and far more radical than her feminist contemporaries in her demands for sexual freedom for women, Goldman figures the ambivalence that Hemmings identifies as integral to the central terms of feminist theory today: gender, race, and sexuality. This kaleidoscopic approach unsettles as much as it re-asserts the importance of Goldman for feminism. And this is partly Hemmings' point: we are left questioning not only why and if we should identify Goldman as a feminist – a term she rejected – but also some of the more routine assumptions of what counts as a feminist issue or object in the present. Hemmings reads these archives against each other in order to bring into view what remains unresolved in feminist and queer theory: namely, the continuing problem of femininity for feminism, the problem of race and racism as historical formations that refuse the clarity some feminists might wish to impose on them in order to 'know' them in the present, and the difficulty, for queer and feminist theory, of conceptualising 'sexual freedom' as something other than a claim to sexual rights.

By focusing on the contradictions in Goldman's thinking and practice, as well as the ways in which it disturbs taken-for-granted preoccupations in feminist and queer theory, Hemmings aims to interrupt 'feminist certainties' and 'expand the range of possible ways of inhabiting feminism'. Here, Hemmings' focus on ambivalence echoes that of other feminist and queer theorists, including Lauren Berlant and Sara Ahmed, both of whom she cites as fellow practitioners of an approach to feminist theory that keeps the impossibilities of its contradictory claims open. Ambivalence, for these theorists, signals a refusal of certainty and an insistence on staying with the discomforts and irresolvability of contradiction. Goldman figures ambivalence for Hemmings, both in terms of her anarchist insistence on privileging the process of politics rather than its goals, and also in her willingness, in her letters especially, to make explicit the disjunctures between her political claims and actions and what she might feel or think (something that is especially resonant in the chapter on sexuality in which Goldman's personal disdain for effeminate men and lesbians contrasts with her public declarations of support for homosexuals).

This is not a book, however, about Goldman the anarchist. The importance of *Considering Emma Goldman* lies elsewhere, especially in Hemmings explorations of the power of attachment in feminist theory and the limits of its contemporary preoccupations. Hemmings is most successful in relation to the latter in her first chapter, 'Women and Revolution', in which she draws out the historiographical and critical implications for contemporary feminist theory of Goldman's antipathy towards women and feminism, despite her simultaneous call for women's sexual freedom and the complete transformation of the public-private system of gender privilege. Goldman's hostility toward women, especially bourgeois women, becomes, for Hemmings, a discordant opening through which the question of why women might disidentify from feminism can be asked. Here, Goldman's 'outsider' perspective helps to clarify some of the failures of feminist thinking. That is to say, it is in her role as a critic of feminism that Goldman has the most to offer feminism in the present.

Hemmings is less successful in using Goldman as a defamiliarising figure in the chapters on race and sexuality. In these chapters the engagement with Goldman seems somewhat arbitrary in relation to current debates. While Goldman's thinking on race, and especially sexuality, offers a challenge to some of the ways both terms have habitually been thought in feminist and queer theory, I remain unconvinced that we *need* Goldman in particular to confront those habits. As I read these chapters I found myself thinking of work not cited by Hemmings which could and does do this work. Hemmings presents us with Goldman's thinking on these issues but does not offer enough engagement with the work of contemporary theorists, which makes her claims about the impasses around race and sexuality seem too narrowly defined, too reductively located in certain niches of feminist and queer theory. Indeed, rather than defamiliarising feminist theory in the present, these chapters return us to Hemmings' attachment to Goldman: it is Hemmings appreciation of Goldman that becomes the most resonant feature of these chapters, an appreciation that is able to take full flight in the fourth chapter in which Hemmings imagines herself as Goldman the correspondent.

The difficulty of the task Hemmings has set herself – to confront the impasses and difficulties of feminist and queer theory in the present through a return to a figure whose attraction, for Hemmings, lies as much in her style of being as in her political writings – is revealed early in the introduction where Hemmings tells the startling (to me at least) story of how her younger teenage self switched the focus of her rebellious admiration from Margaret Thatcher to Emma Goldman. We might think of this story as one of the political reveals of the book: how contradiction and ambivalence in feminist politics and attachment might lead one to move from one strong iconoclastic female figure to another, from an icon of the new right to an icon of the anarchist left. Thatcher and Goldman both knew how to fashion themselves as political figures worth paying attention to. Both enjoyed the drama, the theatricality, of their publicity. And both were skilled debaters and orators. This uneasy symmetry of 'Mrs T' and 'E.G.' is part of the difficulty – and the productive provocation – of Hemmings' approach to Goldman. It invokes the uneasy specter of a political orientation that can morph from a certain kind of libertarianism – 'there is no such thing as society' – to anarchism, in which the state is regarded as an oppressive obstacle to the free expression of human life in all its potentiality. What feminism is – as a politics – remains suspended in these convergences, as it does in the imagined correspondence between Hemmings / Goldman and Almeda Sperry; a suspension that is productive, no doubt, of the 'imaginative archive' that Hemmings challenges her readers to construct and inhabit. But it also raises the question of how we might think about 'style' in relation to feminism (or queerness): does a certain style tell us something about a person's political or theoretical orientation? Put differently, was Emma Goldman's 'panache' immanent in her anarchism, as Hemmings wants to argue, or something more peculiar to Goldman, something in excess of, or beside, her political beliefs and commitments? My reservation here is that 'panache' becomes an unambivalent celebration of a way of being in the world that might just as easily be attributed to someone like Margaret Thatcher as Emma Goldman. The exceptionalism of figures like Goldman and Thatcher become the lure through which we might attach ourselves to their politics, their ideas, but our investments in their exceptionalism also surely reveal the elsewhere of political identification and practice, the nonplace where desire and imagination meet, a place that cannot secure or explain the relationship between one's politics and one's way of being in the world, despite Hemmings' hope that it can.

Victoria Hesford

# Trying to square the circle

Jean-Paul Sartre, Philippe Gavi and Pierre Victor, *It is Right to Rebel*, trans. Adrian van de Hoven and Basil Kingstone (London: Routledge, 2017). xx+334pp. £65.00 hb., 978 1 13874 976 4

In November 1972 Jean-Paul Sartre sat down with two young militants to conduct a series of discussions that could be published as a book, the proceeds from which would help the soon-to-be launched leftwing newspaper *Libération*. The militants were Benny Lévy alias Pierre Victor, the leader of the most influential French Maoist organisation (Gauche Prolétarienne), and a libertarian activist Philippe Gavi, both co-founders of the paper. Translated now as *It is Right to Rebel*, the book has received a new preface from Gavi, the only one of its three authors who is still alive, which discusses not only *Libération* and the immediate context of the discussions, but also touches on the broader situation of militant politics in the early 1970s around Victor's organisation, on the one hand, and Gavi's own, more libertarian position, on the other. The way Gavi ends his preface by personalising Victor's and Sartre's radical 'beliefs', tends to appear symptomatic of the failure that the political moment of the discussions would soon come to suffer.

The book consists of 23 dated discussions (21 chapters, an introduction, and a conclusion) which run chronologically from November 1972 to March 1974 (apart from a discussion from February 1974 serving as an introduction). At times somewhat arbitrarily titled, the sections move back and forth between different topics around socialism and revolutionary politics, including, for example, the Communist Party, legality versus legitimacy, the division of labour, the figure of the revolutionary, freedom, dialectics, the relations between the people, the masses and class, time and history, marginality versus majority.

The broader structure of the book can be seen to unfold roughly through three stages, defined partly by the historical sequence during which the discussions take place. The first few chapters concentrate mainly on Sartre's personal trajectory, from a 'liberal intellectual' to a 'critical fellow-traveller' of the Communist Party in the early 1950s to a friend and co-activist of Maoist militants in the late 1960s. The central theme of the subsequent chapters is the practice of the Maoists belonging to Gauche Prolétarienne, led by Victor. Gradually the main attention shifts to contemporary events such as Chile before and after the coup d'état, the 1973 Arab-Israel War, and, most importantly, the taking over (in June 1973) of the Lip watch factory by its workers. Lip marked a defining moment in the sequence of post-68 revolutionary struggles in France, as the focus shifted to fully autonomous workers' mobilisations, thereby encouraging the self-dissolution of Gauche Prolétarienne. This self-dissolution was duly announced in November 1973, although the occasion goes unregistered in the present book.

The English edition puts Sartre somewhat inadequately at the forefront. Where the original French mentions the authors in alphabetical order, Sartre's name now stands in a bigger font and is followed by those of Gavi and Victor. Sartre's picture also appears on the cover of the book. Understandable as this might be for marketing purposes, there is nothing in the content of the book that justifies Sartre's place at the forefront apart from the early chapters which appear as an interview. Although Sartre approaches the discussions often from the perspective of his philosophical ideas (most notably freedom, but also serialisation, groups-in-fusion, fraternity-terror) these ideas do not have any privileged weight, for, as he's the first to admit, it is collective revolutionary practice, or revolt, which has become the only legitimate source of ideas here. As Sartre himself explains, whereas the classical revolutionaries lamented 'the gap between reality and ideas', ideas are now 'formed in the struggle'. This is the lesson of the movement which had started in May 1968 and whose continuity was at stake in the struggles of the time.

The widely-repeated Maoist slogan which gives the book its title affirms a norm to justify revolutionary politics without providing a preformed guide for specific or local subversive actions. Rather, it validates all such actions by embracing their very illegality. Sartre is unequivocal on this point: 'What must be developed in people is not respect for an order claiming to be revolutionary, but the spirit of revolt against any order.' The central idea of his philosophy is rethought in light of this principle: 'Freedom rebels, and works out a tactic of rebellion.' After years of engagement with the Communist Party and its ideas, 'which passed for thinking', in the Maoist movement Sartre states that he has found a home for some of his old convictions:

> What has changed me is what I see reappearing in new aspects: old things I used to believe in, in my teenage years – ethics, for example – which I gave up in the name of realism when I began to work with the communists a bit, and which I'm finding again now in the anti-hierarchical and libertarian movement. Reality is no longer what is, in other words dead institutions and general facts. ... I am rediscovering, this time materially, ethics as the foundation of realism, or if you like, a materialistic and ethical realism.

This 'living ethics' is the basis on which Victor and his organisation attempt to construct and concentrate a force effective enough to overcome the present order. The aim is 'to pass from a set of heterogeneous rebellions to ... a rallying together, a union, a merger'. Victor explains the ways in which Gauche Prolétarienne has tried to achieve this, by creating and spreading general normative orientations out of particular acts of revolt, 'to make a new rule from what was out of whack in the system of enslavement, to make a marginal action into a central action'. 'Mao Zedong Thought' is the very name of inventing such ways to rally together multiple forces in concrete struggles.

Following the guiding idea of the Chinese Cultural Revolution, Gauche Prolétarienne wanted to combine organised revolutionary action along with decomposition of all hierarchical relations, all relations of command between centralised power and localised acts. This defines the constantly reoccurring problem in the discussions: How to retain 'freedom within organisation' if freedom is understood first of all in terms of revolt against all order? How to construct an overarching unity without compromising the immediacy and directness of revolt? The constant danger is thus that an 'active egalitarian will' loses its immediate basis in those who revolt as it is formed into a more organised collective control of the process; or that the overall process generates forms of knowledge that grassroots activists lack, thus restoring intellectual hierarchies and authoritarianism within the revolutionary movement.

The task inherited from 1968 was to destroy the 'outside synthesisers'; the revolutionary 'must be in a milieu of real rebellion', otherwise there won't be 'any real democratic reflex or reflection'. At the same time, the whole point for the Maoists was to create relations between actions which are not related immediately, and the way the question tends to be presented in absolutising terms – full immediate freedom versus organisatory control which sets limits to it from outside – risks making the problem intractable by definition, the political equivalent of trying to square the circle.

It is nevertheless the leader of the supposedly spontaneist Gauche Prolétarienne who here most determinedly tries to insist on the necessity of centralisation – albeit not without constantly problematising it at the same time. Victor knows that, in one way or another, 'the multiplicity of powers' need to relate to 'the co-ordinating centre of those powers'. It is Sartre and Gavi who tend to criticise Victor for not allowing distinct revolts to keep their autonomy, for not paying enough attention to the multiplicity of contradictions and powers. True, Victor holds onto his more classical revolutionary tendencies only to an extent, and the further we advance into the book, the more cautious he becomes with respect to any 'hasty generalisations'.

This takes us to the ultimate irony of the book. While in its early chapters we read about the inadequacy of the Communist Party, which had only served to render people passive and make them wait for the revolution indefinitely, in the end we return from the other side to a comparable wait-and-see attitude. 'When "Leftism" has matured and is better understood', Gavi explains and the others more or less agree, 'it will be time for the question of building an organisation which unites the revolutionaries according to a new system.' As for now, we should withdraw from organising to avoid any traps of our old authoritarian habits.

As we know, the 'leftist' movement was not given

much of a chance to 'mature', and the radical core of May 68 soon came to be seen as but an ephemeral moment of emancipation. In the coming years and decades, many of the most radical Maoists, Victor included, would find the absoluteness included in the ideas of pure freedom and revolt attainable only in the form of religious thought, while others, such as Jacques Rancière, managed to remain within the earthly sphere only by rethinking revolutionary politics in more modest terms, by stressing intermittent disruptions. Reading these old discussions from the early 1970s gives us an opportunity to revisit the moment which gave rise to currents of radical thought characterised largely by a rejection of any kind of determined and conscious organisational force of synthesis. In so doing, they might allow us to re-evaluate the directions taken by some currents of political thought which would develop during – and fail to challenge adequately – an era defined, in so many ways, by the profound and lasting defeat of radical politics.

Jussi Palmusaari

# Not German enough?

Tom Bunyard, *Debord, Time and Spectacle: Hegelian Marxism and Situationist Theory* (Leiden and Boston: Brill, 2018). 430pp., £123.00 hb., 978 9 00435 602 3

Amid the copious notes taken by Guy Debord on the philosophy of Hegel, the following extract from the preface to the *Phenomenology of Spirit* appears repeatedly: 'By the little which satisfies Spirit, we can measure the extent of its loss.' For Hegel, this was intended as a reproach to the parochial obsession with empirical detail. As to why the fragment held Debord's attention, it is not altogether misplaced to assume its significance lay in his competence as a diagnostician of modern society. An *enfant terrible* among other interventions of the New Left, Debord's 1967 *The Society of the Spectacle* attempted to give inner coherence to the way in which the capitalist economy develops its fetishised and reified character into an objective social form mediated by appearances. The society of the spectacle refers to the social and unitary organisation of appearances embedded with a meaning that contains both the image and the goal of social development under the commodity economy. As a totality, the spectacle both defines that which appears and gives to appearance essential actuality. For Debord, the spirit of the spectacular epoch is thus reduced to a satisfaction afforded by the objectivity of appearance-forms, which had become – under the 'enriched privation' of postwar prosperity – indistinguishable from a base colourless survival.

If the Hegelian and Marxian resonances of this description are readily apparent, they have nonetheless been minimised within most scholarship on Debord and the Situationist International. Instead, one finds Debord as a critic of media distraction, of unrestrained consumerism or as a mere heir to Dada and Surrealism. Yet even a cursory encounter with *The Society of the Spectacle* clearly demonstrates that the spectacle is neither chiefly concerned with visual imagery nor reducible to the advertisements and entertainment that saturate modern society. There have, of course, been exceptions to such readings, although not many. Anselm Jappe's authoritative *Guy Debord* (1993) – which Debord himself considered to be 'the best-informed book about me' – remains unmatched in its situating of Debord within the Hegelian Marxist tradition of Lukács. Nevertheless, most accounts have largely ignored the profoundly Hegelian dimension of Debord's works, at best giving it only anecdotal attention and failing to heed what Debord himself exhorts in a 1971 letter: 'I will affirm to you straight away: I understand *perfectly* what I have written. Obviously one cannot fully comprehend it without Marx, and especially Hegel.'

By contrast, Tom Bunyard's wide-ranging monograph convincingly casts Debord as 'a twentieth-century Young Hegelian' and, through the influence of the young Marx and Lukács, as a thinker of historical praxis. Debord is presented as having incorporated and reformulated elements of Hegel's philosophy across his entire oeuvre, most notably in his concepts of time and history. As Bunyard makes clear, *The Society of the Spectacle* is, from this perspective, 'best understood as a book about history. Or, to put that more precisely: it is a book that describes a society that has become detached from its capacity to consciously shape and determine its own future.' However, interpreted as an estranged form of historical agency, the spectacle itself receives less attention in Bunyard's investigation than does its corrective. Bunyard's Debord is one who affirms a philosophical anthropology – largely informed by Hegelian, existential and early Marxian themes – in which free human subjectivity, dynamically self-constitutive in its dialectical interaction with the objective world, is 'understood in terms of activity and experience in time' and thus knowingly developing in history through the praxis of its own self-determination. Debord's Hegelianism becomes, in Bunyard's words, a 're-figuration of Hegel's claims, in which subject-object unity ceases to be a state of final resolution, and instead becomes the ground of a self-determinate future.'

In this sense, Hegel's philosophy becomes for Debord, above all, a resource – almost exclusively informed by its French reception, and an infatuation with the *Phenomenology*'s Heideggerian and existentialist themes – for articulating the dialectical negativity of human temporality and historical praxis beyond the stultifying and passive conditions of spectacular domination. Bunyard's reading of the spectacle follows as the negative shadow of this philosophical anthropology of subjectivity, as a socially alienated historical agency not reducible to the reification of capitalist society but instead as a broader and transhistorical 'problematic' which capitalism has brought to its most extreme and full expression. Here, the spectacle refers to a condition of separation from self-determinate historical time and praxis, 'as a condition in which individuals become alienated from their ability to shape and direct their own time.' As such, the *society* of the spectacle becomes but one 'instantiation' of this more general problematic of alienated collective agency that can arise within any social formation.

The scope of Bunyard's book and its attention to Debord's archival notes, letters and writings, beyond *The Society of the Spectacle*, unearths a set of inquiries that traverse Debord's entire career, from his investigations in the Situationist International's (or SI's) early avant-garde years, the explicit engagement with Hegelian Marxism during the early 1960s and his work after the upheaval of 1968, through to the dissolution of the SI and his 1988 *Comments on the Society of the Spectacle*. Aside from the aforementioned philosophical anthropology and concept of history, Bunyard identifies three additional themes that give continuity to these various periods in Debord's life: an ethical and normative dimension to the theory of the spectacle for which opposition is grounded against all forms of separated social power; an aesthetic aspect of Debord's interest in the temporal flow of lived experience which entails 'an aestheticisation of finitude, change and temporal process, and [an] identified beauty with conscious, self-determinate action in time'; and finally, the way in which Debord's Hegelianism helps him develop a dialectical conception of strategic praxis, thereby synthesising Hegel with the works of Clausewitz, Machiavelli and Sun Tzu. Along the way, the question is explored of how and to what extent the thought of the young Marx, Lukács, Lefebvre, Sartre and the most prominent French Hegelians (Jean Wahl, Alexandre Koyré, Alexandre Kojève, Jean Hyppolite and Kostas Papaïoannou) each came to inform, whether directly or indirectly, Debord's own thought.

Part 4 of the book offers a more critical engagement with Debord's work, including the latent tension between the SI's call for the abolition of labour – a renunciation of the dignity of labour as something to be redeemed from the fetters of capitalist parasitism – and their affirmation of workers' councils. This is an active tension that extends into the SI's '*theoretical neglect* of labour', which, Bunyard argues, ultimately results in a deficient conceptualisation of capitalism as a consequence of Debord's rejection of economism. Elsewhere in the book, Bunyard impressively examines how the SI's concept of decomposition – as the professed stagnation of modern culture following the failure of the classical workers' movement – amounts to a precursor to the concept of the spectacle; offers an interpretation of Debord's 1978 film *In Girum Imus Nocte et Consumimur Igni* which 'evidences an aestheticisation of temporal flow and movement'; provides a reconstruction of the concepts of 'life' and 'non-life' within *The Society of the Spectacle*; and constructs an argument as to how Debord's interest in strategy and war was not a personal or private idiosyncrasy, but was 'in fact a form of Hegelian Marxism', in which dialectical thinking strategically requires 'recognising and understanding the changing relations between opposing forces.'

There is much to admire, then, in Bunyard's shifting of Debord scholarship towards the theoretical and philosophical foundations of his thought. Nevertheless, the book is characterised by an overemphasis on Debord's normative positions on human subjectivity and temporality that, I think, eclipses the specificity and conceptual determinations of his diagnosis of modern society. For Bunyard, Hegelian thought is important not for the way in which it illustrates the specific logic of the modern spectacle but for the way in which it allows Debord to conceive human practice as self-directed, transitory and free, as an historical unity of subject and substance. While this is illuminating as regards how Debord views the structure of free social activity in general, the spectacle ends up being defined as a derivative of the remedy suggested by Debord's wider philosophical anthropology; that is, it is 'best understood as a condition of historical arrest: as a state of alienation from historical time.' This is a reading overwhelmed by what Bunyard calls the 'ethical dimension' of Debord's thought, an orientation adhering with the passage of lived time from which the spectacle is derived as a contrary counterpart.

Bunyard is certainly right to emphasise the way in which Debord viewed the spectacle as independent of capitalism, or more specifically – as can be found within Debord's scattered comments, mostly within his letters – that there are pre-capitalist origins to the spectacle which has its 'basis in Greek thought', increasing during the Renaissance and in the eighteenth century when 'one opened museum collections to the public'. However, in the absence of Debord having written anything resembling a materialist history of the spectacle, Bunyard is left to generalise an abstraction, dubbed a 'problematic', not reducible to any historical moment and which indeterminately refers to any situation 'wherein social actors become detached from their own collective abilities and agency, and thus from their ability to shape their own lived time.'

As a result, spectacular capitalism is only the 'complete *actualisation* of that problematic', an ahistorical and yet always existing potential for the alienation of collective social power. The movement from *potential* to *actuality* is left unexplained, so inadvertently affirming Bunyard's more general characterisation of Debord as a Young Hegelian. Here, all of the idealist propensities scrutinised by Marx in *The German Ideology* are smuggled into Bunyard's own interpretation of the spectacle without these ever being addressed. Debord ends up a Young Hegelian by inheriting all of that intellectual movement's defects. It is in part a noble approach, one which seeks to open a terrain of political possibility – 'for even if capitalism were to be overthrown, some new form of spectacular separation could emerge.' Yet it is not one which can elucidate the determinate and specific critical purchase that the concept of spectacle might have upon the present moment.

The spectacle emerges as an *idealisation* by which

human beings are subordinated to the results of their own objective activity through a condition of social separation. When Bunyard does describe Hegel's influence on Debord's concept of the spectacle specifically, the analysis is confined to Hegel's notion of representation [*Vorstellung*] along with the antinomies of the *Verstand*. However, Bunyard pays little attention to either the role of appearances [*Erscheinungen*] or the categories of social cohesion outlined by Debord explicitly in the opening thesis of *The Society of the Spectacle*. While Bunyard does concede that 'Hegel's work greatly informs Debord's conception of spectacular representation', this observation is followed by a characterisation of the diremption between subject and object generally thematised within the *Phenomenology*. Bunyard makes reference to the mediations of *Vorstellung* that occupy the separation between a knowing subject and its world, but its determinate elucidation is only given by the example of 'Revealed Religion'. Bunyard does not distinguish between *Vorstellung* as a general immediacy apprehended by consciousness throughout the *Phenomenology* and its particular content within any number of sections in that book. Lost in this reading is the reason why Debord titled his opening chapter 'La séparation achevée', a beginning which traces the general self-moving form-determinations of the social reality of the spectacle as a *unifying force* of organised appearances.

What is important for Bunyard in his account of the Hegelian influence upon the concept of the spectacle is strictly a *generic* condition of the separation between subject and object. Presumably, however, Hegelian thought should have more to say about the deeper more integrative social reality of the spectacle, a point vindicated by Debord's extensive notes on Hyppolite's translation of the *Phenomenology*. While right to say that separation remains pivotal for the spectacle as its 'alpha and omega', single recourse to a Hegelian framework of antinomic division risks failing to grasp the spectacle as 'the social organisation of appearances'. Debord himself composed notes on the *Phenomenology* which exceeded in number those on the 'Revealed Religion' moment of Spirit, such as those on the 'Force and the Understanding: Appearance and the Supersensible World' section, which, it can be argued, does much to clarify the logic of the spectacle in terms of the way in which a dialectic of *Erscheinungen* yields a 'sensuous supersensible' inverted world. Most remarkable in this regard is the complete absence of the concept of *Erscheinung* within Bunyard's analysis, a category that, for both Hegel and Marx, unfolds as the necessary manifestation of essence which cannot but appear at the phenomenal level and whose dynamic, arguably, remains fundamental to the structural determinacy and fluidity of the modern spectacle.

Bunyard is at pains to give determinacy to the unity of contingent forms of separated power, a problem that greater attention to the role of appearances might have resolved. Yet, without a more specific account of how it is that the spectacle, in its specific instantiation, deprives collective praxis of its possibilities, the contours of Bunyard's interpretation of the spectacle remain vague guidelines set at a distance from the actuality of spectacular domination. More attention to the determinations and forms of mediation said by Debord to define the modern spectacle – that is, with a focus on the prominent role of *appearances* – might have allowed Bunyard to give more internal coherence to Debord's disjointed comments on the pre-capitalist origins of the spectacle and thereby incorporated the essentially Hegelian insight adopted by Marx within the *Grundrisse*: 'The anatomy of man is a key to the anatomy of the ape.'

Bunyard's interpretation traces in Debord a heavy debt to French Hegelianism with regards to the centrality of negativity within human history and the temporality of self-determinate social praxis. As a result, the spectacle often appears as a problem of subjectivity, frequently echoing the travails of Hegel's unhappy consciousness and, as such, bearing the strong but qualified impacts of existentialism. In elevating Debord's views on the contingencies of lived historical time, we find a version of Debord not altogether unreminiscent of Lukács' intellectual origins: a thinker whose subjectivism is inadvertently blemished with the stains of *Lebensphilosophie* and whose vitalism affirmed the lived time of subjective self-determination cohering with the flow of temporal and transformative flux. It is odd, in this respect, that Bunyard never once mentions Joseph Gabel's 1962 *False Consciousness*, a book which – synthesising the work of

Lukács and Bergson and existential themes – strongly informs Debord's concluding chapter of *The Society of the Spectacle* and whose theory of reification specifically identifies the '[s]patialisation of experienced duration' and a 'loss of temporalisation' as its constitutive elements.

*Debord, Time and Spectacle* stands out for the unusual manner in which Debord is examined specifically as a part of the tradition of Hegelian Marxism. Yet this also remains an emphatically French Debord, in a fashion which minimises his work as a diagnostician of modern capitalist society by upholding an affirmative conception of historical praxis and deriding the spectacle for failing to live up to that possibility. Despite the limitations of centring a reading of the spectacle on time and history, Bunyard certainly succeeds where this approach serves to develop 'a holistic reading of Debord's oeuvre.' Nonetheless, at a moment when there is such an intense social need to excise ambiguity from a critical theory of society, the determinate mediations contained within the concept of modern spectacle ought to take some precedence over a generalised diagnosis of the deprivation of historical agency. The task therefore remains, one might say, to *Germanicise* Debord against the complaints he himself made about how the theoretical concepts of *The Society of the Spectacle*, 'almost all of which have a German origin', had been 'quietly ignored'.

Eric-John Russell

# Symbolic glue

Roman Kuhar and David Paternotte, eds., *Anti-Gender Campaigns in Europe: Mobilising Against Equality* (London: Rowman &Littlefield, 2017). 302pp., £85.00 hb., £27.95 pb., 978 1 78348 999 2 hb., 978 1 78660 000 4 pb.

What fuels the success of authoritarian populism around the globe and how does the extreme right manage to hijack public debate? We know that 'sex sells', but we also need to learn how 'gender' turns the tables in this context, and *Anti-Gender Campaigns in Europe* is an excellent place to start. The editors, Roman Kuhar and David Patternotte, have gathered reports from thirteen countries following two conferences that took place in 2015 in Budapest and Brussels. Each of the thoroughly researched and accessibly written chapters discusses the discourses, strategies and organisational efforts of the anti-gender movement in one European state, including Russia, often cross-referencing the phenomenon in other places. Most authors have a background in sociology and are prominent scholars of gender studies.

The chapters reveal some local disparities. For instance, the involvement of the Catholic Church varies from great prominence in Italy and Poland to a mere background function in Spain. In Slovenia and Croatia, specific anti-gender parties were established; in France the topic helped boost the existing party on the extreme right, the Front National; while in German a newly founded right-wing party, the AfD, benefited from spreading anti-gender resentment. Most findings, however, corroborate the diagnosis that we are dealing with a coherent and concerted phenomenon across Europe (and possibly beyond) which deserves its own name: 'anti-genderism'. This movement took off from the discursive framing of 'gender ideology' by writers in close association with the Vatican in the late nineties, and peaked in campaigns across many countries in 2012 and 2013.

One of the many things we can learn from the book is that our enemies know us better than we know them. Of course there are a host of projections, lies, exaggerations and false accusations fueling anti-gender campaigns, but, in a certain way, they are about what they claim to be. They are not merely conservative or Christian, not even primarily anti-feminist or anti-LGBTQ (though in consequence they are), but they are about gender. The anti-gender movement opposes the progressive conclusions drawn from the fact that gender identities are historically variable, power-laden social roles and that 'normality' can claim moral authority no more than 'nature' can. As I argued in a previous issue of *Radical Philosophy*, anti-genderism is a very specific type of defense mechanism, one that tries to stabilise corroded sexist and heteronormative ideology (see '*Anti-genderismus* and right-wing hegemony', *Radical Philosophy* 198). In this respect, it is a reaction to left-wing success. Like European anti-semitism at the end of the nineteenth century, anti-genderism comes after (legal) emancipation. In effect, anti-genderism provides a leverage point from which to launch the counter-revolution to May '68 – something which is symbolised, in full historical irony, by the fact that one of the leading German anti-gender journalists, Bettina Röhl, is the daughter of the late Red Army Faction member Ulrike Meinhof.

What makes the anti-gender discourse so effective as a political force, and certainly far more effective than the left so far likes to admit – we want to fight fascists, not anti-genderists, after all – is how, from that focal point ('gender'), an entire conspiratorial web is spun. The term is left untranslated even in European languages in which an equivalent exists. Thus it sounds vague and foreign and can be more easily connected to vast agendas supposedly hiding behind it, tying it to all the hot topics of right-wing resentment in the following ways: Gender is designed to destroy families, because it denies that men and women are different and made for each other. Gender is designed to 'sexualise' children, because it is taught to them in schools in order to confuse them in their natural development. Gender is designed to abolish the national population, because people are stopped from procreating in 'natural' hereditary ways and then are replaced by immigrants. Gender is designed to curb freedom of speech, because whenever one criticises immigration, one is called a racist. Gender is designed to undermine national sovereignty, because it is imposed via EU policies; in fact, the entire EU has been taken over by the gender lobby.

So while, at its clear-sighted, reactionary core, anti-genderism really is about gender, in its obscurantist proliferation, anti-genderism allows resentful and nativist strata of the society to 'explain' all sorts of things which have no causal link to feminist theory, but arose from neoliberalism, urbanisation, shifting forms of labour and foreign policy, in a way that fits a unified right-wing world-view. If 'gender', as almost all articles argue in reference to Eszter Kováts and Maari Põim, serves as symbolic glue, it is a very sticky one indeed. Moreover, as several chapters of this book – and a newer report on Serbia by Adriana Zaharijević – make clear, this 'glue' is deliberately produced and promoted by a few actors and right-wing think tanks, refuting the myth of anti-genderism as a spontaneous 'common sense' upheaval.

The reports in *Anti-Gender Campaigns* could go further in examining the exact link not just between anti-genderism and nationalism, but also the anti-immigration discourses, Islamophobia and racism entrenched in those nationalisms. Is anti-genderism one register, and xenophobia another, of current right-wing fervour? Or are they more intricately linked? Is anti-genderism a sort of dry run for the articulation of outright racist political formations? Anti-genderism produces its own 'witch hunts' against outspoken feminists and gender studies scholars by way of eliminatory rhetorics, but how does it also contribute to the given historical conjuncture in which migrants and people of colour are at highest risk of physical attacks and of a necropolitics?

Even if it doesn't answer all of these questions, Kuhar and Patternotte's anthology provides an encouraging methodological example as to how sociological research into pressing political issues can be conducted. In their sober, account-taking style, the essays provide maximum enlightenment. At the same time, they create the baffling result that this book would serve just as well as a manual for building anti-gender campaigns, or for building one's political career on no expertise except authoritarian anti-gender rhetorics. *Anti-Gender Campaigns in Europe* is neither a blazing ideology critique nor a manual for resistance. But asking for that might be getting ahead of things. The first step is to take the phenomenon of anti-genderism seriously and learn about its dynamics, as this book enables us to do.

**Eva von Redecker**

# Stanley Cavell, 1926-2018

Daniele Lorenzini

Stanley Cavell, the Walter M. Cabot Professor of Aesthetics and the General Theory of Value at Harvard University, was one of the most prominent philosophers of the second half of the twentieth century, who developed over the course of five decades an impressive *oeuvre* characterised by two main quests that define the singularity of his philosophical voice: on the one hand, the quest for the ordinary, originated in Cavell's deep fascination with its uncanny and *extra*ordinary aspects; on the other, the quest for a specifically *American* philosophical tradition, independent of the (mainstream) analytic one. Understanding these two long-standing quests is pivotal to addressing an apparently unclassifiable and tradition-crossing *oeuvre* that might otherwise seem too eclectic and dispersed, with its interests ranging from ordinary language philosophy to aesthetics, from American transcendentalism to psychoanalysis, from post-Kantian continental philosophy to music, from literature and theatre to cinema. Cavell understood philosophy 'as a diverse and democratic activity that cannot be confined to the academy and that naturally extends to all aspects of culture', which, far from being a well-defined academic discipline, consists in a perpetual effort to make sense of our (ordinary) words, practices, and forms of life.[1] As he puts it in *The Claim of Reason*, one cannot teach philosophy without acknowledging that one 'requires education', that is, that one needs to be constantly ready to change, since 'in the face of the questions posed in Augustine, Luther, Rousseau, Thoreau … we are children.' That's why Cavell defined philosophy as 'the education of grownups' – a definition that would later be commented upon and adopted by authors including Pierre Hadot and Hilary Putnam.[2]

Among Cavell's central guides was the Wittgensteinian call to 'return' words from their metaphysical to their everyday use. What really matters is not hidden but lies in plain view, before our eyes; however, it is usually too close or too banal – too *ordinary* – to be perceived. Philosophical jargon contributes a great deal to our inability to see the richness and complexity of our everyday language and practices. Hence, in an original way, Cavell condemns philosophy's widespread refusal to address 'the difficulty of reality', that is, its tendency to flee concrete issues and seek refuge in abstractions, and above all – as Cora Diamond puts it – its ignorance concerning the question of 'how to inhabit a human body.'[3] However, the ordinary is not to be 'discovered': it is rather a place to which one returns thanks to a conversion of one's gaze and attention, and to a radical change in the hierarchy of importance – a change that, according to Cavell, was already prefigured in Thoreau. Thus, by insisting on the transformative powers of the ordinary, Cavell emphasises the essential (but usually downplayed) link between – as well as the critical potentiality of – American transcendentalism and ordinary language philosophy. He also explicitly contests the hierarchies commonly accepted in contemporary academic philosophy that exclude, from the start, the possibility that anything 'serious' could ever be said, for instance, about the Hollywood comedies and melodramas of the 1930s and the 1940s, or that Cary Grant and Bette Davis could occupy the same page as Plato and Kant in a philosophy book.

In the Overture to *A Pitch of Philosophy* (1994), Cavell characterises philosophy in terms of 'the claim to speak for the human', that is, of 'a certain universalising use of the voice', and presents 'the arrogant assumption of the right to speak for others' as the ground of ordinary language philosophy – in particular, of the later Wittgenstein and J. L. Austin's works. Connecting, again, ordinary language philosophy and American transcendentalism in a quite unprecedented way, Cavell discovers the foundations of this 'systematic arrogation of voice' in Emerson's idea that 'the deeper the scholar dives into his privatest, secretest presentiment, to his wonder he finds this is the most acceptable, most public, and universally true.'[4] However, far from constituting a definitive answer, these claims lead to the formulation of one of the most important questions in Cavell's *oeuvre*: the question of the community, haunted as it is – and will always be – by what he calls 'the truth of skepticism.' As Cavell puts it in *The Claim of Reason*, 'to speak for oneself politically is to speak for the others with whom you consent to association, and it is to consent to be spoken for by them'; this means that you constantly risk the rebuff 'of those for whom you claimed to be speaking' and that you risk having to rebuff 'those who claimed to be speaking for you.'[5] Such a risk, formulated here in political terms, has a far more general relevance: it is inscribed, Cavell argues, at the core of our condition of 'creatures of language', of our own form of life characterised by the desire to be acknowledged by others and therefore by the need to make ourselves intelligible to them.

> That my actions are part of the life form of talkers (as Wittgenstein characterises the human, at [*Philosophical*] *Investigations*, §174) makes them open to criticism. That I am open to, perhaps responsive to, the criticism of being insensitive, cruel, petty, clumsy, narrow-minded, self-absorbed, cold, hard, heedless, reckless ... is as much a mystery as my being open to the charge of being imprudent or undutiful or unfair. That we are not transparent to ourselves means that such criticism demands confrontation and conversation.[6]

This is why Cavell is convinced that one cannot find one's own voice – in politics as well as in friendship, love, parenthood, and so on – by speaking for oneself privately. On the contrary, one should take the risk of publicly addressing others within the framework of a community (of language and life) that can never be taken for granted, since it is itself at stake in our words. Thus, Cavell constantly insists on the importance to fight against the temptation of 'empty[ing] out my contribution to words, so that language itself, as if beyond me, exclusively takes over the responsibility for meaning.'[7] This is indeed the only way one has to let oneself matter to the other, acknowledging that 'your expressions in fact express you, that they are yours, that you are in them.'[8] The vulnerability of the human voice – and of our form of life as creatures of language – is therefore far deeper than the power language has to wound. It (also) stems from the fact that it is always possible to deny that my expressions in fact express me, that it is always possible not to mean what I say, and that at the same time to mean what I say exposes me to the risk of being rebuffed, of discovering that in fact I do not matter to the other, that I am unable to make myself intelligible to her. This essential vulnerability of the human voice that Cavell never ceases to emphasise is strictly connected to the vulnerability of ordinary language explored by Austin: ordinary language can always 'go wrong', as Austin argues, since it can not only miss its object, representing or describing it incorrectly, but *fail* just like every other human action. As Cavell puts it, 'if utterances *could* not fail they would not be the human actions under consideration, indeed not the actions of humans at all.'[9]

However, in Cavell's view, the vulnerability of our ordinary (linguistic and non-linguistic) practices is not to be interpreted negatively, as the sign of a radical passivity that would inevitably trap us in a form of determinism. On the contrary, it is precisely because it is vulnerable, because it can always go wrong, that the ordinary can function as a crucial vehicle for change and transformation. This idea constitutes one of the most original contributions of Cavell's work to the philosophy of language. We *do* and we *suffer* things with words: not only because words can wound, but also because, in order to do anything with words, we need to accept the risk of exposing ourselves to various types of failures as well as to the others and their responses – which cannot be known in advance and have the power to profoundly affect our being and life. Therefore, in taking seriously (and extending) Austin's work, Cavell ends up challenging the very idea of a given and unitary subject of speech acts: 'our word is our bond' means that speaking is – also – a way for us to give ourselves a form, not only vis-à-vis the others (with a view to making ourselves intelligible to them), but also vis-à-vis ourselves. Indeed, far from being the external *translation* of a series of 'inner' realities, language as both action and passion is the vehicle for a complex set of processes of (re)constitution of ourselves. These processes are an essential part of our life as creatures of language and deserve to be addressed, as Foucault would have said, from the perspective of a 'dramatics' rather than a pragmatics of discourse.

This is why, according to Cavell, the menace of skepticism 'is not simply that since we may "always" be wrong in our (empirical) judgements, the moral to draw is ... to be cautious in our claims, to measure how far we attach our wills to our words about the world.' It is rather that, 'since I am, as finite, threatened with consequences from unforeseeable quarters, I am at any time acting, and speaking, in the absence of what may seem sufficient reason.'[10] Skepticism, and notably skepticism concerning other minds, is not a philosophical problem that stands in need of a *solution*: it is a fact, Cavell argues, an existential condition entailed by the finitude and separateness of human beings, and which in turn entails the constant need for human beings to change. Thus, far from trying to get rid of it, philosophy should always be kept 'open to the threat or temptation of skepticism.'[11]

Cavell's lifelong interest in the need for human beings to transform or transfigure themselves allows us to explain his discovery of what he calls 'moral perfectionism.' As he explains at the beginning of *Conditions Handsome and Unhandsome* (1990), moral perfectionism is not a *theory* competing with others, but a dimension of the moral life that spans the course of Western thought, running from Plato and Aristotle to Wittgenstein and Heidegger, and including – among others – Augustine, Spinoza, Locke, Kant, Mill and Nietzsche, as well as several (non-philosophical) authors such as Kleist, Ibsen and Wilde. But this 're-gister' of the moral life is also to be found in Emerson and Thoreau, who give it a particularly interesting (and specifically American) form. In *This New Yet Unapproachable America*, Cavell claims that moral perfectionism is exemplified by Emerson's willingness to attract the human to 'the work of becoming human' – which is not a discovery of something hidden, but a *re*-discovery that takes the form of the creation of something new. Indeed, for Emerson and Thoreau, philosophy consists, first, in the loss of the world, and then in the 'returning of it, to it' made possible by the transfiguration of oneself.[12] Moral perfectionism has to do precisely with the acknowledgment that there is always a 'further self' not yet realised, and thus with the effort to attain it, although Cavell clearly emphasises that there is no *final* self to be reached – no Absolute Spirit to be achieved, no true self to be given voice to. Moral perfectionism is rather about the perpetual movement from a state of the self to another, an incessant self-transformation aiming to attain 'the further or higher self of each', signalling that the human being 'is always becoming ... always partially in a further state.'[13] This path is Nietzschean in that it does not go upward – Cavell claims that philosophy is 'a refusal of, say disobedient to, ... transcendence' – but downward: it takes place in the immanence of ordinary human practices, and could also be described as 'the task of accepting finitude.'[14]

Moral perfectionism is thus linked to the ancient (Greek and Roman) conception of philosophy as a way of life, characterised by the effort to radically transform one's way of seeing the world and of living in it. Indeed, the most important question for Emerson is (still) that of 'the conduct of life': How shall I live? It is possible to emphasise here interesting analogies between Cavell's work and other (apparently very different) perspectives such as Pierre Hadot's reading of the history of philosophy in the light of the notion of spiritual exercises or Michel Foucault's late interest in the techniques of the self.[15] And also to bring moral perfectionism closer to a certain conception of the virtues, since they both assign a central role to the formation of the moral character and criticise the idea that morality resolves itself into a series of discrete moments of choice, or that moral reasoning consists in applying a defined set of principles and rules to the 'facts' of a given situation. On the contrary, like Iris Murdoch, Cavell, too, is convinced that moral life is not 'something that is switched off in between the occurrence of explicit moral choices', but rather 'something that goes on continually' – and that what is crucial is precisely 'what happens in between such choices.'[16] It is there that one's self gets formed and

reformed, that the way one sees the world gets shaped, that the 'facts' of a situation gets defined. By speaking of (and studying) moral perfectionism, Cavell thus aims to broaden the traditional philosophical conception of the moral life and to show that moral thought does not take place in 'a situation with fixed, given possibilities' (as Cora Diamond puts it), but consists in a *creative* exercise that transforms the situation, and the moral agent herself. Moral perfectionism is not a moral theory (that's why, ultimately, it should not be considered as a mere variety of virtue ethics), but rather a way to help us to see morality in a different light. Indeed, according to Cavell, morality has to do first and foremost with the way in which we pay attention to things and people, with the hierarchies we build concerning what matters to us, and with the effort to change ourselves in order to reach a higher (but never definitive) state of our subjectivity.

This original conception of the moral life may appear dangerously elitist. However, Cavell claims that it is essentially *democratic* and that, far from being limited to morality, it possesses an explicit political dimension. In addition to (different forms of) moral perfectionism, there is also a political perfectionism – one 'that happily consents to democracy' and gives voice to a 'democratic aspiration'.[17] What we might call democratic – or American – perfectionism is defined by the contrast between conformity and self-reliance; as John Stuart Mill would have said, it consists in the (unconventional) 'exercise of individuality'.[18] Such contrast and exercise define, in Cavell's eyes, a political task: democratic perfectionism emphasises the tension not only between myself as I am and myself as I may become, but also – and more importantly – between society 'as it stands' and society 'as it may become'. As Cavell puts it at the beginning of *Cities of Words*:

> The very conception of a divided self and a doubled world, providing a perspective of judgement upon the world as it is, measured against the world as it may be, tends to express disappointment with the world as it is, as the scene of human activity and prospects, and perhaps to lodge the demand or desire for a reform or transfiguration of the world.[19]

This is why democratic perfectionism is grounded in the self-reliant (public) expression of one's own *voice*. Indeed, the question of democracy, in Cavell's eyes, is the question of the relation between one's personal voice and political discourse: I need to recognise myself in what my society says since I gave it my voice, accepting that it speaks in my name. However, as soon as this relation becomes dissonant, that is, when I no longer recognise my voice in the voice of others, I also need to accept the task of (publicly) expressing my dissent, relying on my sense of what democracy should be. As already noted, Cavell emphasises that the constitution of a (social and political) community relies on the double need to speak for others and to be spoken for by others. And, surprisingly, he addresses this complex issue in his book on what he calls 'the Hollywood comedies of remarriage': what is at stake in them is precisely the possibility for the central pair to overcome the threat of an irreparable rupture (the divorce) and to *re*-establish their mutual relationship (to *re*-marry, that is, to get *back* together, together *again*). Thus, these comedies explore the possibility to create a community based on 'a meet and happy conversation' through which participants acknowledge their shared condition of finitude and separateness, transforming it in the foundation of their life *together*. Indeed, for the central pair, 'talking together is fully and plainly being together, a mode of association, a form of life' whose objective is not to reach a final agreement, but to attain mutual acknowledgment, since – as Cavell puts it – 'we do not have to agree with one another in order to live in the same moral world, but we do have to know and respect one another's differences.'[20]

However, far from drawing a quietist and idealised picture of democracy, Cavell's writings on political perfectionism also suggest that disobedience, as Thoreau first defined it, is (paradoxically) the real foundation of democracy, a sign of health and not at all of decline. Democratic perfectionism is therefore the name Cavell gives to a 'counter way of life', that is, to the establishment of a *critical* relation to one's own society as it is, and to 'the power to demand the change of the world as a whole.'[21] In his eyes, this is an – and probably *the* – essential feature of democracy that, in order to exist, should be incessantly *re*-discovered, as should (philosophy in) America. We will always owe these rediscoveries to the ground-breaking and joyfully unconventional work of Stanley Cavell.

*Daniele Lorenzini is a Marie Skłodowska-Curie 'Move-in Louvain' Postdoctoral Fellow at the Centre Prospéro, Université Saint-Louis Bruxelles, and a Postdoctoral Fellow at the Center for Contemporary Critical Thought, Columbia University. From Autumn 2019, he will be Assistant Professor of Philosophy at the University of Warwick.*

**Notes**

1. Nancy Bauer, Alice Crary and Sandra Laugier, 'Stanley Cavell and the American Contradiction', *The New York Times*, 2 July 2018, https://www.nytimes.com/2018/07/02/opinion/stanley-cavell-and-the-american-contradiction.html
2. Stanley Cavell, *The Claim of Reason: Wittgenstein, Skepticism, Morality, and Tragedy* (Oxford: Oxford University Press, 1979), 125.
3. Cora Diamond, 'The Difficulty of Reality and the Difficulty of Philosophy', *Partial Answers: Journal of Literature and the History of Ideas* 1:2 (June 2003), 13.
4. Stanley Cavell, *A Pitch of Philosophy: Autobiographical Exercises* (Cambridge, MA: Harvard University Press, 1994), vii–viii, vii.
5. Cavell, *The Claim of Reason*, 27.
6. Stanley Cavell, *Cities of Words: Pedagogical Letters on a Register of the Moral Life* (Cambridge, MA: Harvard University Press, 2004), 142.
7. Stanley Cavell, *This New Yet Unapproachable America: Lectures after Emerson after Wittgenstein* (Albuquerque, NM: Living Batch Press, 1989), 57.
8. Cavell, *The Claim of Reason*, 382–83.
9. Cavell, *A Pitch of Philosophy*, 85.
10. Stanley Cavell, *Philosophy the Day after Tomorrow* (Cambridge, MA: Harvard University Press, 2005), 139.
11. Stanley Cavell, *Conditions Handsome and Unhandsome: The Constitution of Emersonian Perfectionism* (La Salle, IL: Open Court, 1990), 35.
12. Cavell, *This New Yet Unapproachable America*, 10, 114.
13. Cavell, *Conditions Handsome and Unhandsome*, 12, 53; *Cities of Words*, 26.
14. Cavell, *This New Yet Unapproachable America*, 46; *Cities of Words*, 4.
15. See Daniele Lorenzini, *Éthique et politique de soi: Foucault, Hadot, Cavell et les techniques de l'ordinaire* (Paris: Vrin, 2015).
16. Iris Murdoch, *The Sovereignty of Good* (New York: Routledge, 1991), 37.
17. Cavell, *Conditions Handsome and Unhandsome*, 1.
18. See Ralph Waldo Emerson, 'Self-Reliance', in *The Portable Emerson*, eds. Carl Bode and Malcom Cowley (New York, NY: Penguin Books, 1981), 160; John Stuart Mill, *On Liberty* (London: Penguin Books, 1985), 119–140.
19. Cavell, *Cities of Words*, 2.
20. Stanley Cavell, *Pursuits of Happiness: The Hollywood Comedy of Remarriage* (Cambridge, MA: Harvard University Press, 1981), 87–88; *The Claim of Reason*, 269.
21. Cavell, *This New Yet Unapproachable America*, 115.

# Paul Virilio, 1932–2018
Paolo Fabbri

The disappearance of Paul Virilio is my concern.* It provides an opportune moment for a 'spontaneous declaration', as well as for some clarification with respect to a series of apodictic interventions.

1. The personal facts. Memory – transformed recollections and changed expectations – delivers to me a Virilio who was, alongside Michel de Certeau, Louis Marin and Jean Baudrillard, editor of *Traverses,* the review of the Centre de Création Industrielle (CCI); on the scientific board of the *Cahiers d'Etudes Stratégiques* of the Centre Interdisciplinaire de Recherches sur la Paix et d'Études Stratégiques (CIRPES/EHESS); contributor to the debate on 'the nuclear state' in the special 1984 issue on war in *Change International*; co-director of the CIPH, Collège International de Philosophie. Virilio also presided over the series *Images et Politique, Rencontres Internationales de la Photographie*, Arles, 1997, which I participated in with my own article 'Faire de l'Image un Monument?'[1]

2. Explications. Turning too hastily towards such a productive author – translations abound – runs the risk of consigning him to the Hades of forgetfulness, something that befell our common friend Jean Baudrillard – though such fate is undoubtedly preferable to cheap embalming procedures: the inventor of dromology, the sprinter-visionary of technology, the theorist of catastrophes and, *absit iniuria verbis*, the mass-mediologist. Above all, there is the Philosopher, a commendation of thought that Virilio was never awarded, at least in the French philosophical tradition – torn between Sartre and Merleau Ponty, on the one hand, and Koyré and Bachelard, on the other – not even philosopher in the sense of a scientific anthropology (Serres) or empirical philosophy (Latour). If anything, he was closer to Guattari, with whom he experienced May '68 – Deleuze's absence was excused! – for whom a philosopher was a concept synthesiser. Rather than suspending him from the protean hanger of pop-philosophers – whom he would have likely accused of philo-*folly* – it is best to recognise his Dreyfus-like role as an intellectual. A strong thinker, critical in content, an essayist of a writing both graphic – books, reviews, collections – and visual, as manifest in important exhibitions: *Vivre à l'Oblique* (1970), *Bunker Archéologie* (1975), *La Vitesse* (1991), *Ce Qui Arrive* (2002) and *Terre Natale, l'Ailleurs Commence Ici* (2008-9). Visible experiences of thought and of '*Revelatory Art*'!

2.1 An intellectual marked by war. Son of an Italian immigrant, Virilio experienced the German *blitzkrieg* before and after the disappearance of the city of Nantes during the 'liberation' bombings. From world war and total urban destruction, he developed an original perspective on velocity and architecture, the city and techniques of war. In 1987, Virilio received the *Grand Prix National de la Critique Architecturale*: he was an urbanist first and foremost, an architect who was passionate about the spatial arts – theatre and dance – and who was gifted with an international vision of culture. Director of the École Spéciale d'Architecture in Paris, his interest in the German bunker of the Atlantic Wall – the Valhalla of Bauhaus monoliths in military space – derives from his preference for the Cave – as opposed to the fortified Tower – as a primary space of survival, and for cement as the

---

* The following text is a translation of 'Il gusto di Paul Virilio per la parola penultima', *alfabeta2*, published 7 October 2018, https://www.alfabeta2.it/2018/10/07/il-gusto-di-paul-virilio-per-la-parola-penultima

material of resistance. Theorist of an Oblique Architecture made of seamless interiors through the concatenation of oblique and horizontal planes, he built a bunker-church in Nevers (St. Bernadette in Banlay) and influenced architecture stars such as Jean Nouvel. Obliquity is a strategic propensity to diagonally flee the opposition between vertical and horizontal, an ideogram that gradually led him to its opposite: the contemporary de-materialisation of virtuality.

After the radical experience of 1968 – Virilio had joined the occupation of the Sorbonne and the Théatre de l'Odéon – and the disillusionment that ensued, he founded the review *Cause Commune* with Georges Perec who, like him, had been deeply affected by the war. For both of them, May '68 was a cultural more than a political event, and its implosion posed questions to a left-wing realpolitik and the necessary safeguard of common spaces. Virilio analysed the shape of buildings and, in his inquiries into urbanism, studied the *detournement* of places – churches turned into garages, barracks into museums, warehouses into theatres. Above all, like Perec, he noted the infra-ordinary character of banal signs that are neither ordinary nor extraordinary, in order to give a language and meaning to the 'daily anti-spectacle that newspapers fail to talk about'. Perec joined the *Ouvroir de Littérature Potentielle* (Oulipo) in 1967, but Virilio refused to reduce this to mere language games, pointing out its tragic violence, which affected his own work also. For Virilio, Perec's new voyeurism was, unlike Alain Robbe-Grillet's, that of an urban nomad who, with writing, exhausted space both sociologically and politically. Perec's *Espèces d'Espaces* (1974) was the first publication in the series 'L'Espace Critique', curated by Virilio for Éditions Galilée, which aimed to reflect upon the new branch of knowledge he named 'Dromology'. As a discipline of trajectories replacing metrology, or the geometry of objective forms, dromology was necessary to an investigation of the greatest catastrophe of the twentieth century – the 'omnicities' of millions that we are going to leave behind, Virilio thought, just as peasants once left behind their land.

2.2 After 1968, the notion of the Event imposed itself, focused upon the works of Deleuze and Guattari. In the landscape of events, Virilio grasped the accidental dimension of a planetary acceleration of technique first and technologies second. The Accident, which he transversally considered in his research, points not only to the absolute unpredictability of the event, but also to a breakdown or failure [*guasto*]: the inevitable and unimaginable outcome of any technical making (*'it is the ship that invents the shipwreck'*!). His reflection upon the always-new accidents that occur whilst avoiding accidents resulted in a definition of the catastrophic 'Integral Accident': rupture points such as Seveso, Chernobyl, Fukushima and the destruction of the (hated, Babelesque) Towers. Catastrophes are outcomes inherent not to technical failure but to technical success: the more performative the invention, the more traumatic the event. The ecstasy of acceleration that marks the Golem-like gait of science and the technical arts not only demands principled precaution, but also a political and ethical rethinking, including the urgent need for de-growth and dis-invention (as in the case of plastic and cars). This is especially so because the unfolding of technique in a military-industrial society is always oriented to, when not dictated by, the logic of war, the invention of deadly prostheses (already nuclear and now cybernetic). War advances under the guise of the 'freedom' of liberated and costless [*libera e gratuita*] interactivity. For Virilio, even means of communication – from the telegraph to photography and cinema, from the radar to the internet – are devices of optical and electronic domination, homologated and adopted in techno-systems of strategic interaction. The postmodern arsenal, ready for deployment, now relies on three macrosystems of bombs: nuclear, informational and genetic – the deliberate, sinister mutation of human nature.

2.3 The value of speed – whose discovery Virilio ascribed to the warmongering vanguard of Futurism – guided his last reflections.[2] From space to time, from topology to 'nano-chronology': means of transport and tourist flows put an end to local time and jetlag. This upturns the relationship between the Sedentary – who is communicatively equipped and always knows where he or she is and is going – and the Nomad, who is out of place anywhere.

For Virilio, temporal synchronisation pollutes distances and reduces the very perception of the Earth itself, its dimension and ecosystem. This is the root of the ongoing planetary re-population, a diaspora against which it is futile to furnish space with walls.[3]. Simultaneity creates new inertias and insecurities, not only spatial, but temporal too – terrorism is indeed ubiquitous and omnipresent. In his late works, Virilio pointed to the phenomenon of an instantaneous synchronicity of affects as the matrix of new collective and political flows and intensities. Concurrent emotions that play out in real time have replaced the reckoning of interests that formerly standardised public opinion in representative democracies. The synonymy of information and disinformation (so-called 'fake news') is, in this respect, among the effects of globalisation: 'the largest-scale transmutation of public opinion ever attempted in peace time'.

A 'futurism of the instant' is the 'here and now' of a radical presentism that catastrophically alters the meaning of history, though without marking its end. It is a different history, accidental, free of any civil religion of progress that would be added to the regime of events [événementielle] envisaged by Braudel.

3. This multiform and radical oeuvre, recalcitrant by default, and beyond disciplinary labels, has been met with virulent critique: like the notorious, laughable 'Sokal Hoax' which was mobilised against those who define themselves as critics of the art of science, as well as the pamphlets of sociologists for whom Virilio, like his friend Baudrillard, 'did not take place'. The benevolent defence that ascribes to him the Fourierist title of 'visionary' only aggravates his position. Through the drafting of documentary dossiers on technology and war, Virilio grasped accidents as signs that anticipate tendencies and premonitions of collective orientations in the process of being realised: like the shift from the Cyclops's gaze of Orwellian dictatorship to the countless eyes of contemporary capitalist surveillance. Digital prints and eye scans, DNA data, facial recognition security cameras, doppler radar, drones, number-plate recognition: from panoptical observation to the most private of traces.

Unlike failing econometric models, Virilio sent out probes and sounded warnings: in the pragmatic and neorealist world of the *matter of fact*, he sought to invest in difficult questions and general problems: he did not search for pre-packaged answers and solutions. The ire his proposals provoked – a Museum of the Accident, a University of Disaster, a Ministry of Temporal Planning, the inclusion of the night in the lists of the world heritage of humanity [*Patrimonio dell'Umanità*]– was deliberately and ironically calculated.

More surprising is the general refusal of an idiosyncratic aspect of his style: the creation of neologisms. Virilio did not use keywords ready to be put into search engines. With varying success, he tried to take responsibility for new events and situations, to place writing at the same level as the infra-ordinary disasters he investigated. *Claustropolis, Dromosphere, Meteo-politics, Megalopolis, Nanoworld, Post-intimacy, Trajectography*, but also *endo-colonisation, telepresence, conditioned reflex, photosensitive inertia*, and so on and so forth. An experimental writing in intent is no different from avant-garde literature, or from the optically 'incorrect' [*scorretto*] work of artists – Baj, Beuys, Pollock, Turrell, etc. – whom Virilio liked because they had abandoned the atelier for the workshop.

As an experimenter, Virilio had a taste for the penultimate word: he did not warn of a final catastrophe, instead he was apocalyptic in a 'revelatory' way. A fervent catholic, he would quote St. Paul: 'Hope against all hope'.

**Translated by Arianna Bove**

**Notes**

1. Paolo Fabbri, *Images et Politique*, Actes sud/AFAA, Arles, 1998. https://www.paolofabbri.it/image_monument/
2. See, 'Futurismo dell'istante' [Futurism of the instant] in the first issue of *Alfabeta2*, 2010.
3. See the exhibition, *Terre Natale, Ailleurs Commerce Ici* [Native Land, Stop Eject], 2008-9. https://www.fondationcartier.com/en/exhibitions/terre--natale-ailleurs-commence-ici

www.ingramcontent.com/pod-product-compliance
Lightning Source LLC
Chambersburg PA
CBHW041809070526
44586CB00026B/2816